D1250411

Nazi Propaganda

OTHER BOOKS BY Z. A. B. ZEMAN

Germany and the Revolution in Russia 1915–1918:
Documents from the Archives of the German Foreign Ministry

The Break-up of the Habsburg Empire:
A Study in National and Social Revolution

The Merchant of Revolution:
The Life of Alexander Israel Helphand (Parvus) 1867–1924
(with W. B. Scharlau)

Prague Spring:
A Report on Czechoslovakia 1968

A Diplomatic History of the First World War

Twilight of the Habsburgs

Nazi Propaganda

SECOND EDITION

Z. A. B. ZEMAN

OXFORD UNIVERSITY PRESS
London   Oxford   New York
1973

OXFORD UNIVERSITY PRESS

London   Oxford   New York
Glasgow   Toronto   Melbourne   Wellington
Cape Town   Ibadan   Nairobi   Dar es Salaam   Lusaka   Addis Ababa
Delhi   Bombay   Calcutta   Madras   Karachi   Lahore   Dacca
Kuala Lumpur   Singapore   Hong Kong   Tokyo

Copyright © 1964, 1973 by Oxford University Press, Inc.
Library of Congress Catalogue Card Number: 72–96614
First published by Oxford University Press, London, 1964,
in association with The Wiener Library
Second edition published as an Oxford University Press paperback,
London and New York; 1973

Printed in the United States of America

For Leonard Wolfson

Contents

Illustrations

Introduction

Hitler's speech to the party rally on 12 September 1936 struck a high note of self-congratulation and compliment to his audience. The Germans were lucky to have found him, he said, as he was lucky to have found them; what obstacles might they not surmount when he himself had 'come from nothing to the head of a nation'?[1] This is not the place to consider the irony, or the accuracy, of the double piece of good fortune Hitler referred to. However, it is beyond dispute that his personal rise to power from obscurity was a notable achievement. As an aspiring politician, Hitler was badly placed. He entered the jungle of German postwar politics with so many handicaps that anyone versed in its ways would have advised him against embarking on a political career at all. His family background was undistinguished; his education was negligible, and it did not provide him with the still highly-prized *Verbindungen* — connexions that would have eased his ascent through the remaining traditional channels; his political attitudes alienated him from the new order established in Central Europe after the Great War. Although his military career in the war was distinguished by the award of an Iron Cross decoration his service, as an Austrian by birth, in the German army did not even secure him German citizenship on the conclusion of hostilities.

Yet Hitler's rise to political power was amazingly rapid. He ran a public conspiracy against the Weimar Republic; he was a revolutionary only in the sense that he despised the Weimar 'system' and that he never thought in terms of the possibility of a compromise with it. He had no revolutionary tradition behind him comparable with that of, say, the Russian Bolsheviks. It may be argued that Hitler and his party revolutionized their country's political life. That process—it went on for some twenty-five years—was not based on a coherent ideology. With their particular bundle of ideas, the Nazis travelled light. In the last instance National Socialism was a standing invitation to an elect nation to indulge in the pursuit, and the worship, of naked power. We shall have opportunities to remark on the poverty of Nazi ideology and the ways in which it affected the fortunes of their movement. Despite Hitler's claims to the contrary, the National Socialist ideological equipment would bear no comparison with the philosophies which informed great universal movements and affected European history, be it Christianity or Marxist socialism.

There were, however, two aspects of political activity in which the Nazis excelled, and which were analysed in great detail for them in Hitler's *Mein Kampf*. They were party organization and propaganda.

Problems of organization had occupied European political leaders before Hitler started taking an interest in politics. The controversy in the German Social Democratic party in the eighteen-nineties, and then again the split of 1903 in the Russian Social Democracy had shown that the shape of a political party was closely bound up with its functions. Revolution and conspiracy on the one hand and, on the other, reform through parliamentary means required different kinds of organization. In simple terms the choice was between a small, closely knit party of revolution and a mass organization of reform.

From its beginnings until the *Machtergreifung* in 1933, the National Socialist party stood in a middle position between conspiracy and reform. Hitler never intended to come to terms with the established régime; neither was he prepared, or effectively constrained, to renounce the advantages of running a mass organization. In fact two divergent impulses shaped the *Nationalsozialistische Arbeiterpartei*. It was a party of conspirators as well as of the masses. Hitler had originally seen it as an exclusive élite group; later an official distinction was made between *Altkämpfer*, the old Nazis, and *Parteigenossen,* the regular party members. With the exception of the S.A. purge in

1934, the old Nazis had on the whole an easier time under Hitler than did the old Bolshevik guard under Stalin. In Nazi Germany old conspirators were transformed, without serious difficulties, into new bureaucrats.

In the political situation in the Weimar Republic Hitler was not compelled to make a clear-cut choice between revolution and reform, and the two different types of party organization which accompanied the two activities. He probably was unaware of the difference. He understood instead the connection between party organization and propaganda. In *Mein Kampf* he wrote that 'the task of propaganda is to attract followers; the task of organization to win members. A follower of a movement is one who declares himself in agreement with its aims; a member is one who fights for it'.[2] He did not want the party to grow too large because 'a movement which enlarges itself *ad infinitum* would necessarily some day be weakened by this procedure'.[3] In this respect, however, he realized that his propaganda itself acted as agent of natural selection: 'the more radical and inciting my propaganda was, the more it frightened off weaklings and irresolute characters and prevented their pushing into the first nucleus of the organization'.[4] Propaganda spread the conspirators' message to the masses, and it helped to widen the 'first nucleus' into a broad organization.

Though organization and propaganda were closely linked in Hitler's mind, he had no doubt which came first on the Nazi scale of priorities. After the end of the First World War, young Hitler arrived in Munich in time to witness the rise and fall of the Bavarian Soviet Republic in April and May 1919, and for a few months he acted as a "political education officer" to the First Bavarian Rifle Regiment. He had earned a reputation among his officers as a man of sound, nationalist ideas, who could make those ideas attractive to the men in the ranks. Hitler's task as a political commissar was to convert disaffected troops many of whom were under the influence of revolutionary Marxist slogans, to becoming once more good Germans.

At that time Hitler came in touch with a small political group called the German Workers' Party and took charge of its propaganda activities. His skill and interest in the practice of propaganda had raised him from the ranks: it also became the foundation of his party's fortunes.

Hitler used propaganda in his own way. In the original meaning of the word, propaganda was the vehicle for a religious faith or a political doctrine. Pope Gregory XV used the term in this sense when he founded the *Congregatio de Propaganda Fides* in 1622, which supervised missionary activities. Later, the Marxist parties in Europe used the term in a similar way. Their leaders had in their possession a doctrine, and propaganda was a means of giving it wider currency. The Russian Bolsheviks, for instance, made a sharp distinction between propaganda and agitation. Their agitation aimed at influencing the masses, at producing the ephemeral mood of the moment; propaganda was meant to pass on the doctrine down the ranks of the party.

The Nazis did not find it necessary to make that distinction. Josef Goebbels, the only intellectual in the top ranks of the party, who became the Minister of Propaganda in 1933, put it this way: 'Propaganda has no policy, it has a purpose.'

In the years of his apprenticeship as a politician in Munich, most aspects of political activity were synonymous, to Hitler, with propaganda; it was a way of pulling himself out of 'nothing' into prominence. There are two chapters dealing with propaganda in *Mein Kampf*:[5] on these pages Hitler achieved a level of clarity unequalled in other parts of the book.

Although Hitler rightly regarded the First World War as the proper starting point for an examination of propaganda, the first tentative steps were taken before 1914; young Hitler had an opportunity to observe the pioneers of mass propaganda at work in Vienna before the war. He acknowledged his debt to the 'Marxist Socialists' who, he said, had mastered the instrument and 'knew how to handle it in a masterly way and how to put it to practical uses. Thus I soon came to realize', Hitler added, 'that the right use of propaganda represents an art which was and remained almost entirely unknown to the bourgeois parties. Only the Christian-Socialist movement, especially during Lueger's time acquired a certain virtuosity with this instrument and it owed much of its success to it'.[6]

In this connexion, Hitler had a revealing observation to make. When discussing the uses of propaganda before the war, he compared two politicians prominent in the Vienna of his youth: Karl Lueger and Georg Schönerer. They were both antisemites—the former only in public, the latter in private as well—but whereas Lueger was a Catholic and a loyal Habsburg subject, Schönerer became a Protestant who worshipped the Prussian dynasty. Although Hitler approved of Schönerer's politics, he did not let this influence his judgement of the respective worth of the two men as politicians. Schönerer was playing up to upper-middle-class Germans: he lacked 'the force and understanding . . . with which to transmit the theoretical knowledge to the masses'.[7] Lueger, on the other hand, had a 'rare gift of insight into human nature and he was careful not to take men as something better than they were in reality'. He ran a mass movement and he realized the value of propaganda: to him, Hitler awarded the higher marks.

The last lesson on the subject of propaganda, before Hitler embarked on his political career, was administered by the Allies during the First World War. He was highly critical of German propaganda during the war and gave all the credit to the Allies. But there is no indication that Hitler made an effort to understand the political and social realities that lay behind the work of the propagandists. As far as propaganda to their own countrymen was concerned, the Germans faced a more difficult task and they were less skilled then their opposite numbers among the western Allies. In Britain especially, the wartime Ministry of Information produced some noteworthy results. It was run by the presslords—Beaverbrook, Northcliffe, and Rothermere—who were assisted by a large number of journalists. These men not only had an intimate knowledge of their public, but their public was more homogeneous than that in Germany, and even more so than in Austria—Hungary. The tensions that rent the Habsburg monarchy in October 1918 and brought about the revolution in Germany in the following month had existed during the war. National hostilities in Austria—Hungary; in Germany social antagonisms and profound political dissensions and, ultimately, military failure did not make the work of the propagandists in Vienna or Berlin easy.

Nor was Hitler much concerned with the actual content of propaganda: the fascination the subject exercised on him was largely of a technical nature. He saw propaganda essentially as a problem of political salesmanship in a mass market; he understood the similarity between selling a product and a politician to the people. For his pur-

poses he had to form a precise estimate of the quality of the material
he was going to work with. He appreciated the possibilities offered
by the entry of hitherto apolitical, uneducated masses into political
life. He knew that the 'masses' were indispensable for his aims: he did
not believe, as Jefferson had, that they consisted of individuals capable of directing their own political destinies, nor did he regard them
—as the Russian *narodniki* had done—as a noble moving force of
national salvation.

Hitler thought of the masses as malleable, corrupt, and corrupt-
ible; their sentiment was 'not complex but simple and consistent'.[8] He
answered the question 'to whom has propaganda to appeal?' in an
emphatic manner: it 'must always address itself to the broad masses
of the people'.[9] There was no point in trying to influence the intellectuals: Hitler conceded that they would be capable of forming their
own opinions. The proper task of propaganda, he argued, was to
bring certain subjects within the field of vision of the masses.[10] He
knew that a politically uneducated mass public was bound to be
receptive to emotive appeal rather than to rational argument. Propaganda had to concentrate on as few points as possible, it had to hammer them home repeatedly, it had to present them in terms of black
and white. It could afford to make no concessions to the other side.

But all this was not enough. Hitler knew that the kind of propaganda he had in mind required stiffening with a large dose of intimidation and terror. According to his own testimony, he had first noticed
this technique in Vienna before the war: pressure was brought to
bear on the workers to join the trade unions, and character assassination of political opponents was, in Hitler's view, one of the main
features of the Social Democrat press.[11] Hitler therefore resolved,
early in his political career, 'to fight poison gas by poison gas';[12] he
argued that lies had to be countered by still bigger lies, and that terror
cringed only when confronted with a still more frightful terror.

By the time Hitler left Landsberg prison in December 1924, the
foundations of National Socialist ideology, as well as the basic views
on the party's two main concerns—propaganda and organization—
had been formulated. Superficially, they did not change much in the
subsequent years. The Nazi theorists produced little but glosses on
Hitler's views; party organization and propaganda continued to be

regarded as forming the hard core of the Nazi scheme of things. In fact all these three aspects of National Socialist activity underwent considerable changes. The ideological content of National Socialist agitation of course followed the demands of political circumstances; the party and its propaganda both gained and suffered, after 1933, from their close connexion with the state. Hitler always avidly grasped at every new instrument of power, be it the army or the administrative machinery of the state. The position of propaganda therefore depended largely on Hitler's main preoccupations at the time. It was only during the *Kampfzeit*, the 'period of struggle' which lasted until 30 January 1933, that propaganda retained its privileged position as the highway to power in the state.

This study is an examination of the part played by the manipulation and control of public opinion in the National Socialists' capture and exercise of power in Germany, as well as of the manner in which Hitler's government employed propaganda in its bid for power abroad. The concept of propaganda is understood here in its broadest sense: in the same sense, in fact, the National Socialists themselves employed it.

Lenin's dictum that the Soviet state rested on a balance of persuasion and coercion applies to Hitler's Germany just as much as to all the other one-party states Europe has seen in this century: both coercion and persuasion were, and still are, used to make the state acceptable to its citizens. It appears that the coercive aspects of one-party states exercise a certain fascination on writers and readers alike. In comparison with the vast literature descriptive of coercion, be it in Nazi Germany or the Soviet Union, the attempts of such states to persuade either their own citizens or those of other countries have received little attention. Herein lies the main justification for adding this book to the already voluminous literature on National Socialist Germany. But there are other considerations: the history of National Socialism is now a self-contained unit; in its course a massive attempt at persuasion was made: it is the only one on which documentation is available;[13] because of its lack of ideological content propaganda can be seen to operate, as it were, in its pure form. Also, this was the first time in the history of Europe that propaganda by a one party state was carried out in a highly industrialized society.

Nazi Propaganda

I
The Conquest
of the Masses

On the morning of 20 December 1924, a large Daimler-Benz was parked opposite the entrance to Landsberg prison. The driver and Heinrich Hoffmann, a photographer, were sitting in the car, watching the prison gates. Soon Hitler walked out, a free man after thirteen months of incarceration. Hoffmann was not allowed to photograph him leaving the prison; the three men drove off and then stopped at the gate of the old town wall. There, Hoffmann took several photographs of Hitler, next to the imposing motor car, wearing the familiar belted mackintosh. On the same day, the keen photographer sent the picture to a number of newspapers, with the ambiguous caption: 'Adolf Hitler leaves Landsberg fortress'. It easily lent itself to misinterpretation; indeed, the following day all the newspapers that printed it provided it with dramatic captions, such as 'The first step to freedom' and 'The fortress gate has opened'. Remembering the incident, Hoffmann wrote: 'When I received my copies, I could not help laughing'.[1] The first small dishonesty by propaganda was committed a few hours after Hitler's release from prison.

After the failure of the Munich *putsch* in 1923, the party was in a bad way. It had been banned by the Bavarian government; some of its founding members were left behind in prison; some had not been able to return from exile; a few had died. The Nazis who remained at large quarrelled and had proved themselves incapable of piloting

3

the party safely through the difficult period. Hitler had to start all over again; he returned from prison rested and full of energy.

He had to revive the party and gather the threads of power once again in his own hands. First of all he had to get the ban on the Nazi movement and its newspaper lifted; he succeeded in doing so a fortnight after his release from prison, during a short conversation with the Bavarian Prime Minister. On 26 February, the *Völkischer Beobachter*[2] appeared for the first time after a gap of more than fifteen months. Hitler's name was given as that of the publisher. It printed a proclamation by the Führer on the front page, and an announcement of a great public mass-meeting at the Bürgerbräukeller on the following day, to which all former party members were invited; it was stressed that no Jews could be admitted.

Some four thousand Nazis crowded into the large hall from which the ill-fated *putsch* in November 1923 had been launched; the rivalries among their leaders who came as well as among those who stayed away were deadly. Nevertheless, Hitler's first political meeting was carefully stage-managed. A lot of handshaking took place on the platform, and smiling faces bore witness to the good chances for the rebirth and unity of the party. No discussion or questions were allowed; Max Amann had done a lot to make smooth proceedings possible, and he said that Hitler alone was capable of leading the movement. During a speech that lasted over two hours, Hitler proved that he had not lost his touch as an orator. The audience fell under his spell, and it is possible that some of the more prominent members of the movement, who had resented Hitler's ambitions, came round while he spoke.

Indeed, public speaking was, at the time, Hitler's main propaganda weapon. Although he usually put down 'writer' as his profession at this time, he could not hope to make any political capital out of political writing: it was not a suitable means for the kind of persuading Hitler wanted to do, and anyway he was not very good at it. He was convinced that all the important revolutionary events had been brought about not by the written, but by the spoken word. But Hitler had in mind the relation between the orator and his audience; his inability to sway a small number of *individuals* has often been contrasted with his supreme skill in bending large crowds to his will.[3]

Hitler was at his most effective when his message reached the listener through a haze of mass hysteria; he preferred covincing individuals through the masses rather than the other way round.

By 1925 Hitler's public speaking had acquired all the qualities that put him into a class of his own. He was not an impromptu speaker: usually, he prepared his speeches in advance. They do not read well: their contents alone are not an adequate indication as to the effect they actually created at the time of their delivery. Hitler's power as a speaker lay mainly in the *rapport* he established between himself and his audience. The opening moves of every speech he made were hesitant. The attitude of his body was stiff, he was feeling his way like a blind man; his voice was muted and monotonous. After a few minutes, this apparent unwillingness to communicate gave way to a steadier, louder flow of sentences; the speaker's muscles visibly relaxed, and he was soon to begin using his right arm in gestures that resembled blows aimed at an invisible nail. Then the flow increased into a torrent; the punch-line was delivered in a loud, sometimes hoarse, high-pitched voice; the end was abrupt. A new paragraph, another train of thought, was then introduced in a softer voice, though not in the same halting manner as the opening of the speech; the clockwork was again seen by the spellbound audience to unwind itself, the *crescendo* was once more achieved, and wiped out by a wide sweep of the right arm. The onslaught on the eardrums of the audience was tremendous: it was estimated that the frequency of Hitler's voice in a typical sentence was 228 vibrations per second, whereas 200 vibrations is the usual frequency of a voice raised in anger.[4]

His audiences, whose critical powers were only indifferently developed, were soon battered into a state of passive receptiveness by the torrential flow of Hitler's words. During the two hours or longer, he conducted them through a number of highly emotive states; at the conclusion of the speech, they had shared a profound experience with the speaker. He appealed to the emotions rather than to the reason of his audience; in the words of Hjalmar Schacht, he could play like a virtuoso on the well-tempered piano of the lower-middle-class hearts'.[5] But what Hitler said mattered far less than how he said it; he found the right mould for his speeches early in his career, and he never had to recast it.

During his conversation with Bavaria's Prime Minister in January 1925, Hitler doubtless had made a promise to conduct the activities of the party within the limits of legality: no more revolutions and revolutionary agitation. He was, however, used to moving on the border-line of legitimate political activity and conspiracy; as soon as he mounted the speaker's rostrum, he was unable to control his sentiments against the established authority. On 9 March, ten days after his first appearance in the Bürgerbräukeller, Hitler was forbidden to make public speeches in Bavaria, and soon the governments of other federal states followed suit. In the end he was able to speak only in Thüringia, Braunschweig, and Mecklenburg. This did not mean that the movement entirely lost its most effective means of agitation; meetings were arranged in the three states that had not placed the ban on Hitler, or, if they took place elsewhere, they were advertised as closed meetings for party members; the party publishing house printed Hitler's speeches in pamphlet form in large editions.

Nevertheless, the first concentrated Nazi propaganda campaign was in fact occasioned by the ban on Hitler's public speaking. On 20 April 1926 a meeting in celebration of Hitler's thirty-seventh birthday took place in Munich; at the same time, the party organ published a rather flattering drawing of Hitler's head, with two pieces of sticking plaster across his mouth, bearing the inscription 'Ban on speaking'[6] and the caption: 'Alone among 2,000 million people of the world he is not allowed to speak in Germany!' Hitler put in an appearance at his birthday meeting in Munich, but he remained silent; Julius Streicher spoke on the subject 'Why is Hitler not allowed to speak?', and a letter from the Nazi-organized 'Action Committee for the Organization of People's Protest Against the Ban on Adolf Hitler's Speaking'[7] was presented to Hitler. According to the text of the letter, 1,234 propaganda cells of the *NSDAP* had collected signatures for the protest.

In the following years the Nazis used every means to get the ban lifted. Early in 1927, the legal committee of the *Reichstag* turned down a petition by Dr. Frick, a Nazi deputy; the responsible civil servant said that although the ban was unconstitutional, foreigners could not claim any benefits granted by the constitution.[8] Such pronouncements of course aided the Nazi campaign. It was typical of the corrupt federal government and of the contemptible *Reichstag*, they loudly complained, to treat as a foreigner a man who had been born in the '*Ostmark*'—a term for Austria which reduced that country to the status of a German province—and who had spent four and a half years as a front-line soldier in the German army. After two years, the campaign began paying dividends. On 11 February 1927, Saxony, the last state to have imposed the ban, lifted it; the Bavarian government allowed Hitler to speak in public from 5 March, and, finally, the Prussian authorities did the same in September 1928.

Apart from the ban on Hitler's speaking, the regional governments took a variety of administrative measures against the Nazi movement in the twenties. In June 1925, for instance, public collection of contributions for party coffers was forbidden in Munich; in May 1927 the party was banned in Berlin; in July 1929 the police banned the opening ceremony of the Brown House, the new party headquarters in Munich; at the end of the summer, a trial on charges of high treason of several junior army officers with Nazi leanings took place in Leipzig. But such sporadic attempts as were made never seriously threatened the party's existence; they were only too easily exploited by the Nazi propagandists, who presented them as administrative chicanery directed against a respectable patriotic movement.

The Nazis were not seriously disturbed in their pursuits in the last years of the decade. Their mass-meetings were frequent and carefully arranged around a speech by Hitler or other prominent members of the movement; they did away with any semblance of democratic procedure. The rank-and-file members of the party were always presented with one voice and one opinion; no questions were ever asked. Mass-meetings usually took place, on weekdays and weekends alike, late in the evening—they usually began at 8 p.m.— when, as Hitler knew, man's suggestibility was high, and his resistance at its lowest ebb. The pattern of the Nazi assemblies was developed during these years; their programme was arranged with the precision of a railway time-table. The *Parteitag*—the party rally—was the sum total of the various forms of Nazi meetings, and it was designed to be the crowning experience of party life for the rank-and-file members.

The first and last of these congresses before the unsuccessful

Munich *putsch* had taken place in January 1923; by the middle of
1926, the party had recovered sufficiently to hold such a rally. The
second *Parteitag* in the history of the *NSDAP* took place in Weimar,
on 3 and 4 July. In the afternoon of the first day, some 10,000 Nazis
assembled in Marktplatz, the main square in Weimar, and the meeting was concluded by a parade of the party para-military organizations, the *SA* and the *SS,* before Hitler. In the evening of the first day
of the Weimar rally, Hitler spoke at the National Theatre on the
subject 'Politics, Idea, and Organization': the meeting ran on customary lines. First, the rank-and-file members walked in and took their
seats; then the uniformed troopers, carrying their standards, arrived
and took up their positions— they were there for decorative purposes
and to maintain order—then the leaders of the movement walked
down the centre passage and, last of all, Hitler himself. The tension
that had been built up among the audience by the introductory proceedings lasted through the first hesitating sentences of his speech;
it was released by the increasing torrent of words.

In August of the following year, another *Parteitag* was arranged,
the first of the famous Nürnberg rallies. According to the estimates
of the local railway officials, more than 100,000 Nazis were brought to
Nürnberg in special trains;[9] fifty members of the Berlin *SA* had marched all the way from the capital to Bavaria. The main programme of
the rally was opened by a 'congress of delegates' on Saturday morning, 20 August; the day was closed by an effective innovation: a torch-
light procession of the *SA.* Many of the visitors to the rally spent the
night sleeping on the floors, thinly covered with straw, of the vast
exhibition pavilions at Luitpoldhain; early on Sunday morning they
were rewarded by watching their Führer present colours to twelve
detachments of the *SA.* Shortly before 11 a.m., some 30,000 *SA* and
SS troops, together with contingents from Austria and Czechoslovakia marched past Hitler in the main square.

Year after year the party celebrated its high mass at Nürnberg: as
one of the National Socialist leaders put it, the Nürnberg rallies were
meant to transmit "new spiritual strength." Some of the important
events took place at night when the assembled Nazis were at their
most receptive. Those were the sacred hours for the party and its
members, and they were meant to remember them. They did. Profes-

sor Beno von Arent, a theatrical director who later received the title of *Reichsbühnenbildner*—the imperial producer of stage sets—was responsible for many such spectacular events.

The Nürnberg rally in the summer of 1927 had all the basic features of Nazi stage management. The leader and his speeches, the open-air demonstration and the large indoor meeting; the flags, the insignia, the songs, the *Heil* greetings. These were by no means brand-new techniques of political agitation; what was new, however, was the intensive and calculated use that was made of them.

Hitler took a close interest in the *façade* his movement presented to the outside world. As a young man he had been turned down by the school of architecture of the Viennese Academy and instead painted postcards and advertising posters to earn his living. As a politician Hitler could play out the frustrations of his youth on a big scale.

The flag was the centrepiece of the Nazi decorative scheme. It remained for them, as it had been in the past, a military rallying point; it was the subject matter of many of their songs: it provided the hypnotic, repetitive pattern for the backcloth of their public meetings. Hitler wrote that he "laid down, after countless attempts, its final form". The red background stood for socialism: the white of the central circle for nationalism. But the significance of the swastika—a Sanskrit word for good fortune and well-being—the main part of the emblem, was less certain.

It became the symbol of infinity, of the sun, of recreation; it was found on the textiles of the Incas, on relics in the excavations in Troy, in the catacombs in Rome. It was one of the sacred signs of Buddhism from where it passed into European literature. Kipling knew the sign well: it was also imprinted on the books published for the circle of Stefan George. In the Austria of Hitler's youth at least one crank, Adolf Lanz von Liebenfels, took it for an Indian—and therefore, in his racial theories, Aryan—symbol. On a Christmas day around the turn of the century a swastika flag apparently flew from the tower of a derelict castle on the Danube, where Lanz briefly attempted to run a colony of racially pure blue-eyed blondes. For Hitler, the sign had similar racial connotations, symbolising the victory of the Aryan man and of creative work, which "in itself has been eternally antisemitic". When, in 1921, the first Nazi flag was unfurled the effect was so

profound that Hitler himself was pleased and surprised. It survived
until 1945: between 1933 and 1935 the *Hakenkreuz* flag flew side by
side with the German national colours, replacing them as the sole
emblem of the Third Reich in September 1935.

Every National Socialist organization had its own flag: the war
flag (*Reichskriegsflagge*) was developed from the imperial war flag
of 1871-1918, and it had the Iron Cross at its centre; the Hitler Youth
Flag had red-white-red stripes as the background to the swastika; the
German Labour Front's (*Arbeitsfront*) swastika was placed inside a
cogwheel. The head-piece on the Roman-style *SA* standard was a
three-dimensional replica of the design on the front page of the
Völkischer Beobachter. It incorporated the eagle: apparently Hitler
had found it described as the 'Aryan in the world of animals' in an
antisemitic encyclopedia: it was also important for him that the eagle
was 'Striving upward'.

On the Nazi flags and emblems red and white predominated; only
the association of German Young People (*Deutsch Jungvolk*) had
a black flag with white runic signs. The preoccupation with perspectives, the preference by Nazi organisers for nocturnal events and
their technical mastery of the play of light and darkness: they were
setting the stage for an opera by Wagner. The Nazi music—their
song-books contain a large collection of National Socialist pop—
underscored the irrational element of the movement. The shouted
primitive tune, the shabby lyricism of the text, the total lack of hu-
mour, the insistent beat of drums and the thin, reedy sound of pipes
provided the answers to Hitler's followers: no questions had to be
asked. The postwar despair and degradation of the people; the freedom to rearm, loyalty to the nation or to the movement and punishment for dissent; the trumpet call to renewed struggle; such were the
favourite themes of Nazi songs.

Many of them were taken over from the postwar *Freikorps* repertoire; Dietrich Eckart, a friend of Hitler's, gave the Nazis the first song
of their own. It was a *Tonpoem* rather than a song; it was first sung at
a rally in 1923 and carefully rehearsed by Hitler himself. It began with
the line '*Sturm, Sturm, Sturm*' and ended with '*Deutschland er-
wache!*'—Germany awake!—which became the Nazis' favourite
battle-cry. The *Horst Wessel Lied*, the ponderous march which

celebrated the movement and its flag, the struggle of the 'brown battalions' against both the *Rotfront* on the Left and *Reaktion* on the Right, joined the Nazi repertoire in 1927. Six years later it became the second part of the German national anthem.

Another favourite sound effect of the movement was the *Heil* greeting. It had been used by the *Wandervögel*, the back-to-nature movement before the First World War, as well as by some nationalist elements in such variations as '*Im deutschem Namen Heil*' and '*Sieg und Heil*'. The Nazis later reduced it to the more succint '*Sieg Heil*' which was used as a chant at mass demonstrations. The alternative greeting *Heil Hitler*, more appropriate for encounters between two party members, had first appeared on banners in the Munich municipal elections in 1924. It was just as well that, when young Adolf was twelve years old, his father had changed his name from Schickelgruber to Hitler.

Hitler was not interested in converting the intellectuals. When he was in power, and talking about the kind of people he wanted to grow up, he said 'I do not want intellectual education. Knowledge would spoil my youth. I should most like to let them learn only what they absorb freely through play. But they will have to learn self-control. They will have to learn it for use in the toughest trials to win over the fear of death. . . .' [10] He had nothing to say to men like Karl Kraus, the inventive Viennese satirist, who dismissed Hitler tartly— 'In regard to Hitler, nothing occurs to me'. When Hitler spoke he wanted men to grind their teeth and women to sob. We have evidence that, quite often, they did. He tapped a deep well of emotion in German life.

The enthusiasm in 1914, the demand and the necessity for national unity in the following four years, the excitement of the World War was followed by the Versailles treaty, and a frightening silence. Hitler broke that silence: compared with the dull, hopeless speeches of the middle class politicians of the Weimar Republic—the men who had to cope with the practical consequences of defeat—Hitler's message was one of hope. He saw the National Socialist era as a watershed, the beginning of the history of the Great German Empire—the *Grossdeutsche Reich.*

In the years after the war the defeat which had bemused Germany,

and the role of Hitler in breaking the spell, was the centrepiece of
Nazi propaganda. National resurrection had to be fought for hard;
for Hitler and his followers fight was the purpose of life. They did
not see it, at first, in terms of a military campaign, conducted by
armies and divisions. Hitler had personally experienced the struggle
of a young lower middle class man down on his luck; he had witnessed
the decline of political influence of the Germans in the Habsburg
Empire before the First World War; he had lived through the defeat
of the German army. In that way Hitler's determination to struggle
against misfortune took shape. The social Darwinists, who had made
their contribution to European thought late in the 19th century by
translating the struggle to survive from the world of animals to the
world of people, came to his aid. In the minds of Hitler and his followers, the struggle to survive became confused with class and racial
theories.

The invention of the blond, blue-eyed beast—the most likely
animal to survive—was borrowed from Nietzsche. In National Socialist imagination, it had the dynamic will to expansion, essential for the
colonisation of the new territories, especially of the Slav East. Somewhere along the line, the attributes of the new breed of man became
confused. On the recurrent image of the Norman and his mode of
operation—sudden assault, incendiarism, plunder, swift withdraw-
al—there was superimposed the figure of the Teutonic knight, with
the appropriate virtues, pushing the Slav barbarians beyond the
eastern marshlands.

Though the National Socialists did not have, as we have already
noted, a coherent ideology, there was a certain consistency in their
ideas. Antisemitism was an extension of their racial theories which
could be put to important propaganda uses; the confused romantic
images were backed up the teaching of the German *volkisch*—
populist-philosophers. Their targets had been many: taxes and
capital, stock exchanges and industry, economics and politics.[11]
They all derived from a common source: the urban life of the 19th
century. Its complexities puzzled the new arrivals from the countryside in the fast growing suburbs, as much as the populist philosophers.
Most of them were teachers who belonged to the lower half of the
middle class; they advocated return to the ideals of old German

patriarchal society. Hitler had witnessed in Vienna the activities of politicians like Lueger before the First World War, and the uses the Mayor of Vienna had made of the discontent of the new immigrants into his town; here, German populism was translated into political action. And the Jews, the town-dwellers in that part of Europe, could be blamed for the abuses of modern urban life.

The emotion generated by Nazi propaganda and the show the movement presented to the Germans stood out against the drabness of everyday life in the Weimar Republic. It was a splash of bright colour on the subdued background of postwar Germany.

But these were the gentle means of persuasion used by the Nazis. Propaganda alone was not enough for them: we have already noted Hitler's views on its connexions with violence.[12] The same idea was stated openly and concisely by Eugen Hadamovsky, who later became the chief of German broadcasting: 'Propaganda and the graduated use of violence have to be employed together in a skilful manner. They are never absolutely opposed to each other. The use of violence can be a part of propaganda: it was their "hard sell" technique'.[13] This axiom had far-reaching practical consequences for the Nazis. They knew that, if they wanted to carry out their propaganda successfully, they had to dominate the streets. In the words of the *Horst Wessellied*. 'Free the street for the brown battalions'.

When the Nazi movement embarked on its public career early in the decade, the streets belonged to the Communists and the Social Democrats. The National Socialists showed themselves in the public thoroughfares of Munich only fleetingly, being conveyed on lorries to their meetings at one or other of the beercellars. But in order to be able to break out into the streets, they had to gain strength as a powerful para-military organization. We have already seen that any disturbance, even mild heckling, had no place in Hitler's conception of political meetings; since the early days of the movement, there were always *Ordner* present, men whose task was to ensure smooth proceedings: they were the chuckers-out of political enemies.

In addition, the bloody encounters played, especially in the early history of the party, an important role in securing publicity for it. In an official textbook for German youth which appeared in Berlin in 1938, the author flatly stated that 'The greatest difficulty of the party lay in the fact that . . . nobody took any notice of it'. Rough methods of keeping order at meetings helped. 'Now at last', the author went on in his bright manner, the party had found the means to shake the newspapers from their icy reserve! Here was the rope by which it could pull itself from the depths of being ignored to the daylight of 'public opinion'. The criticism of its endeavours made in the press was very acid and unfriendly, because its wishes and aims were never touched upon. From now on, therefore, every opportunity was grasped to answer even the most insignificant provocation by a neat chucking-out. And lo and behold! From this time on, the bourgeois and the Red press dealt with the bad Nazis almost every day.[14]

The meeting at Munich Hofbräuhaus on 4 November 1921 was officially regarded as the foundation date of the *Sturmabteilungen*.[15] On this occasion, a large number of 'Marxists' came to listen to Hitler's speech, and a clash occurred between them and the Nazis. This was the first *Saalschlacht*—a battle in a political assembly hall—in which the Nazis took part, and there were many bloodly engagements to come; it was a gang warfare with its own rules. At this time, the Nazis were not only unable to show themselves in public but they also had a difficult time of it protecting their own meetings against hostile intruders from the street.

The *SA* troops were originally divided into groups of one hundred men, the *Hundertschaften*; by September 1922, eight 'hundreds' were in existence in Munich; on 23 November, the organization of the eleventh unit was completed under the leadership of Rudolf Hess. Hitler intended these units to show the 'Marxists' that National Socialism is 'the future ruler of the street just as it will eventually become the ruler of the state'.[16] Indeed, the domination of the street was, for the Nazis, the key to political power in the state.

In August 1922, several *SA* units demonstrated, together with other extreme right-wing groups, against the law for the protection of the Republic; in October, they ventured unaided into the streets of Coburg, during the celebrations of the *Deutsche Tag*. Hitler arrived in a special train, together with some eight hundred *SA* troopers on 14 October, and they marched into the streets of the provincial town in North Bavaria; after some short, sharp clashes they succeeded in clearing the streets of their political opponents.

This was a memorable day for Hitler: ten years later all the surviving participants of the Coburg march received a special decoration.

In 1922 and early 1923, the foundations of Hitler's para-military organization were laid. The first application forms for entry into the *SA* were printed, and they put special stress on enquiries into the military experience of the applicant; a rudimentary uniform made its first appearance. Early in 1923 their first standards, designed by Hitler, appeared at the *SA* congress in Munich; two months later, Hermann Göring, the last commander of the famous Richthofen flying squadron in the First World War, took over the command of all the *SA* units.

At this time—in March 1923—a group of eight men was separated from the main body of the *SA*, and set up as Hitler's personal bodyguard under the command of Julius Schreck. It became known as *Stosstrupp Hitler*, the forerunner of the *SS*. When Hitler re-established the party in February 1925, the *SA* was still banned; in the following year, the ban was lifted and the stormtroopers reappeared at the Weimar rally. For the time being, the small *Schutzstaffel* took over the original duty of the *SA*, namely that of *Ordner* at political meetings. In the circumstances, the task of the early *SS* men was extremely difficult, and they had to be recruited from the toughest members of the former *SA*. Hitler was allowed to speak in Saxony and Thüringia,[17] and a large number of meetings were organized there; the two states had strong Communist parties—they were 'at the time entirely red Saxony and Thüringia' in Nazi terminology[18]— and the *SS* often found it difficult to prevent the enemies of the Nazi party from breaking up its meetings. Nevertheless, when the *SA* re-emerged in the course of 1926, its members once more took care of the party meetings, and the *SS*, some two hundred strong at the time, was incorporated into the older organization, and placed under the authority of its Supreme Command. Only three years later, early in 1929, the future began to look brighter for the *SS* men when Heinrich Himmler was asked by Hitler to built the organization into an *élite* corps of the party.

In the meantime, however, Hitler placed his reliance on the *SA*. On 1 November 1926, its Supreme Command was established in Munich, with Franz von Pfeffer, the party leader from the Ruhr area, as its head; in the following months, a thorough reorganization of the *SA* was carried out. At the rally of 1927, the stormtroopers arrived in full strength: no dissentient voice was heard either at the party meetings or in the streets of Nürnberg. The Nazis were able to take over the town for the duration of the *Parteitag*. Nevertheless, the place for the meeting had to be carefully chosen, and Nürnberg was a highly suitable location. It was not the capital of a state, and it was surrounded by the provinces with strong Nazi party organizations: it was easily accessible, for instance, to party members from the neighbouring Bayrische Ostmark.[19]

Indeed, the varying local conditions profoundly affected the life of the party in these years. Its main strength was still concentrated in Bavaria; in many other German states the Nazis found themselves faced with a hostile attitude on the part of both the local authorities and the population. There was no question of holding the 1927 *Parteitag* in, say, Berlin, instead of Nürnberg. In May that year, the Prussian authorities banned the party and the *SA*; in a number of other German states, the ban on the *SA* uniform also became operative. The *SA* leaders tried to circumvent these bans as best they could It was quite simple to ignore the ban on uniforms, and to exploit it for the purposes of propaganda. The National Socialists were able to publicize yet another example of 'chicanery' by the administration; the *SA* troops arrived at their meetings in white shirts, or half naked, or in their underclothes. After May 1927 Dr. Goebbels coined the slogan for the Berlin *SA* '*Trotz Verbot, nicht tot*'—not dead despite the ban ; many of the Berlin stormtroopers went to the Nürnberg rally, and they put on their uniforms in the special trains on the way to Bavaria; some of the forgetful enthusiasts who omitted to change into their civilian clothes on the return journey to Berlin were arrested when they got off the train.

In Berlin, the characteristic *Saalschlachten* of the 'period of struggle' took place just as in other German towns; the battle in the Pharus assembly hall, the 'fortress of Berlin Communism,'[20] on 11 February 1927, was the first of many fierce engagements. But here, in the German capital, the stormtroopers developed a new technique of offensive warfare. In the late twenties they were faced with powerful opposition, Social Democrat and Communist, among the Berlin workers; they split up into small groups, which met in private flats and then, anonymous in dark streets, proceeded to break up any Communist or Socialist meeting going on. Such commando tactics were suitable and successful in the circumstances; for an effective terrorist activity a small number of men was sufficient, and they could operate regardless of official bans. In the words of an official Nazi pamphlet, the *SA* became 'the fist and the propaganda arm'[21] of the movement; apart from providing very useful publicity for the party, and formation of a political army injected an element of violence into the propaganda effort, an element that appeared indispensable to the Nazi theorists.

In terms of numbers, however, the party was far from being a formidable movement in the years before the economic slump; in 1927, only 72,590 Germans paid their membership dues to the *NSDAP.*[22] But Hitler knew how to display the comparatively small numbers to their best advantage: the overall impression created by the Nürnberg rally was one of a highly disciplined, powerful movement. This was largely due to the *SA* organization which amounted, at this time, to nearly half the total registered membership of the party. And with good stage-management, the march-past of some 30,000 stormtroopers could be spun out to last five hours, and create the impression that the stream of partisans of the new movement was indeed endless. The marchers themselves, on the other hand, achieved a still more intense emotional state than the onlookers. They were proud to be marching under the swastika flag; they were self-assured, superior; they belonged to a select community.[23] Their intoxication bound them more closely together; if marching could have such a powerful effect, fighting the common enemy proved a still stronger tie. The *Saalschlacht*, the street battles, the sudden commando raids, were not merely a means of intimidating political opponents. On this subject, Otto Strasser, a Nazi who had to flee Germany in 1935, wrote from his Canadian exile: 'The battle, however, rather than destroying the purpose of our meeting, actually strengthened it enormously. All those who still remained in the hall after the fight had taken our side in a sort of spontaneous partnership. The bitter struggle had brought about that spirit of *camaraderie* which is engendered when men go through physical conflict together. A short time before they had been doubtful of us, suspicious, as are all human beings of an offer of something for nothing. Now that attitude was changed. We had become allies if only by force of circumstance'.[24]

While Hitler was on his way to supreme power, the Nazis transformed the streets of German towns into a battlefield. Theirs was, of course, not the only movement that had 'political troops' at its disposal. *Reichsbanner*—an association for the protection of the Republic—commanded a strong fighting section; there was the ex-servicemen's *Stahlhelm* and the Communist *Rotfront-Kämpferbund* and the *Antifaschistischer Kämpfbund*; the Bavarian People's Party was a latecomer with its *Bayernwacht*. Indeed, in the words of Mr. Clark, a contemporary observer of Germany's political scene:[25] 'if one had the military imagination, the parties seemed like phantoms and these [i.e. the para-military organizations] the only realities. If they were all let loose the Thirty Years War would rank as a minor catastrophe'. As a weapon of propaganda, the *SA* came to rank perhaps higher than Hitler's speeches. To stimulate emotion and violence, and to benefit by their interaction, were the first aims of Nazi propagandists. They were, however, less successful in translating this method into the terms of the printed word.

We know that writing took for Hitler a much inferior second place to speaking; it was clear that the effect of his speeches, when printed in pamphlet form during the official *Redeverbot*,[26] fell far short of the impact of the actual speech. But Hitler believed, possibly quite mistakenly, in the necessity of owning a newspaper; after all, every political movement ran its own organ. A newspaper was for him a sign that the movement was prospering; it was an advance from the time when the party had to rely on meetings and leaflets only. He developed his views on the press early in his career, and they were those of a rabid nationalist. One of the points of the party programme that was first expounded at a meeting in Munich on 24 February 1920 dealt exclusively with the press: 'We demand a legislative fight against conscious political lies and their spreading by the press. In order to make the creation of a German press possible, we demand that (a) All editors and writers on newspapers printed in the German language must be compatriots (*Volksgenossen*). (b) State permission will be necessary for the publication of non-German newspapers. They must not be printed in the German language. (c) Every kind of financial backing of German newspapers or influence on them by non-Germans will be forbidden by law, and we demand as punishment for its breach the closing down of the newspaper as well as an immediate deportation of the foreigners who participated in it. Newspapers which oppose public welfare are to be forbidden. We demand a legislative fight against such trends in art and literature that have a corrosive effect on our national life and the closing down of institutions that run counter to the above-mentioned demands'. [27]

Some months after the publication of this programme the party acquired the *Völkischer Beobachter*. The National Socialist organ was some thirty-two years older than the party. In January 1887 a Munich printer began to publish a weekly, the *Münchener Beobachter*, as the trade journal of the local butchers' guild. After an eventful but obscure existence it became, in August 1919, the *Völkischer Beobachter*. It was then run on *völkisch* and antisemitic lines, until, in December 1920, the National Socialist party bought it for 120,000 Marks. [28]

The early history of the Nazi press is closely connected with the development of this paper. The issue of 25 December 1920, which brought the announcement that the paper had been taken over by the *NSDAP,* was printed in 800 copies only; its first Nazi editor was soon succeeded by Dietrich Eckart, the poet, and Alfred Rosenberg, the ideologist of the movement, as joint editors. During the first two years as the organ of the party, the *Völkischer Beobachter* frequently ran into difficulties; it was often confiscated or banned. When it became, in August 1923, a daily, it was still a local Bavarian newspaper; its circulation had, however, risen to some 25,000 copies. After the failure of the *putsch,* the *Völkischer Beobachter* disappeared from the Munich newspaper stands until 26 February 1925; in its special number on that day — the official date of the 're-establishment' of the party — it printed Hitler's exhortation to its readers for the setting up of a press fund. 'If one can judge the value of a newspaper by the hatred of its enemies, then it was the most valuable paper in Germany', Hitler wrote, and he added: 'The hatred of Jews, of the Marxist criminals, of racketeers like Barmat and Kutisker, was poured out on no other newspaper as much as on the organ of the *NSDAP*, the *Völkischer Beobachter*'. [29]

When the newspaper reappeared in February 1925, 10,000 copies were printed; from 4 April onwards, it again became a daily, and its circulation climbed, albeit slowly, until it reached in 1929 the figure of 26,715 copies.[30] In July 1926, the *Illustrierter Beobachter,* the party organ's sister publication, began to appear in the course of the rally in Weimar. The oldest ally of the official Nazi newspaper was Julius Streicher's weekly, *Der Stürmer,* the first numbers of which appeared in Nürnberg in November 1923, shortly before the Munich *putsch*; it also suffered a temporary eclipse after the ban on the party and its press. The circulation of these three newspapers was largely confined to South Germany in the nineteen-twenties; in Berlin, the Strasser brothers, Gregor and Otto, ran their own organ, the *Berliner Arbeiterzeitung.* Hitler disapproved of the *Arbeiterzeitung* as much as he did of its publishers; the balance on the press front in Berlin began to change in Hitler's favour when Goebbels—he had deserted the Strassers and was now giving his full support to Hitler[31]—launched his small weekly, *Der Angriff,* in July 1927. From 1 October 1929, it started to appear twice a week, and from November of the following year daily.

Indeed, until the Nazi success in the elections in September 1930, the party press did not do at all well. In the summer of that year, only six Nazi dailies were printed in the whole of Germany; five of them appeared in Bavaria, and one in Schleswig-Holstein. And of the Bavarian daily newspapers, only the *Völkischer Beobachter* had some tenuous claims to be described as a national newspaper. It was then printing a Berlin, as well as a Munich, edition; its circulation was, however, still rather low—84,511 copies were sold in 1930.[32] Apart from the dailies, there were some forty-three weeklies and other periodicals; they commanded—apart perhaps from the *Illustrierter Beobachter*—little influence and a small readership.

The failure of the Nazi press could not be explained by financial and technical difficulties only. Although it had a certain prestige value for the Nazi leaders, it was not a very suitable vehicle for their propaganda. As late as January 1932, Goebbels complained in his diary: 'Only a few flames are burning in Germany. The others only reflect their light. With the newspapers it's worst: we have the best speakers in the world, but we lack nimble and skilful pens'.[33] There was a good reason for this: the movement did not attract many writers and journalists, and anyway, the translation of Nazi propaganda into the cold columns of the printed word was far from easy. The Nazis of course had to make the attempt, and they produced some interesting innovations.

In all their publications, the leader was short, hard-hitting, calculated to attract immediate attention, to strike a responsive chord rather than to stimulate reflection in the reader. The Nazis did not indulge in the long thoughtful leading articles, the hall-mark of the German Socialist press; nor were they tempted to follow the earlier practice of the Social Democrat organs of printing learned tracts on academic subjects. The *Illustrierter Beobachter* was intended to be a popular tabloid newspaper; in its early issues, it exhibited the characteristic features that were to be found, to a greater or lesser extent, in all the Nazi press. It contained news items of course but they were largely dedicated to the greater glory of the movement: the paper first appeared immediately after the rally in July 1926, and it contained impressive photographs of the proceedings in Weimar. Political *reportage* continued to be confined, almost exclusively, to one subject: the National Socialist movement marching forward. Pictures of meetings, demonstrations, and processions were always present: reporting on other topics, insofar as it took place at all, was heavily slanted, and since no demand for objective reporting was ever formulated by the Nazis, there was no need to distinguish between fact and comment.

Violence, death and sex also found their place in the Nazi press. Although the party journalists were no prudes, their treatment of these subjects was prudish in a special sense. The London tabloid newspapers, for instance, deal with such items on their own merits: they are reported because they are starkly dramatic and they have an obvious appeal. The Nazi journalists gave them a new twist. The murder of a peaceful citizen caused by jealousy, desire for gain — any of the 'civil' motives — was of no interests to them; the death of an *SA* trooper in a beer-hall fight, on the other hand, was a highly charged subject, which was invariably given a lot of space. Scandalous gossip about the Jews also rated high on the priority list — this form of journalism had been introduced by Julius Streicher in *Der*

Stürmer. 'Ritual murder', for instance, was a hardy perennial; it combined antisemitism, violence, and sex in equal proportions.

Neither truth nor objectivity were regarded as ideals worthy of achievement. The political struggle, the social scene, had to be presented in the simplest terms of black and white. Nevertheless, the Nazis did not rely only on generalizations; both Streicher and Goebbels preferred to concentrate their attacks on individuals instead, and to invest them with all the hateful qualities they could think of. Goebbels in particular developed this technique in *Der Angriff.* He would pick on a member of the Weimar Republic's 'establishment' — Dr. Weiss, the Jewish deputy chief of the Berlin police, was his favourite target — and then heap abuse upon his head, involve him in scandals, and denigrate his character. Goebbels was fortunate in having the services of '*Mjoelnir*', the *Angriff* cartoonist and a poster painter, at his disposal who drove home the simple political points.[34]

Goebbels's influence on Nazi propaganda was not confined to *Der Angriff.* He had been associated with the Strassers, and he had worked for them in the Rhineland, when the two brothers were building up the party organization in that area and in North Germany. They did so independently of Hitler; although he succeeded in avoiding an open breach with them in 1926, theirs was an uneasy truce. Hitler soon began making his own arrangements in the capital: late that year, he appointed Goebbels the *Gauleiter* in Berlin. When he arrived in the capital, Goebbels was entirely Hitler's man; two years later he was appointed the director of propaganda, a key position in the Nazi hierarchy.

When he arrived in Berlin, there was a copy of *Mein Kampf* in his suitcase, personally inscribed by Hitler. We have no reason to suppose that he disagreed with any of the views on the subject of propaganda expounded in the book. He was a more professional speaker than Hitler. His effects were calculated, he was highly adaptable with regard to the mood of his audience, he could switch emotion on and off. He was an accomplished and successful orator, and there was a high charge of cynicism in his performance. In Berlin he faced a difficult taks, and in some respects he improved on the high standards of political agitation set by Hitler. He had to break the hold of

Communist and Social Democrat organizations on the working-class population of the capital: in Bavaria, Hitler had never faced such a stark situation. Violence and the fight against 'Marxism' went hand in hand as far as Goebbels was concerned, and they were the main features of the bitterly contested 'Battle for Berlin'. Goebbels had no choice but to carry the struggle into the camp of the enemy: the party organisation he took over on his arrival was weak, and he had to build it up in the heat of the battle. The shock tactics he used in furthering the Nazi cause in Berlin made the activities of his friends in Bavaria appear leisurely and gentlemanly pursuits.

Goebbels wasted no time in joining the battle. Early in February 1927, he began to advertise a meeting to take place on 11 February, in the Pharus-Saele in the working-class district called Wedding. Glaring posters in red and black ink announced: 'The middle-class state [*Bürgerstaat*] is approaching its doom. A new Germany must be forged: workers of the brain and of the hands, you can decide the fate of Germany On Friday 11 February, at the Pharus-Saele: Subject: The Break Down of the Bourgeois Class-State.'[35] The suggestion that the middle-class state was on the way out could hardly have sounded incredible to a Communist; the announcement itself was not very offensive, even to the opponents of the Nazis, and it did not introduce any distinctly Nazi political jargon. But the movement was already known in Berlin, the first blows had been exchanged, and neither side was in doubt as to what exactly the advertised meeting meant. It was a declaration of war.

The Pharus-Saele was a large, suburban emporium of entertainment; it contained a cinema, a theatre, an assembly room, a beer-garden. And so far the Communists had used it for their general meetings; their local organization met there nearly every week. Shortly before 8 p.m. on 11 February, an excited and impatient Goebbels arrived at the meeting; the *SS* leader reported to him that the hall had been closed by the police at 7.15 because it was too full, and that two-thirds of the audience consisted of members of the Red Front fighting organization. 'This was what we wanted', Goebbels later wrote in his book of recollections. 'The decision must be made here. This way or that. And we were ready to give all we had'.[36] The atmosphere in the hall, filled with tobacco and beer fumes, was tense when

Goebbels entered. There were cat-calls and abuse from the audience as soon as it recognized the Nazi *Gauleiter*; there was no doubt that his supporters were in the minority. Some twenty *SA* troopers surrounded the speaker's platform; when their leader attempted to open the meeting, he was unable to do so. The din in the hall continued and soon fighting flared up. The battle was short and bloody; there are two accounts of what happened after its conclusion. Goebbels himself wrote that the Nazis succeeded in clearing the hall of their enemies unaided. The noise of the *Saalschlacht* was followed by an icy silence, interrupted by the groans of the wounded; there were some Nazi casualties lying on the speaker's platform. According to Goebbels, there were no Nazi first-aid men present.[37] 'Workers-Samaritans' had to be relied on; they were not very sympathetic, and they abused even the stormtroopers who had been seriously wounded. According to another account,[38] the police intervened and the Communists dispersed. When order was restored, Goebbels had the Nazi stretcher-cases brought to the platform, and then proceeded to make a speech against the gory background. Be that as it may, there can be no doubt that Goebbels made his speech surrounded by the Nazi wounded, and that he developed, on this occasion, the concept of the unknown *SA* stormtrooper—the martyr and the hero.

Until 1929, the technical equipment at the disposal of Nazi propagandists was rather primitive. The means of mass communication —large-circulation press, films, radio, and television—instruments that now appear indispensable to totalitarian régimes—were usually absent during the rise to power, both in Russia and in Germany, of the totalitarian parties. The Nazis had their 'propaganda lorries', which carried posters and people shouting slogans; they advertised the *Völkischer Beobachter* by means of mock armoured cars. But until the Nazi election victory in 1930, their press and other printed matter did not command mass circulation and, apart from their meetings, the Nazis had no other way of reaching their public; even microphones were not available for their speakers until the later nineteen-twenties. The end of the decade marked the turning point in their fortunes. In October 1929, Stresemann died, and soon afterwards the Young Plan for reparations was ratified by the *Reichstag*; then the economic slump put an end to Germany's short-lived prosperity.

While these momentous events were taking place, Hitler entered into an alliance with Alfred Hugenberg. Hugenberg had a varied career behind him: he began it as a civil servant in German Poland; soon after the turn of the century he found his way into industry through family connexions; when he was thirty-seven years old, he was appointed chairman of the directors of the Krupp consortium. He joined Ullstein and Mosse as one of the three largest publishers when he bought the Scherl Verlag in 1916; ten years later he acquired the controlling interest in UFA, the film company which ran its own weekly newsreel as well as an extensive chain of cinemas. He was, however, thwarted by the government in the attempt to bring under his control the nascent German broadcasting system. He developed his political interests at the same time; a man without strong political convictions, he was, in the view of a contemporary of his, a 'political calculating machine, completely cold, thinking in relative terms only. The point of his endeavour is to possess political power'.[39] Shortly before he met Hitler, Hugenberg became the chairman of the German National Party; the alliance, dating from the autumn of 1929, was highly attractive to both men. Hugenberg had connexions in the world of industry and finance as well as his communications empire on his side; Hitler had direct access to the masses. On the crucial points, their political views did not differ, both men abhorred the Socialists as much as the Versailles Treaty or the Young Plan. Although Hitler was to break this alliance, it fulfilled a very useful purpose for the Nazi movement while it lasted. The *Berliner Lokalanzeiger*, the *Tag*, and the illustrated weekly the *Woche*, were among the newspapers controlled by the Scherl Verlag; Hugenberg also owned influential news and feature agencies. They all gave Hitler favourable publicity; in the *Ufa Wochenschau*, the weekly newsreel, the Nazi movement often found its way, during the Hitler-Hugenberg alliance, on to the screens of the German cinemas.

Despite the efforts of the Nazi leadership, the party had done only moderately well in the years between 1925 and 1928. At the end of 1928, it commanded a following of 108,717 registered members;[40] at the general elections on 20 May, it polled 809,939 votes, and it sent twelve deputies to the *Reichstag*. Its advance showed considerable regional variations: the number of local party organizations in Essen rose only from 9 to 11 and in Düsseldorf from 20 to 21 in those three years. In Berlin the picture looked brighter, largely due to the energetic work by Goebbels; here 28 local organizations existed in 1928 as compared with 9 in 1925. Nevertheless, Bavaria still provided the best recruiting ground for the Nazis. In Franconia, a district that included Nürnberg, the number of local organizations rose from 18 to 36 between 1925 and 1928; in Upper Bavaria from 16 to 23; the Bavarian Ostmark—a district which bordered on Czechoslovakia—registered a record growth from 57 to 115 organizations.[41] In these years the foundations of the party organization were broadened; the two para-military organizations, the *SA* and the *SS*, were joined, at the time of the Weimar rally in 1926, by the *Hitlerjugend*, the Nazi youth organization; the *Frauenorden*, the women's society, was officially incorporated into the party in January 1928.

The characteristic brand of Nazi radicalism had no great appeal to the Germans during a time of comparative prosperity. This was already apparent during 1924—Hitler was in prison at the time—in the course of the two *Reichstag* elections in that year. In May the party still benefited from the aftermath of the inflation, and it received 6.5 per cent of the total poll; in the winter, the number of votes cast for it declined sharply to 3 per cent. After 're-establishment' of the party in 1925, those sections of the population which derived no benefit from the improving economic situation—salaried men, former officers, white-collar workers as well as small artisans and shopkeepers and the permanently unemployed—continued to be a receptive audience for Nazi propaganda. In those years, the party remained largely confined to the discontented sections of urban population, without making any significant impression in the countryside.

This situation began to change towards the end of 1927. The break-down of the price structure of agricultural produce then occasioned a feeling of panic among small farmers, and the *NSDAP* began to identify itself with their interests. The first moves in this direction were made by the Nazi leaders during the election campaign in 1928; two years later, in the campaign of 1930, their agitation in the countryside was in full swing. Working on the principle that the memory of the masses was exceedingly short, the Nazi propagandists disregarded their previous declarations on agricultural policy; their propaganda effort was nimble and completely opportunist. On 6 March, an 'Official party announcement on the attitude of the *NSDAP* towards the peasantry and agriculture' was published. It quietly dropped the demand for land reform (although the large land-owners in East Germany had at first proved impervious to the attractions of the Nazi movement, the alliance with Hugenberg made it necessary for Hitler to protect their interests as well), and it formulated a policy of lighter taxation, the lowering of rents, and the creation of co-operatives under state patronage: a policy that put the task of making agriculture profitable squarely upon the shoulders of the state. At the same time, an 'agricultural department' was formed inside the party, and on 1 June, Walther Darre was made responsible for the organization of the peasantry; three months later, the *NS Landpost*, a special party organ designed for the countryside, appeared for the first time, and an expert adviser was attached to local and district party organizations in the rural areas. The campaign paid a completely satisfactory dividend: in 1930 the peasants supplied the party with 13.2 per cent of its total membership.[42]

During the five years since the 're-establishment' of the party, the Nazi net had been cast over Germany. It could be used to catch more supporters for the movement when a suitable opportunity presented itself: it came in the shape of the economic slump. Before 1930, the party had been a refuge for the socially and economically underprivileged and for the outcasts; now, the isolated islands of discontent were submerged in the flood. In the elections to the *Reichstag* on 14 September — a fatal date in the annals of the Weimar Republic — members of the middle class joined the peasants as the new supporters of the Nazi movement. The republican party system began to break down; the middle class, including those of its sections that had shared in the economic prosperity, began to search for a new political platform. The Nazi movement offered them this.

Although the *NSDAP* claimed to be a socialist party, it did not make an equally spectacular advance among the German working class. Significantly, there were no Nazi trade unions; only when the ranks of the unemployed rose to 4,380,000 at the end of 1930 were the Nazis moved — in January of the following year — to set up an 'economic-political' department. It was led by Otto Wagener, and it absorbed the organization of industrial cells[43] together with its organ, *Das Arbeitertum.*

In a sociological break-down of the German society into its component parts (excluding housewives, pensioners, and students), the workers accounted for 45.9 per cent of the employed population in 1930; they supplied the Nazi party with 28.1 per cent of its membership.[44] But the features of the party that repulsed the workers attracted the big industrialists. For this, the ground had been prepared in 1928, when the party leadership banned the formation of Nazi trade unions; when the industrialists saw themselves threatened by the slump, they found the Nazi party, among the radical movements, by far the most congenial.

At the general elections in 1930, 6,407,397 votes were cast for the *NSDAP*, and it sent 107 deputies to the *Reichstag*, compared with the twelve deputies who had been elected two years earlier; it became the second largest party in the parliament. Indeed, as the slump gathered momentum, the membership of the party continued to grow at a fast rate. The following table shows the rate of increase:

YEAR	NUMBER OF REGISTERED MEMBERS	RATE OF INCREASE, PER CENT
1928	108,717	149.3
1929	176,426	161.5
1930 (September)	293,000	—
1930 (December)	389,000	221.0
1931	806,294	207.2
1932	1,414,975	175.5[45]

The sharp increase in Nazi membership exactly followed the growth of the numbers of the unemployed until 1931, from then on, the jobless masses of Germany continued to provide the Nazis with their recruiting ground.

The growth of the party was also reflected in the sudden jump in the circulation figures of its press; the number of copies sold of the *Völkischer Beobachter* rose, between 1929 and 1932, at the following pace:

1929	26,715
1930	84,511
1931	108,746
1932	126,672[46]

During the same period, the number of Nazi newspapers rose to 121, and they commanded a total circulation of well over a million; in January 1932 a press agency, the *Nationalsozialistische Partei-Korrespondenz,* was set up.

During the period of sharp increase in their following, the Nazis were by no means forced to overhaul their methods of propaganda. Speeches, meetings, and rallies still headed the list of priority, and they had precedence over any other form of agitation. The press still remained relegated to second place; only when Nazi activities were jeopardized by one or other of Brüning's emergency laws, did the press—when it was not banned itself—become more important as the only available means of propaganda. Violence in the streets and at political meetings grew more frequent and intense; civil war raged in full view of a powerless government. In addition to the feeling of belonging to a strong and resolute community, the *SA* could now offer food and shelter to thousands of its unemployed members. When all political uniforms were banned on 8 December 1931, the *SA* and the *SS* continued to meet, wearing white or no shirts; in Munich they staged a sit-down demonstration when mounted police attempted to break up their meeting. Since the ban on uniforms was clearly not very effective, the government banned the *SA* and *SS* on 13 April the following year; their homes, kitchens, and other property were impounded. Although it came late, the ban was a serious blow to the Nazi leaders; at this time, Goebbels recorded in his diary: 'When the *SA* troops once again march in their brown shirts, then the whole depression will be overcome, and the enemy will soon fall under our blows.'[47] His wishes were fulfilled: the ban was lifted on 14 June, and violence flared up once again. During the month after the stormtroopers' return to the streets in their uniforms, some thirty of them were killed; one Sunday at Altona, near Hamburg, sixteen people lost their lives and fifty were seriously injured.

The lethal combination of propaganda and terror was carried on in the same manner—although on a larger scale—as in the twenties. But now, after the turn of the decade, Hitler began to lay his hands on the really heavy artillery of technical equipment for propaganda. At first his alliance with Hugenberg helped, both financially and in the field of public relations; Hugenberg's press and film empire rendered Hitler useful services. But the flow of money from German industry into Nazi coffers continued even after Hitler turned, early in 1932, to attack his former ally.

Indeed, in the final stage of Hitler's way to power, circumstances conspired to make the ascent easy for him. The technical means for propaganda had been developed, and they became available to Hitler at a time when he disposed of adequate financial resources and when a highly receptive audience existed. During the year 1930 microphones and loudspeakers became the standard equipment of Nazi meetings; without them, the monster meetings—such as those at the Sportpalast in 1932—would have been impossible to organize. The formidable armoury of Nazi propaganda came into play during the two presidential election campaigns in 1932, when Hitler competed for the highest stakes yet of his political career. He was in close consultation with Goebbels, who relieved him of the cares of the detailed organization of propaganda, as well as making a considerable contribution himself to its general direction. Early in February, Goebbels was able to write that 'the election campaign is ready in principle. We now only need to press the button, to set the machine into motion'.[48] The Nazis ran some 34,000 public meetings during the first campaign; they distributed 8,000,000 pamphlets and printed large editions of the party newspapers; striking coloured posters hammered election slogans home. They were simple and effective— a drawing of the profiles of three grimly determined *SA* men, for instance, carried the text: 'National Socialism, the organized will of the nation'.[49] Since the highest office in the state was being contested, the Nazi propagandists soft-pedalled party differences, and concentrated on identifying their movement with the nation. They also produced, for the first time, their own films, which were usually shown at open-air meetings, as distribution through the usual channels was still proving difficult.

In the first election on 13 March, Hindenburg did not acquire an absolute majority, but he led Hitler by more than 7,000,000 votes. Goebbels was desperate; Hitler announced that the second election campaign would be launched at once. The propaganda machinery was overhauled, and new directives were worked out. Many party

Auschläge: Ebenhausen. Langewiesche-Brandt Verlag 1963

I.   The string-puller. 1924

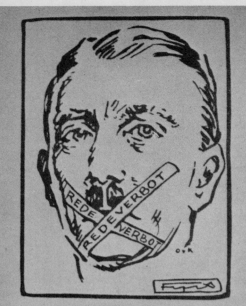

Einer allein von 2000 Millionen Menschen der Erde darf in Deutschland nicht reden!

IIa. Hitler: he alone is not allowed to speak in Germany. 1926

IIb. SS Troopers are forbidden to wear their uniforms. 1930

workers were sent to reinforce the propaganda department in
Munich; in his speeches, Hitler switched from carping criticism of
the evils of the Weimar 'system' to painting a picture of a happy
future for the Germans; Goebbels, on the other hand, promised to
devote himself to combating the 'lies' and slander heaped on the Nazis
by their opponents.[50] He was not quite happy about the part the
Nazi press played in the campaign; on 1 April, he complained in his
diary that journalists had made many mistakes, and that they were
'mostly very badly suited for propaganda'.[51] He also imitated the
Social Democrat *Sturmvogel* squadron in the course of his campaign. He had already discussed, early in January, the possibility of
using aricraft for the speedy delivery of principal speakers from one
city to another;[52] the idea was put into practice only between 3 and
9 April during the second election campaign. Hitler flew in a Junkers
D 1720 plane piloted by Captain Hans Bauer, and he visited twenty-
one towns in six days. Apart from its practical advantages, the first
Deutschlandflug had a high propaganda value: the slogan 'Hitler
over Germany' had an effectively ambiguous meaning. The speaker
who commanded the largest audiences in Germany was ubiquitous;
the energy, the power to hypnotize, the speed of movement, all
belonged to a human being with superhuman attributes. As early as
February 1932, Goebbels's department distributed 50,000 gramophone records; during the second presidential campaign, the Nazi
propagandists made an extensive use of recorded speeches, which
were played from vans carrying loudspeakers. Five days after the
election of the President—when the election campaign in Prussia
was being launched—a speech by Hitler was played at the beginning
of the meeting at the Sportpalast on 15 April; Goebbels described
the experiment as a 'tremendous success'—*Bombenerfolg*.[53]

Nevertheless, such practices were mere substitutes for radio propaganda. Broadcasting was under government control, and time for
political broadcasts was sparingly allocated. Aside from two talks—
a part of a discussion programme—delivered by the party ideologist
Gottfried Feder in 1930 and 1931, the Nazis did not gain access to the
German broadcasting system until the summer of 1932. Their protests in the parliament were frequent but ineffective; they followed
the Communist example in creating disturbances at public functions

which were broadcast. In August 1932, for example, after the opening speech of the Berlin wireless exhibition, the two party radio functionaries, Hadamovsky and Dressler-Andress, sprang to the microphone and shouted 'Long live National-Socialist radio! Heil Hitler!'[54]

Hitler's bid for the highest office in the state failed again in the second presidential election. Nevertheless, the Nazis were now preparing to take up the reins of government; after a year of continuous election campaigns, punctuated by hard political bargaining, Hitler achieved his ambition. On 30 January 1933, the aged President Hindenburg entrusted him with the office of Chancellor. During the eight years since his release from the Landsberg Prison, the rise of Hitler and his movement to prominence and finally to power had been spectacular. Despite the frequent bans on various forms of Nazi activities issued by the governments of the federal states, the central government in Berlin had proved itself incapable of co-ordinating and directing the fight against a movement that threatened the very existence of the democratic system. It was perhaps too late when Chancellor Brüning began to pass one emergency decree after another. By then the Nazis commanded the largest political organization in Germany. It was built up from insignificant beginnings and its early growth — by no means striking compared with the growth of the party after 1929 — was largely due to the skilful exploitation of propaganda techniques. By and large, the themes of Hitler's agitation were not as impressive as their delivery. Certain subjects recurred: the Nazis were anti-parliamentary, anti-Marxist, anti-Communist, anti-Liberal, anti-Jewish. They exploited national humiliations: the Versailles Treaty, and the Yound Plan for reparations; they placed the blame for the defeat and humiliation squarely on the Weimar 'system'. But their propaganda, especially when dealing with current political problems, was quick to grasp the main chance, and it remained unhampered by any ideological considerations. It was firmly based on the principles Hitler had developed early in his career. It was not intended to persuade by reasoning; it appealed to the emotions, and it was reinforced by a considerable dose of violence. Although the theory and practice of Nazi propaganda were derivative to a certain extent, Hitler and his star pupil Goebbels had a sure touch in its execution; its cumulative effect has never been surpassed. Finally, in the first three years of the new decade, the Nazis benefited by the economic crisis; the party had a long tradition behind it of being the refuge of the discontented, of the outcasts. And at the time when it was becoming a truly mass-movement it began acquiring the technical equipment for the conduct of mass propaganda. By the end of 1932, the *NSDAP* was ready to assume the highest responsibility in the state.

II
The State
and Propaganda

'It is like a dream. Wilhelmstrasse belongs to us. The Führer is already working in the Chancellery. We are standing upstairs at the window, and hundreds of thousands of people are passing by in the flaming light of torches before the grey President and the young Chancellor, and they are gratefully acclaiming them. . . .'[1] When Goebbels recorded the events of 30 January he was no less surprised than moved. The young man who had come to the hostile city six years before was now witnessing its final conversion to the true faith: at long last, Germany had awakened. The future promised unlimited possibilities.

Josef Goebbels had made an important contribution to Hitler's success. As the leader of the Berlin *Gau* he had wrested the control of the streets of the German capital away from the Communists and the Social Democrats. He was a tough, dedicated, malicious Nazi. He has been described as the only intellectual in an anti-intellectual movement; his intelligence never interfered with his loyalty to the party and its leader. He highly prized the party and his own career in it. He preferred times of crisis to times of peace; he liked playing with words and arguments, and, best of all, he liked lying. 'Any lie, frequently repeated, will gradually gain acceptance,' Goebbels echoed Hitler.

Though he never pushed hard the concept of the master race—

Goebbels was small, dark, and had a clubfoot—he hated the Jews and was unswervingly loyal to his master. He had a deep admiration for Hitler, whom he probably saw as a man of instinct who had no intellectual doubts. Goebbels's greatest achievement as a propagandist was the creation of the Hitler myth—the *Führerkult*— a line which became a big national industry. In this respect alone did Goebbels come very near to believing his propaganda.

He had started work on that task when he was still an unknown party official in the Rhineland, and Hitler the leader of a small and obscure party. His pamphlet *Die Führerfrage, Die Zweite Revolution —Briefe am Zeitgenossen* (The Leadership Question, The Second Revolution—Letters to Contemporaries) was published in Zwickau in 1926. Goebbels described in it the advent of the new German Messiah, 'a meteor before our astonished eyes', 'the fulfillment of our mysterious longing'.[2] Miracle, mission, Messiah were the terms Goebbels frequently used: they were underscored by the more secular view of Hitler as a spokesman for a hard-pressed generation. Like Napoleon, Goebbels later stressed the need, for a charismatic leader, of luck: the masses forgave their leader everything 'except the lack of good fortune'.

By November 1932 most of the components of the Hitler personality cult had been assembled. The necessary double image of Hitler as a superman and a man of the people had been evolved by Goebbels and then driven home in two articles in *Der Angriff* on 1 and 4 April 1932. They were entitled 'Hitler as a Statesman' and 'Hitler as a Human Being'.

Hitler was presented, in the first article, as a farsighted planner of Germany's reconstruction; in the second one as a nonsmoker and teetotaller who was far from tyrannical because he did not impose his personal tastes on others. The link between the two articles was the view of Hitler as an artist who went into politics because of the suffering of the German nation.

The process of construction of the Hitler myth went on after 1933. Goebbels then dropped most of the quasi-religious imagery; there was no longer any need to present him as a symbol of a generation engaged in a hard struggle. Instead he emerged as a great national symbol. Goebbels again took up the theme of Hitler as the 'Greater

German'—an Austrian who had desired all his life a great German Reich. He was about to complete the work begun by Bismarck. His personality was now enhanced by success: he had a sure touch and he 'alone was never mistaken'. Hitler had been proved right and therefore was infallible. In addition, the ruler had to be identified with the ruled. References to loyalty to his friends and old comrades-in-arms were interspersed with the various aspects of the father image. His kindness to children, the way he never abandoned the many millions who were dear to him. For that they owed him undying loyalty and obedience.

By the outbreak of the war the personality cult of Hitler, as constructed by Goebbels, contained so many layers that only a dedicated expert was able to pick his way through them. The basic features of the image remained: the colouring depended on the political exigencies of the time. Goebbels knew that the memory of his audience was short. He gave it the right image at the right time, and that was what mattered.

Hitler as a military expert who was about to complete, sword in hand, the work begun by Bismarck, was, when the need arose, substituted for by the picture of a polished diplomat who could sit down at a conference table with other European leaders and overwhelm them with facts and figures. At one point Goebbels even started introducing an element of the mother image into the purely masculine imagery:'The whole nation loves him because it feels safe in his hands like a child in the arms of its mother.'[3]

The aim of all this iconography also remained the same. It was the complete identification of the followers with their leader. In 1933 Goebbels knew that he had to be careful not to identify Hitler's followers with the whole German nation: five years later, after much hard work by the Minister of Propaganda, underscored by Nazi successes at home and abroad, Goebbels did not seem to be constrained in that way. At the outbreak of the war many Germans were prepared to die for 'Our Hitler', for the synthetic symbol so carefully constructed for them.

In technical terms, the foundations for the manipulation of the German people by the state and its propaganda machinery had been laid down sometime before the day of Goebbels's exultation on 30

January 1933. He had become the *Reichspropagandaleiter* of the party on 9 January 1929; his chance to strengthen his own position and to extend the powers of his office came in 1932. Its activities overlapped to a great extent with those of the *Reichsorganisations-leitung*—the department of party organization—headed by Gregor Strasser. And when the ever-present problem of Gregor Strasser's position inside the party flared up again in the autumn of 1932, Goebbels seized this chance to reorganize and strengthen the administration of propaganda. He was convinced that Hitler was getting ready to take over power in Germany, and he carried out the reorganization of the propaganda apparatus with this end firmly in his mind. Its main function had been, until then, the efficient transmission of directives down the hierarchy of local organizations; now, Goebbels's main concern was the broadening of the central organization and the dividing of it into specialized sections that could look after every aspect of propaganda.

The section dealing with 'active propaganda' (*Amt I*) formed the core of the organization: it dealt with the execution of political agitation, from the monster meetings with their problems of architectural design, accommodation, transport, etc. (there was a special subsection for *Grossveranstaltungen*: the organization of the party rallies was run, however, by an independent permanent office in Nürnberg, which came under the direct supervision of the *Reichspropagandaleiter*) to the small meetings in the countryside. The main subsection, which had a comparatively long history behind it, was concerned with *Rednerwesen*, the direction of public speaking. The office of 'active propaganda' also distributed its own newspaper, *Unser Wille und Weg*, which had been founded in 1931.

Then there were sections dealing with 'culture'—including architecture, Hitler's special sphere of interest—with radio, film, and 'liaison with offices of the state'. These sections were expanded after January 1933; until then, they existed only in a rudimentary form. The same division was perpetuated on the lower levels of party organization: the *Gaupropagandaleiter* was responsible for five sections corresponding to those in the central office on the provincial level; lower down in the hierarchy, there were the *Kreispropagandaleiter*—the district director of propaganda—the *Ortsgruppenpropaganda-*

leiter, who worked on the level of local party organization, and finally the *Stützpunktpropagandaleiter*—the cell-leader. All these ranks
led a separate existence from the rest of the party organization; the
hierarchy was used for transmitting orders downward, and passing
information—situation reports, 'audience research', etc.—upwards.
Regular monthly situation reports were passed on from the lowest
level through the same hierarchy. By 1934, the party propaganda
apparatus employed some 14,000 people.[4]

Nevertheless, the machinery that controlled Nazi propaganda
activities was carefully concealed from public view. The marion-
ettes were there for all to see, but the strings, and the stringpullers,
would have spoilt the illusion. On one occasion, Goebbels had a fit
of blinding fury because an illustrated magazine published a picture
of a man putting on a record of a triumphal bell chime after a special
announcement; at a press conference in Berlin selected journalists
were informed that 'problems of stage management [*Regiefragen*]
should not on principle come before the public. All that goes on
behind the backcloth belongs to stage management'.[5]

Although the internal structure of party propaganda apparatus
was often reshaped, and although its functions frequently overlapped with those of other party or, after 1933, state departments, it
gave Goebbels a unique position of power. He used it to the full.
In addition, coercion could be substituted, when necessary, for
persuasion; the terror that had been inflicted on the Germans by
the stormtroopers before 1933 could now be meted out by the state.

On the evening of 27 February, fire raged inside the *Reichstag*.
It is immaterial whether it was started by a demented Dutch Communist pyromaniac or by the Nazis themselves, or independently by
both; the fact remains that the Nazi action against their political
opponents was swift and ruthless. By no means partisans of parliamentary institutions, the Nazis used the *Reichstag* fire as a pretext
for their first move towards large-scale political repression. They
declared it to be a Communist plot, the beginning of a Communist
revolution. On the day after the fire, Hindenburg was made, by
Hitler, to sign a decree for the protection of 'the People and the
State', which suppressed those sections of the constitution relating
to civil liberties, and authorized the central government to assume,

whenever necessary, complete power in the federal states.

The *SA* troopers now acted as defenders of the state. They were used as a supplementary police force for arresting thousands of their fellow-countrymen; the first concentration camps were set up. The Communists suffered first and foremost; the Social Democrats, and the leaders of the liberal parties, soon joined them in the camps. The last semi-democratic elections took place in an atmosphere of terror. The Nazis had suppressed most of the newspapers run by their political enemies; they now had all the available mass media at their disposal. Despite these advantages and their attempt to extract the full propaganda value from the threat of a Communist revolution,[6] the Nazis did not gain a clear majority. They polled 43.9 per cent of the total vote. Only when the fifty-two deputies of Hugenberg's German National Party were added to the 288 National Socialist deputies did Hitler's government achieve a marginal majority in the *Reichstag*.

Soon after the elections, Hitler saw the Enabling Law through the *Reichstag*; it gave his government dictatorial powers. In these circumstances, the main aim of Nazi propaganda was to achieve the identification of the party with the state. The opening of the new *Reichstag,* on 21 March, served this purpose admirably. It was stage-managed by Goebbels, and the garrison church at Potsdam provided a suitable setting. The place had powerful historical associations: Frederick the Great was buried here, it was a reminder of Prussia's past. Among such memories there was no place for democratic, parliamentary ideals; the tradition was authoritarian, underscored by past military glory. The Nazis turned up in force, and so did the living relics of the Empire in their splendid uniforms of a bygone age. Hindenburg made a speech to the deputies assembled in the garrison church; he was followed by Hitler. Again, the same image as on 30 January occurred to Goebbels.[7] The grey, old President with the young Chancellor: the past and the future of Germany were united in the present moment; Germany's honour was restored, and the shameful memories of recent past were safely buried.

A few days after the elections Goebbels was appointed, on 13 March, the Minister of Popular Enlightenment and Propaganda. This was no routine appointment. The Ministry—*Promi* as it became known—was a new institution. Goebbels was a busy man in the first months after the formation of Hitler's government. The Nazi leaders no longer saw their party as one of the competitors in the political arena; the point now was to eliminate all competition, while completing a watertight *Gleichschaltung* of every aspect of political activity. And not only that: every facet of national life had to be inspired from a single source and directed by a central authority.

Propaganda occupied, as we have observed, a focal position in the Nazi scheme of things when the party was still on the road to power; after 1933, Goebbels's Ministry was placed in a corresponding key position. According to Hitler's decree, published in June, the Minister was responsible for 'all tasks of spiritual direction of the nation'.[8] This vague directive gave Goebbels's Ministry a wide scope. Other departments of state had to give up a variety of their former functions in its favour. The Ministry of the Interior handed over to Goebbels the supervision of radio, films, press, theatre; the protection of works of art and memorials, and the regulation of state celebrations and holidays; the Foreign Ministry had to give up—at any rate in theory—the control of the whole range of propaganda abroad. The organization of the Ministry and the division of tasks inside it corresponded closely to that of the party department of propaganda (*Reichspropagandaleitung*). Apart from the sections for active propaganda, radio, films, press, there were sections dealing with theatre, creative arts, music, and writing. (In the *Reichspropagandaleitung*, all these latter activities came under the direction of the *Kulturamt*.) There were also special sections dealing with propaganda abroad, foreign press, and the *Fremdenverkehrsabteilung*. The last section looked after tourist traffic; for a National Socialist this did not simply mean going abroad for holidays, or foreigners coming to Germany for the same purpose. Although the Nazis erected no 'iron curtain' around Germany, tourism became a political exercise that was closely linked with the overall propaganda effort.

Most of the top positions in the Ministry and in the *Reichspropagandaleitung* were held by the same men; the two institutions in fact merged, at many points, into one apparatus. The key *Abteilung II* acted as the general staff of the Ministry; policy was formulated here, ideas were discussed and worked out in detail; it also included sections dealing with specific tasks, such as the fight against Marxism, the Versailles peace treaties, antisemitic propaganda, eastern and borderland problems. The head of the whole department was Wilhelm Haegert, who also managed the liaison section of the *Reichspropagandaleitung*; Leopold Gutterer, who looked after the section which dealt with large meetings (*Grossveranstaltungen*) inside the party propaganda organization, also acted as a principal (*Referent*) in the *Abteilung II* in the Ministry; Hans Kriegler was head of the departments of broadcasting both in the Ministry and in the *Reichspropagandaleitung*, as well as acting as the President of the *Reichsrundfunkkammer*. Division of labour between the two organizations was purely functional, and it did not affect questions of general policy. The Ministry was, for instance, responsible for state visits and state celebrations, whereas the *Reichspropagandaleitung* carried out the celebrations of the various party anniversaries.

Centralization of all propaganda activities implied, for Goebbels, the elimination of every alternative source of information In this respect, his most difficult task lay in the *Gleichschaltung*—the achievement of uniformity—of the press. When Hitler became the Chancellor of the Republic there existed some 4,700 newspapers in Germany; their political make-up was highly differentiated, they had a long tradition behind them, and some of them had acquired, in the course of the years, a nation-wide reputation. They all made heavy demands on the pool of skilled journalists: Hitler and Goebbels had not been very successful in the competition for their services.[9] The Nazis ran only a small section of the very diverse press; at the beginning of 1933 they had 121 dailies and periodicals—most of them with low circulation—at their disposal. By the end of 1934, the situation had drastically changed. The party then controlled some 436 newspapers directly, and indirectly all the German press.

But the uniformity achieved in those years was by no means obvious at a first glance. Only the extremists in the movement advocated a radical suppression of all the former democratic press, which would put the party, at once, into a monopoly position.[10] Goebbels was well aware of the difficulties involved in such an operation. He maintained that direction behind the scenes should continue to flow through a variety of channels. Goebbels in fact preferred to advance along the line of least resistance. In this way, the readers' habits would not be suddenly broken, and the Nazi journalists would not be faced with a task beyond their powers. The long-term views on the development of the German press—Goebbels very likely shared them with Max Amann, the party publisher, and with Rudolf Hess—were that the *NSDAP* press would eventually come to dominate the field, not so much because of its intrinsic value and merits, but because of the help the party authorities could render it.

The slow erosion of the independence of the German press was carried out gradually. The *Reichstag* fire served as a pretext for the suppression of all Communist newspapers, and a ban on those run by the Social Democratic party. The elimination of hundreds of newspapers was followed by a more oblique step. The *Wolff Telegraphenbüro* was transformed into the *Deutsches Nachrichtenbüro*, and the other agencies were also brought into line. As well as regulating the flow of news at its very source, Goebbels tackled the problem from the other end, on the editorial level. Official press conferences had been introduced in Germany during the First World War, and in 1919 they became a regular feature of a journalist's life in Berlin. They were run by the *Reichspressechef* or his deputy, and their main purpose was to explain the official attitude of the government on the most important issues of the day to the newspaperman, and to answer their questions. The press department of *Promi* controlled the admission of journalists to these meetings, as well as the information that was dispensed to them. And under Goebbels's régime, the conference gradually lost its original function—to inform the journalists. Instead they were given the party commentary: the *Deutsches Nachrichtenbüro* issued the hard news. The agency also provided a small circle of Nazi journalists and party functionaries with strictly confidential material intended for their personal use. When the system began to function smoothly, *Promi* orders were issued at the press conference. They came from Goebbels, and he had the whole apparatus of the state behind him if he wished to enforce them.

The Nazis attempted to create their own image of an ideal editor: a man who was not a mere technician, but a fighter for their ideals. They had a romantic picture of such a person, which they derived from the 'period of struggle' before 1933; Weiss, the editor of the *Völkischer Beobachter*, described him in the following manner: 'A National Socialist editor never was a journalist exclusively but always and foremost a propagandist, very often a newspaperman, a speaker, and an *SA* trooper in one person. We want editors who will support their Führer and the new Reich not because they have to do so, but because they want to'.[11]

In the meantime, however, Goebbels did not rely on cynical journalists being willing to accept his 'ideals'. In the autumn of 1933, the Nazis reinforced their press policy by legislation. The *Schriftleitergesetz*— the law of 4 October— followed the lines that Hitler had first expounded in the party programme some thirteen years earlier. [12] The law declared the office of an editor to be an official position, which could not be held by a person without German citizenship, or who had been deprived of his rights as a citizen, who was a Jew, or who was married to one. When discharging their functions, editors were placed under a variety of restrictions. They were bound by law not to confuse their 'private [good] with the general good in a manner misleading to the public',[13] they were not to print anything that might harm Germany's ability to defend herself, her economy or culture or indeed anything that broke the rules of 'good conduct'. Certain paragraphs of the law, especially those concerning the functions of the editor, entirely ruled out editorial independence. The right to criticize the government was denied to the German journalists. The law gave the Ministry of Propaganda an instrument for the achievement of a complete uniformity of the press: there was no need for censorship because the editor's most important function was that of a censor.

Goebbels defended the press law in a speech to the journalists on the day of its publication. He argued that the free expression of opinion could seriously threaten the state, and that personal liberty depended on the degree of freedom that 'can be enjoyed by the nation, and the freedom of the individual will be the narrower the greater the dangers are that temporarily threaten the state'. Only much later— in 1942— did Goebbels explain what he meant by temporary danger: he said that freedom of opinion could be established only when the German nation reached the 'maturity' of the English people, a process that would take at least a century.[14] At the conference on 4 October 1933, Goebbels further argued that the state was not able to give up the means of controlling the press, because of the tendency, among the Germans, to take the printed word much more seriously than the spoken word. He talked to the assembled journalists as one of them; he attempted to make the law acceptable to them by pointing out that it raised their professional status, and that it strengthened their position in relation to the publisher.

_ Nevertheless, even in this respect— the relation between the editor and the publisher— the freedom of the journalist to choose his own employer was being gradually whittled down. The operations of Max Amann constituted another line of attack on the independence of the press. He may have disapproved of those clauses of the law that downgraded the relation between the publisher and the editor to a purely contractual basis: nevertheless, by the autumn of 1933, Amann was well on the way to becoming a dictator of German publishing. In the early years of the party's activity in Bavaria, Max Amann had been its business manager as well as the director of the Franz Eher Verlag, the official Nazi publishing house. As Hitler's personal friend, the proprietor of the Eher Verlag, the chairman of the Union of German Newspaper Publishers, and as the Secretary of the Press Chamber (*Reichspressekammer*), Amann was, by 1933, in a unique position. He used it to bring, gradually, a large part of German publishing under his control. His first opportunity came when all of the Communist and Social Democrat press was banned after the *Reichstag* fire: by the end of the year, some 1,500 publishers were deprived of their business. The decrees issued in April 1935 for the 'preservation of newspaper publishing', for the 'extirpation of newspapers dealing in scandal' etc., offered Amann new opportunities. Before Amann started building his empire under Hitler's patronage, some 80 per cent of all publishing houses were run as family businesses; their number decreased rapidly, constantly harassed and decimated by the government and by Amann. Even the newspapers run by the Scherl Verlag and controlled by Hitler's former ally Hugenberg, were gradually swallowed up by Amann's organization. In 1933 the Nazis ran only 2.5 per cent of all German newspapers: in 1944 82 per cent of the remaining 977 newspapers were controlled, directly or indirectly, by Amann.[15] In 1939 the Amann concern employed 600 editors-in-chief of publishing houses and 3,000 journalists, apart from many thousands of administrative employees.

On the occasion of Max Amann's fiftieth birthday in 1941, Hitler congratulated his friend on the superlative work in the field of publishing he had done for the Nazi idea. Nevertheless, the *Gleichschaltung* of the German press had been a slow, costly, and laborious process. By comparison, the control of the film industry and of broadcasting was easier of achievement, and, from the Nazi point of view, more rewarding. Both the privately owned film industry and the staterun broadcasting system had been only recently developed as the means of mass communication; they possessed neither the traditions nor the wide diversity of the press. Although the Nazis had gained little first-hand experience of these media before 1933, Goebbels prized their importance very highly, and he had begun plotting their capture some time before the Nazis came to power.

It has been suggested that the productions of the German film industry in the Weimar Republic prepared the ground for the establishment of the Nazi régime. Mr. Siegfried Kracauer, for instance, concluded his study of the German film *From Caligari to Hitler* with this perceptive paragraph: 'Irretrievably sunk into retrogression, the bulk of the German people could not help submitting to Hitler. Since Germany thus carried out what had been anticipated by her cinema from its very beginning, conspicuous screen characters now came true in life itself. Personified day-dreams of minds to whom freedom meant a fatal shock, and adolescence a permanent temptation, these figures filled the arena of Nazi Germany. Homunculus walked about in the flesh. Self-appointed Caligaris hypnotized innumerable Cesares into murder. Raving Mabuses committed fantastic crimes with impunity, and mad Ivans devised unheard-of tortures. Along with this unholy procession, many motifs known from the screen turned into actual events. In Nürnberg, the ornamental pattern of Nibelungen appeared on a gigantic scale: an ocean of flags and people artistically arranged. Souls were thoroughly manipulated so as to create the impression that the heart mediated between brain and hand. By day and night, millions of feet were marching over city streets and along highways. The blare of military bugles sounded unremittingly, and the philistines from the plush parlours felt very elated. Battles roared and victory followed victory. It all was as it had been on the screen. The dark premonitions of a final doom were also fulfilled.'[16]

Although it is true to say that some films reflected various Nazi tendencies in German life in the pre-Hitler era, and that many of the people connected with the making of films gladly accepted the patronage of Goebbels, German cinemas had largely been showing commercial films, free from any political tendency. High production costs had to be covered by adequate box-office return: Goebbels attacked precisely these films in a speech to the representatives of the industry in February 1934. He sharply critized the manner in which German film-making was 'debased' by the dictates of capital, and the low level of the routine film produced purely for the sake of box-office returns; he said that German film-makers must learn to regard their profession as a service, and not as a source of profit.

Some time before this speech, the law for the establishment of a 'Provisional Film Chamber' was published:[17] it was mainly concerned with bringing the film industry into the 'general economic framework' of the state. The film companies began to be heavily subsidized from official funds, and then one after the other were taken over by the state; the largest of them—Hugenberg's UFA company—was acquired in 1937. In less than five years the film department of the Ministry of Propaganda acquired a monopoly in film production; this policy was accompanied by the gradual elimination of foreign competition for the favours of the German filmgoers. No one could compete with Goebbels as an independent producer.

The Minister rated the value of films as a weapon of propaganda very high indeed; he also had a liking for the world of film, and he gave it a good deal of personal attention. Even well-known directors had to tolerate Goebbels's interference with their business; they often had to make changes in their casts and re-shoot whole scenes at the Minister's bidding. Apart from the propaganda documentaries—films of party rallies, of the Berlin Olympic Games and the heavily slanted newsreels—a number of films with strong political tendencies were made. *Jud Suss* put across the antisemitic message; *Hitlerjunge Quex* glorified the party and its youth; *Friesennot* underlined the trials of the Germans living outside the frontiers of Hitler's state. Indeed, in this *genre*, the Nazis scored some popular successes, which they attempted to match on the stages of the German theatres. The achievement and the technique of film-producing collectives could not however be employed in traditional theatre; individual authors could be neither discovered nor coerced as easily. In theatre, the Nazis had to be content to rely on the old repertoire, and to select from it the plays that suited them best.

Quite apart from his personal taste for actresses, Goebbels was attracted to films because they were easier to make and mould and because they reached much wider audiences than live theatre. Nevertheless, their limitations as an instrument of propaganda soon became apparent. Although box-office considerations were done away with, not all the films made in Germany could carry a high charge of Nazi propaganda. A large sector of the industry went on producing entirely apolitical films: indeed, the initial enthusiasm of the Nazi film-makers to put across their message gradually cooled off. Although the Hitler Youth Quex had mercifully perished at the hands of Communist thugs, he was revived during the war. Now a fully grown man, he appeared as Pilot Quex, a figure of comedy rather than of high-minded drama. In this respect, Goebbels failed: the kind of films he criticized in February 1934 continued to be made; the German public had to be amused.

When Goebbels became the Minister of Propaganda, the newspaper and film industries were privately owned: the broadcasting system was, on the other hand, state-run. It had some ten years' history behind it; although it had eluded the grasp of the Nazis before 1933, the imposition on it afterwards of centrally directed uniformity proved comparatively simple. For the Nazi propagandists, the control of broadcasting was the most coveted prize. Indeed, in June 1932 Hitler made his support of von Papen's government conditional on the grant to his party of broadcasting facilities; after that, numerous pronouncements by high party functionaries bore witness to their interest in the medium. At the opening of the radio exhibition in Berlin in August 1933, Goebbels quoted Napoleon, who had described the press as the 'seventh Great Power', and he continued: 'What the press was for the nineteenth century, wireless will be for the twentieth. One could alter the words of Napoleon, and call it the eighth Great Power.'[18]

In Germany, as in other industrialized European countries, the two powers initially clashed. Mass-circulation press and broadcasting catered for the same public, and their functions—especially as far as the dissemination of news was concerned—were similar. Their rivalry had by no means been resolved before Hitler became Chancellor: the Nazi propagandists later favoured broadcasting at the expense of the press; Goebbels regarded it as a much more effective means of influencing the masses. In a small circle of his collaborators, he expressed the view that the press was an 'exponent of the liberal spirit, the product and instrument of the French revolution', whereas broadcasting was 'essentially authoritarian', and, therefore, a suitable 'spiritual weapon of the totalitarian state'.[19] Since Hitler hardly ever listened to wireless, Goebbels had a greater freedom of action in this than in any other field of propaganda; he also valued the fact that it was immediate, and that it penetrated. The spoken word disappeared without trace: he often allowed his broadcasters to exploit this liberty. Yet though broadcasting was the pampered child of Nazi propagandists, the principle by which it had to give way to the claims of the press to bring important news first—this had been established in the Weimar Republic—was continued. In this respect, Max Amann's influence was decisive: until the outbreak of war speed in the dissemination of news was sacrificed in favour of the established prerogatives of the press.[20]

The new masters of the German broadcasting system laid special stress on the development of 'political broadcasts'—from dramatic poems set to music, composed to glorify the past of the party, to Hitler's speeches. Indeed, the latter were the focal point of Nazi radio programming. In 1933 fifty speeches by Hitler were transmitted. But in this respect the Nazi broadcasters had a lot to learn. Hitler's first radio message was followed by a flood of complaints from all parts of Germany; another recording had to be made, this time slower and less slurred, and it was broadcast the following day with better results. The Nazi propagandists learned their lesson; from October

III.   Election poster. 'National Socialism the organized will of the Nation.'
       1932

MONTAGE
BAUER
MÜNCHEN

DER MARSCHALL UND DER GEFREITE

KÄMPFEN MIT UNS FÜR FRIEDEN UND GLEICHBERECHTIGUNG

Auschläge: Ebenhausen. Langewiesche-Brandt Verlag 1963

IV.   The Field-Marshal and the Corporal. 1933

1933, when the Führer announced Germany's departure from the League of Nations, until late in the war, Hitler made no studio broadcast. The contact with the 'masses' was the essential stimulus of his speaking, and its effect was further strengthened by the 'acoustic backcloth': the applause, the rhythmic chant of *Sieg Heil,* the offstage noises of the large meeting. Without the direct *rapport* with his audience, and without the background it provided, Hitler was a failure as a speaker. He was unable to learn the technique—President Roosevelt in his 'fireside chats' was its master—which confined the speaker in the studio and left him to address a mass audience, but one composed of individuals in the privacy of their homes.

The most impressive achievement of the Nazi broadcasters lay, however, in the creation of this mass audience. In May 1933, German radio manufacturers undertook to produce a cheap, uniform set, the *Volksempfänger.* A few months later, the first 100,000 of these sets reached the market, and in 1934 the power of the transmitters was increased by 30 per cent. When the war broke out, some 3,500,000 sets had been sold.[21] In 1939, 70 per cent of all German households owned a wireless set: the highest percentage anywhere in the world. But the Nazi policy-makers were not quite satisfied with this situation: they did not regard the housewife and her family as a safe enough audience. Compulsory listening was developed alongside the compulsory attendance of meetings and the purchase of Nazi newspapers. Loudspeakers were introduced into factories, and production stopped when an important party or state broadcast was being transmitted; the completion of the plan for the installation of 6,000 'loudspeaker pillars' in the streets (here the Nazis imitated the practices introduced by the rulers of Soviet Russia early in the nineteen-twenties) was interrupted by the war.

In addition to all the practical advantages of broadcasting for the audience at home, there existed the attractions of broadcasting abroad. Broadcasters could not be controlled by foreign governments as easily as other agents of propaganda; indeed, wireless broke down the customary definition of international law concerning 'sovereignty of air space', and it enforced the formulation of the opposite principle of the 'freedom of the ether'.

Soon after Hitler came to power, Alfred Lau, the editor of the

Preussische Zeitung who later become the head of the Königsberg station, suggested that an hour should be devoted daily to a broadcast to territories in the East inhabited by Germans. Problems of foreign policy were of course mentioned on German home transmissions, and radical solutions were suggested for them. But they were either inspired by over-confidence on the part of the new rulers of Germany, or they were intended to probe the mood abroad: on one occasion, such a broadcast elicited a protest from the Polish government. Only on one occasion, in 1934, the Nazi leaders showed themselves willing to limit their freedom of action in foreign broadcasting. Following the treaty of friendship with Poland, signed in January, the official radio organizations in Warsaw and Berlin came to an agreement—on 13 October—that was to limit mutually hostile propaganda. The National Socialist broadcasters undertook, for instance, to omit all references to the oppression of the German minority by the Polish government. The order affected the German press as well, and it remained valid—and it was in fact enforced—until 1939.

The Germans in Poland received enough attention from the Nazi propagandists later, in the months that preceded the invasion of Poland on 1 September, 1939. There existed, however, *volksdeutsche* minorities elsewhere: they became the first, and they remained the most important, targets for German foreign broadcasts. The National Socialists were able to carry on the programming practices that had been established under the Weimar Republic, and designed to maintain contact with Germans abroad. But after 1933 the content of these broadcasts began to change. The Germans abroad had to be convinced of the merits of Hitler's state, they had to be drawn into organizations sponsored by the *NSDAP*; they had to be prepared to further, at a later date, concrete political demands.

The campaign took place under the sign of the misleading emotive slogn *Heimkehr ins Reich* (neither the Austrians nor the Sudeten Germans were in fact 'returning' to the Reich), and its intensity was indicated by the increasing numbers of long-and medium-wave broadcasts—the former from the *Deutschlandsender*, and the latter from Leipzig, Breslau, Königsberg and Munich stations—to the Germans on the other side of the frontier. The number of *volksdeutsche* broadcasts rose from 236 in 1933 to 924 in 1937 and then to 1,500 in the following year,[22] In an essay on the role of wireless in the creation of Great Germany[23] Hans Kriegler, the chief of the broadcasting department in the Ministry of Propaganda, wrote: '. . . the year 1938/39 must be regarded as the most active time of our broadcasting work. For long weeks and months of momentous political events, wireless was the centre of popular interest as never before. There were days, even weeks, when in the whole of Germany, as well as among the Germans on the other side of the frontier. . . the wireless receivers were in almost continuous use'.[25]

The first Nazi broadcasting onslaught was aimed against Austria: the famous 'radio war' developed in the summer of 1933, soon after Dollfuss banned the Austrian National Socialist Party. We shall have an opportunity to discuss Hitler's propaganda in Austria later;[24] at this point the second big broadcasting campaign—it preceded the Saar plebiscite—will be examined. Under the Versailles Peace Treaty, the future of the Saar territory was to be settled in 1935: the area had been receiving some attention from German broadcasters before Hitler came to power. In 1930 the Cologne station arranged a series entitled 'Saarland', and in August 1932 the 'Saarland Frontier Report' was broadcast, which contained an interview with the Chancellor, von Papen; in November 1932 all German stations transmitted a speech on the Saar problem that was made at the meeting on the theme 'German Frontiersmen in Distress'.[25]

During the first year in power, the National Socialists continued to produce similar broadcasts: their purpose was to remind the inhabitants of the Saar territory that they had not been forgotten by their mother country. Nevertheless, the broadcasts that originated from Cologne, Frankfurt or Stuttgart were never properly co-ordinated; sometimes the speeches by local party functionaries, with their exaggerated demands, cut across the foreign policy of the Berlin government.[26]

A systematic propaganda campaign to the Saarland was launched at the beginning of the year 1934. Early in January, Goebbels ordered the setting up of an office for the co-ordination of broadcasting to the Saar area. It was officially given the unrevealing name of *Westdeutsche Gemeinschaftsdienst*, and Adolf Raskin, who had worked in the Saarland as a journalist and who, immediately before his latest appointment, had looked after music and light entertain-

ment for the West German broadcasting network, was appointed
the head of the new office. Its function was to approve every broadcast relating to the Saar territory before transmission; Raskin himself enjoyed the full confidence of the Minister of Propaganda.
Goebbels was content to inform Raskin of his views on the situation
at occasional meetings, otherwise leaving him to work on his own.
At the same time, close co-operation between Raskin and *Gauleiter*
Bürckel, the government plenipotentiary for the Saar, ensured that
propaganda would remain in line with foreign policy.

From 25 April 1934, every Wednesday evening, the series 'Our
Saar—The Way to Understanding is Clear'[27] was networked
throughout Germany. A few days later, Raskin's organization
demanded that 6 May should be set aside as the 'Day of the Saar', and
that all German broadcasts on that day should be devoted purely to
Saarland. *6 May* was a Sunday, and the programming relentlessly
drove home the Saarland motif.

6 a.m.	'Reveille from the Saar.' Networked
6.15— 8.15	'Hamburg Harbour Concert with Guests from the Saar.' Networked.
9.00— 9.30	Protestant Service from Saarbrücken. Transmitted by Cologne, Stuttgart, Frankfurt, and Munich.
9.30— 9.35	Bell-chimes of all the Saarland churches. Networked.
10.15—10.45	Catholic Mass from Saarbrücken. Cologne, Stuttgart, Frankfurt, Munich.
10.50—12.00	Music. Short stories from the Saar.
12.00— 1.00	A miners' brass band from Saarland. Frankfurt, Stuttgart, Cologne, Munich.
2.15— 2.45	Children's hour: 'Kasperl visits the Saar children'. Frankfurt, Cologne, Stuttgart, Munich.
3.00— 4.30	Transmission of the Zweibrücken meeting, with a speech by the Minister of Propaganda. Networked.
4.30— 6.00	Marches of the former Saarland regiments, popular music, etc. Stuttgart, Frankfurt, Deutschlandsender.
6.00— 6.20	'Foreigners speak about the Saar question.' Frankfurt, Stuttgart, Deutschlandsender.
8.45—10.00	'Jakob Johannes. A Story of the Saar.' A radio play by Willi Schaeferdiek (based on a true event). Networked.
10.45—12.00	An evening of entertainment with Saarland wit, anecdotes, jokes, etc. Stuttgart, Frankfurt.

Until the plebiscite in January 1935, the so-called 'National Hour'[28] as well as school and youth broadcasts were frequently employed for Saar propaganda. In the last broadcasting hours of the year 1934 all German stations transmitted a programme entitled '1935—in thirteen days—the Saar Returns Home'. The final concentrated onslaught on the German listeners was made on the first Sunday of the new year. The composition of the programme ran on similar lines to those of 6 May: the morning masses were celebrated by high Saarland ecclesiastics; bands from the Saar provided the music; the day culminated in a transmission from a mass meeting at the Berlin Sportpalast.

The National Socialist propagandists left nothing to chance. They had provided the programmes; they were determined to see that there should be enough listeners. Compared with the territory of the Reich, where there were 77 listeners to every 1,000 inhabitants at the time, the density in the Saarland was considerably lower at 24 to 1,000.[29] The local National Socialist circle of listeners [30] looked after the supply of the *Volksempfänger*, cheap receivers produced in Germany; in the months between January 1934 and April 1935 some 4,000 sets were distributed in the Saarland, and the number of listeners went up from 28,000 to 40,000. In addition, the National Socialist listeners' associations organized community listening to transmissions of important party events; about fifty such meetings were organized during the Saar campaign, and the total number of listeners attending meetings throughout the area often exceeded 100,000. In conformity with broadcasting practice inside Germany, the National Socialists preferred community to individual or family listening in the Saarland; a group of people was more receptive to propaganda effects produced, say, by Hitler's speech.

There can be no doubt that broadcasting played the decisive role in the success of the National Socialist campaign. The Germans were of course unlikely to lose in the plebiscite: but they would never have won by such a clear majority without an effective propaganda campaign. [31] It must be borne in mind that the task of the National Socialists in the Saarland was not a simple one. Before 1933, the Catholic Centre, the Social Democrats, and the Communists had run the biggest organizations: in January 1935 the voters in the plebiscite had to decide the return of their province to a National Socialist Germany. There were, however, certain circumstances that favoured National Socialist propagandists. The French made only a belated attempt to counter German broadcasting to the Saar. When the Strasbourg station began to be employed, it could not hope to affect the hold over the Saarland audiences already gained by the Nazi broadcasters.

In addition, Nazi-inspired whispered propaganda—*Flüster propaganda*—aimed at convincing the German voter that the party knew exactly how he voted and would therefore punish or reward him accordingly. It was reported, for instance, that Max Braun, the Socialist leader who favoured the preservation of the status quo in the Saarland, had fled the province. Soon after the announcement Braun drove through the streets of Saarland in an open car, but the harm had been done.

The Nazi agitators did not, however, concentrate on the Saar alone. The aim of their technique was to create a *Saar-atmosphere* in Germany as well: a feeling of national community of interest that transcended former party divisions. The National Socialist leaders were of course aware of the important role broadcasting had played in the Saar campaign, and especially in creating the link between the Reich and its former province; they were to use the same technique on a number of occasions before the outbreak of the war. Soon after the conclusion of the campaign Goebbels wrote: 'German broadcasting in particular put its far-reaching powers at the disposal of the successfully concluded Saar struggle. In about fifty large networked broadcasts and over 1,000 individual broadcasts the living connexion between the Reich and the Saarland, which was still detached at the time, was maintained, and the basis was laid for the great plebiscite victory on 13 January.'[32]

The following big broadcasting campaign—it was connected with the 1936 Olympic Games in Berlin—was of an entirely different type. The Saar campaign had been arranged for the purpose of national expansion; the Olympic Games for that of national representation. Before the arrival of the foreign guests in Berlin, the Nazis had to undertake an extensive 'Potemkin village' operation. All such notices as 'Jews not admitted' were taken down from the entrances to hotels and restaurants; Streicher's newspaper *Stürmer* could not be bought in the streets, and many other aggressive Nazi propaganda devices either disappeared or were toned down.

The effort was successful. The Olympic Games were an ideal vehicle for propaganda, and the transmissions from Berlin made an indelible impression on foreign audiences many times larger than those in attendance at the capital. At the previous Olympic Games — at Amsterdam in 1928 and at Los Angeles four years later — no arrangements were provided for simultaneous reporting; in 1936 the Germans took great pains to make available as many facilities as possible. Indeed, the technical achievements alone of the planners were impressive.

A special allowance of 2,000,000 Marks for broadcasting was made: 450 additional wireless workers were ordered to Berlin in the summer of 1936. Three hundred microphones, 220 amplifiers, 20 transmitting vans were put at the disposal of foreign broadcasters. The arrangements for broadcasting the Olympic Games — they started being made early in the year 1935 — first came to test during the ten days' winter sports events at Garmisch-Partenkirchen, when some 300 reports and commentaries were broadcast to 19 countries.[33] This output was supplemented by the productions of the German short-wave network.

Some time before the beginning of the summer Games, language courses in German were transmitted on the short waves; the Berlin station, on the other hand, ran courses in English, French, Italian, and Swedish for the benefit of German hotelkeepers and other interested people. Foreign broadcasts also contained detailed advice on travel in Germany, on excursions in the environs of Berlin and other topics of interest; the periodical *Olympia Dienst* was printed in four languages, and it enlightened foreign journalists on the arrangements made for broadcasting and its employment at the Olympic Games.

The facilities provided in the summer of 1936 were used by 19 European and 13 overseas countries; 92 foreign reporters described races and other competitions, while provisions were made to record

62 reports simultaneously. About as many German as foreign reporters were at work, and of these 17 were on the staff of the German
short-wave transmitter. During the 16 days of the Olympic Games
2,500 reports were broadcast in 28 languages. The effort and the
accomplishment of the German broadcasters was indeed impressive, and they did not go unnoticed. The majority of the foreign
radio representatives sent telegrams to Goebbels, full of admiration
for the achievements of the German broadcasters; a director of the
American NBC said in his concluding report from Berlin that 'the
work done by the *Reichsrundfunk* remains without precedent in the
history of broadcasting'.[34]

The short-wave system which the National Socialists used during
the Olympic Games, both to supplement the reports of foreign
broadcasters and to enlighten those countries that did not send their
own reporters, had first gone into operation in 1926. On Christmas
Day that year the first musical programme was exchanged between
the United States and Germany; in February 1930 Solf, Germany's
former Ambassador to Japan, spoke on the problems of disarmament, and his speech was transmitted to America and networked by
NBC in a coast-to-coast broadcast. The short-wave programmes
transmitted by the authorities of the Weimar Republic were, however, largely non-political; anyway more people read about the
technical achievements in the press, than heard the broadcasts
themselves.

The National Socialists regarded 1 April 1933 as the birthday of
the German short-wave broadcasting. At first, they concentrated
on the United States and on the countries of Central America; the
programmes transmitted during the day were selected from suitable
home broadcasts: the night programmes, on the other hand, bore
the characteristics of National Socialist short-wave broadcasting
from the very beginning. The new rulers of Germany needed political credit as well as markets for their goods. Apart from these tasks,
the short-wave transmitter never neglected the Germans abroad.
The broadcasts were used to instruct members of the Nazi *Auslandsorganisation*, to strengthen them in their faith, and to bring new
members into the organization. The National Socialist broadcasters
soon learned the rules of this type of work, and they made a consid-

erable contribution to perfecting the short-wave technique. Only a few sets were equipped with short-wave bands at the time; 'fading' made reception usually unsatisfactory. There were no mass audiences: an average listener could not be expected to put up with all the difficulties; the usual type of listener to short-wave broadcasts was one with some special technical or political interests.

When the National Socialists came to power, they inherited from the Weimar Republic only one short-wave transmitter that beamed broadcasts to America. The enterprise was run by seven employees who had neither an official chief, offices, nor studios they could call their own. In the middle of April, Kurt von Böckmann—he had run the Bavarian network for eight years— was appointed the head of short-wave broadcasting; in June a second newscast in English was started, and soon afterwards news was broadcast for the first time to Central and South America in Spanish. The Christmas message in 1933 was read by Hess; it was broadcast by three new transmitters. The world was divided into four zones—North America, Africa, Asia and Australia, and South America; the first broadcasts to the three new zones went out on the first three days of February. The National Socialist authorities recruited diplomats based in Berlin to send messages to their own countries.

The network of German short-wave broadcasts was completed early in 1935, when a transmitter for South Asia and another for Central America went into operation. At the time of the Olympic Games eight stations were in working order, and they were serviced by more than a hundred men. At this point the Germans overtook the overseas services of the BBC, and they continued to improve their position until the outbreak of the war. In 1939 ten transmitters were looked after by some 250 people, who produced more than seventy hours of programmes every day (see table on page 58).

With the increase in broadcasting time, the number of languages that were employed also went up: English was used for North America, Spanish for Central and South America and, from 1937, Portuguese for special regional purposes; English, Portuguese, and Afrikaans in Africa, as well as Arabic for the Mediterranean regions within the reach of this transmitter; English, and from 1937 Dutch, were used for broadcasts to Asia and Australia. German was

	1933	1934	1935	1936	1937	1938	November 1939
United States	2.00*	5.15*	5.45*	5.55*	6.55*	7.00*	11.55*
Africa	–	4.45	4.30	6.55	7.50	7.45	8.10
East Asia	–	4.45	7.00	10.15	10.55	10.55	11.10
South America	–	4.00	4.15	7.55	7.55	7.50	9.15
Special area—Brazil	–	–	–	–	–	–	4.10
South Asia—Australia	–	–	7.00	10.15	10.55	10.55	11.10
Central America	–	–	5.45	6.55	6.55	7.00	2.50
Europe	–	–	–	–	–	–	11.00
Special broadcasts in Arabic	–	–	–	–	–	–	1.50
Total hours and minutes	2.00	18.45	34.15	48.10	51.25	51.25	71.30†

* All times shown are hours and minutes broadcast daily.　† Heinz Pohle, op. cit., page 428.

of course employed in all the four zones; broadcasting became the most important means of keeping in touch with the Germans overseas.

More time was allotted to music than to any other feature of the programmes; it linked the news, political commentaries and economic reports, in which special attention was given to European prices for the main overseas export products. Plays and serials—many of them on famous men from the age of discoveries, colonization, or of the wars of liberation—were popular with the programme planners in Berlin. A special stress was laid on the pioneering work done by the Germans; the achievements of the National Socialist regime also received mention. But an attempt was made to exclude the more obvious forms of propaganda; a good deal of care was devoted to the 'German Study Circle', a series of programmes on a variety of academic subjects.

We have noted that short-wave broadcasts could not be designed for mass audiences; the individualism of this kind of broadcasting could, however, be used for the creation of the closest possible personal contact between the broadcaster and his listeners. The aim was to produce an 'atmosphere of friendship and confidence' that was different in kind from the emotive relationship between the speaker and his mass audience. It was a process that took a long time, but the German broadcasters thought the results justified the expenditure, especially in the case of their compatriots abroad. In the first year of its operations under National Socialist direction, short-wave broadcasting devoted special attention to the national festivities of the various countries: they often asked their diplomatic representatives to the broadcasting house in Berlin; at the same time, the country in question was asked to make arrangements to transmit the broadcasts on its own network. Nevertheless, addressing a particular country was too broadly based an operation: very often a particular town, school or a wireless club was singled out and addressed by Berlin. Greetings to individual listeners became very popular, and a special period of five to ten minutes daily was made available for them; the same intimate contact was also maintained by reading the listeners' letters, answering their enquiries and organizing discussions of topics selected by the listeners.

The speakers also did their best to maintain a high level of cosy chumminess. They addressed their listeners as their good friends, they told them of their private joys and sorrows. An announcer, for instance, broke off while making a joke to go and shut the window— he, of course, described this action—because there was a dog barking outside the studio, and he did not want it to interfere with the reception of the programme in some remote part of the Brazilian forest. Indeed, one of the listeners in Brazil wrote to the broadcasting house in Berlin: 'I believe that one must live in a primeval forest in order to learn to appreciate the wireless.' [35]

Nevertheless, the spoken word would have been soon forgotten without support from the printed word, and the National Socialist broadcasters developed the 'zone service' which was designed to inform the listeners of forthcoming programmes and to remind them of past ones. Every month 75,000 copies of bilingual programme sheets were distributed to various clubs, listeners' groups and to individuals; some 3,000 matrices were also sent out to interested newspapers abroad. All these services were provided on request, free of charge. Until America's declaration of war on Germany, the programmes of the German short-wave transmitter were published in all specialized radio magazines in the United States as well as in some of the daily newspapers; the 150 German-language papers often published detailed reports on the content of the broadcasts.

The attempt to establish an intimate personal contact with the listener was by no means a revolutionary innovation in broadcasting: American radio-commercials had been trying to do precisely the same thing for many years. Nevertheless, the National Socialists employed the technique, for the first time, for political rather than commercial purposes. It later spread from short-to medium-and long-wave bands; during the war, the personal touch was indispensable to broadcasters who ran the various military stations as well as those designed to maintain the links between soldiers and their relatives and friends at home.

There can be no doubt that the German short-wave broadcasts achieved some remarkable successes. The listeners' letters to Berlin bore witness to this: although their contents were often questionable, the fact that they arrived in large numbers at least showed that the broadcasts had aroused interest. The Americans were especially sensitive to this form of propaganda: the Institute for Propaganda Analysis—the only institute of its kind—was founded in New York in 1938 partly as a countermeasure to German broadcasts. In the same year, an American radio commentator described the short-wave transmissions from Germany as the 'biggest and most powerful propaganda machinery in the world', and as 'the most frightening institution for the spread of political doctrine'. [36] The success was due, to some extent, to the element of technical surprise; many listeners were attracted by the technical accomplishments and by the novelty of the broadcasts. Nevertheless, some of the credit must go to the planners of the short-wave transmissions. Only on this channel of propaganda the National Socialists used a 'soft-sell' technique. The political contents of short-wave transmissions remained moderate even when other forms of Nazi propaganda began to assume an aggressive tone; at no time did the broadcasts contain a high charge of offensive agitation.

A difference in kind between the contents of the short-wave broadcasts—indeed, this was true of National Socialist broadcasting as a whole—and the general tone of Nazi propaganda certainly existed, and it was made possible by a conspicuously autonomous development of broadcasting under Goebbels. There were some purely administrative reasons for this: the Minister of Propaganda was in sole and undisputed charge, his collaborators were handpicked, and they were more easily controllable than, say, the journalists. The new broadcasting techniques had to be developed empirically, and they sometimes did not correspond to the broader phases of Nazi propaganda. At a time when Hitler's régime was mainly concerned with the achievement of recognition and respectability abroad, the broadcasters indulged in an aggressive radio war against Austria [37] and, soon afterwards, in the expansive Saarland campaign. Nor were the powerful anti-Soviet blasts of 1936 adequately echoed in the short-wave transmissions; the Nazi broadcasters were also trying hard to make their régime internationally palatable during the Olympic Games in the summer of 1936, at a time when the broader campaign for international acceptance was being quietly superseded by other pursuits.

Although broadcasting was sometimes used in an independent manner, it cannot be said to have run counter — perhaps with the exception of the Austrian radio war — to the general aims of Nazi propaganda. Indeed, there were certain idiosyncracies of National Socialist publicity that were fully shared by broadcasting. The Nazis employed foreign languages on the short-wave bands only; but even here, news and other spoken programmes were usually bilingual, using German plus the regional language. On the medium-and-long-wave bands — best suited for short-distance transmission in Europe — the National Socialists did not develop a foreign-language service before the war. During the Czechoslovak crisis in 1938 and 1939, for instance, they did not bother to set up a Czech-language service. On the whole, broadcasting, like other expressions of National Socialist propaganda, was circumscribed by the view that the German nation was the most suitable vehicle for the Nazi revolution.

In certain circumstances, however, this weakness could be converted into strength. In the Saarland campaign, the greatest achievement of the National Socialist broadcasters was the complete identification of National Socialism with German nationalism. The former party structure in the Saar territory was ignored and obliterated; the aims of the Germans in the Saar and those of Hitler's government were presented as being identical. The creation of the *Saar-atmosphere* inside Germany on the one hand, and on the other of a feeling in the Saarland that the whole nation stood united behind the demand for reunification, was a propaganda technique that came to be employed by other media as well, and that was used on several fateful occasions before the outbreak of the war.

III
Propaganda Abroad: The Instruments

In the six years of peace they allowed themselves, the Nazis interfered in every aspect of public and private life to an extent unknown in their country's history. The Germans were to have no private lives: their work, their holidays, the new buildings in their towns, the education of their children, the newspapers they read, the films they saw, the radio programmes they listened to, all carried the Nazi stamp. Newly married couples were presented with free copies of *Mein Kampf.*

Nevertheless, after two years of Hitler's rule, the propagandists were able to point to some solid achievements. While many European governments were still struggling with the aftermath of the economic crisis, the Nazis claimed to have solved it in Germany; the Jews, in Nazi eyes the main solvent of the national community, had been deprived of German citizenship. And in the background, there existed powerful means of coercion: the *Gestapo*, the secret police, and the concentration camps.

Many of the original aims of the National Socialists had been achieved and power and success were now living realities for them. This, of course, strengthened the hand of the propagandists. The Germans were trapped in their Nazi state, and they had to listen to incessant sermons on the excellence of their capture.

Imperceptibly, the actual value of propaganda as a political

weapon changed, and perhaps declined, after the National Socialists had achieved power. Before 1933 it had served as the main
instrument for laying the foundations, by winning over the masses,
for the conquest of power in the state. But once he achieved power,
the state, rather than the party, became Hitler's chief interest. The
creation of *Promi*, the department given in gift to Goebbles, sym-
bolized the continued prominence of propaganda in the National
Socialist system: its main task was to gain the maximum popular
support for the Nazi state. At the same time coercion, the officially
sanctioned violence of the pre-1933 era, became available. From a
private army that had operated on the fringes of legality, the *SA*
became an executive organ of the state. But outside Germany,
new horizons opened before the Nazi propagandists.

When the attention of the Nationalist Socialist leaders turned to
the foreign scene, their limitations became more apparent than
ever. Their nationalism and parochial view of life, the poverty of
their ideology, did little to enhance the international appeal of their
party. Unlike the Russian revolutionaries, the Nazis had never been
given an opportunity to acquire, in exile, a cosmopolitan background. Hitler's acquaintance with the outside world was only slight;
his service as a lance corporal in France during the First World War
was his only excursion outside Austria and Germany before 1933.
Goebbels's experience of the foreign scene was still more limited,
and many other high-ranking Nazis were no better off. Such igno-
rance put expert knowledge of foreign affairs at a premium. The
few leading Nazis with a foreign background, men like Alfred
Rosenberg and Rudolf Hess, tended to be automatically regarded
as experts on the subject. Nevertheless, Hitler's government created
a formidable propaganda apparatus abroad; although it often failed
in its mission, it had certainly made its mark on the world before the
war broke out.

We shall have occasion to observe that, even abroad, the National
Socialist propagandists preferred to employ Germans, and especially the German minorities. These were not always available:
there were, however, certain constant factors that worked, almost
everywhere, in the Nazis' favour. In a way the Nazi movement and
its propaganda abroad acted as a catalyst bringing out the critical

state of European life since the conclusion of the First World War. The conflict had drained the resources of the victorious and defeated states alike: the process of Europe's decline from prominence in world affairs had set in. In addition there were the political and economic complications in its eastern outposts that followed the break-up of the Habsburg Empire. The adoption—and the transformation—of Marxist Socialism by the Russians as the official doctrine of their state, and finally, the economic slump at the turn of the decade: all these factors produced a certain *malaise*, especially among the middle and lower-middle classes of Europe. There was a need for some kind of a message of hope, and the Nazis attempted to supply it. Nazi propaganda abroad was mainly directed at the discontented, as it was in Germany.[1] The state of post-war Europe, and especially the existence of German minorities abroad, facilitated the work of the propagandists in Berlin in their attempt to lift the Nazi movement out of the confines of Germany's frontiers.

After Hitler's seizure of power, the first aim of Nazi propaganda was to make the new régime acceptable abroad before embarking on a more ambitious course, and preparing the ground for expansionist moves. For both these tasks, the new rulers of Germany regarded propaganda, rather than diplomacy, as the more suitable instrument. The Nazis shared with other new owners of political power in Europe, including the Bolsheviks immediately after the November 1917 revolution, a distaste for traditional diplomacy and a distrust of the diplomats. Those movements carried a message that could hardly be contained in diplomatic channels. Hitler described the Foreign Ministry as an 'intellectual garbage dump';[2] jolly Hermann Göring, after posing a rhetorical question to a frightened legation counsellor as to what he did the whole day, said: 'In the morning he sharpens pencils, in the afternoon he goes out to tea somewhere.' Attacks on the conduct of foreign affairs came from several sides—they were launched by Goebbels, Rosenberg, and Hess. They all believed in the efficacy of propaganda, and their belief was reinforced by the fact that the diplomatic apparatus was largely in the hands of men who were not party members.

Hitler inherited the Foreign Minister, Baron Konstantin von Neurath, from Schleicher's cabinet: Neurath was a close friend of

President Hindenburg, who asked him to continue serving under Hitler. Although—or perhaps because—he did not, in 1933, expect the Nazi revolution to accomplish a great deal, Neurath became a useful servant of the new régime. He was an easy-going man, probably too easy-going: he combined diplomatic skill with laziness and an inability to resist pressure. Until 1936 he was assisted by the State Secretary, von Bülow, another diplomat of the old school. In the nineteen-twenties, the Social Democrat governments had made some unorthodox appointments: by the time Hitler came to power the German nobility had the Foreign Ministry, once again, firmly in its grasp. Few personal changes occurred in 1933; the missions abroad remained virtually untouched. One of the few remaining Social Democrat appointees, Adolf Müller, the German Minister to Berne, served Hitler's régime for more than six months.

Indeed, the Nazi threat that, after their takeover of power 'heads would roll', was received quite stoically in the Wilhelmstrasse: wits inside the Ministry maintained that, as there were no heads in evidence at the office, they could hardly roll.[3] They were not far wrong. The penetration of the Ministry by the National Socialists in the early years of their régime was so slow as to be insignificant. This was true even on the highest level: not until early 1938 did Ribbentrop, a party member, take over the direction of Germany's foreign policy. But just as there were few out-and-out Nazis in the Foreign Ministry, so there were few determined opponents of Hitler. By the end of 1935, Neurath himself had made his peace with the Nazis; professional diplomats were deeply impressed by the easy initial successes of Hitler on the international scene, and they gave him ungrudging support. And although many leading National Socialist politicians did not see it this way at the time, the continuity of the diplomatic service was of the greatest propaganda value to them. They were trying to make their régime respectable abroad: the services of the diplomats were priceless for this purpose. Had the new Nazi government had to create an entirely new representation abroad—as the Bolsheviks had to do after November 1917, when their seizure of power was followed by wholesale resignations in the diplomatic service—the impression abroad of a break with the past would have been much deeper, and it would have taken much longer to repair.

Goebbels was, of course, more interested than von Neurath in the subject of propaganda abroad and he was the first leading Nazi to begin sniping at the established positions of the diplomats. A conference concerning propaganda abroad took place at the Chancellery on the afternoon of 24 May 1933. Goebbels opened the meeting by remarking that its purpose was the delimitation of duties between the Ministry of Propaganda and the Foreign Ministry; he pointed out that influencing public opinion abroad was the chief task of his Ministry. He needed large funds for this purpose; larger, indeed, than for propaganda at home. He said that agreement existed on his proposal to send to German missions attachés whose relations with the official representatives and with the domestic authorities would be similar to those of the Military Attachés. But the position of the Press Department of the Foreign Ministry still remained to be clarified.[4]

Neurath had no particular liking for Goebbels, and he resented his attempts to encroach on the functions of the Foreign Ministry. He did not want it to become a clearing house for propaganda and espionage activities;[5] his Ministry had to have its own press department, and if this were incorporated into the Ministry of Propaganda he would have to create a new office for the Foreign Ministry. He suggested that it should therefore remain intact, and that it could enter into a personal union with the Ministry of Propaganda through Walther Funk, the Press Chief and a State Secretary in that Ministry.

At this point Hitler intervened. He agreed with Neurath that the Foreign Ministry could not do without its Press Department, as this furnished the Ministry with the basis for the taking of political decisons. But he was really on Goebbels's side: since public opinion abroad was to be influenced, an entirely new organization had to be created. The Ministry of Propaganda would have to concern itself with the 'most varied methods of aggression propaganda' and it would have to execute the directives from the political leadership.

Neurath, who spoke again after Hitler, said that the problem of jurisdiction could be solved quite simply: the officials of his Press Department would furnish factual information, but they would not engage in propaganda; the two Ministries would, he suggested, co-operate closely. The Foreign Minister must have known, however, that his position was weak and that Goebbels would eventually get his way. Later in the discussion, the distinction that the Foreign Minister was trying to make was blurred by Hitler's and Goebbels's remarks; von SchwerinKrosigk, the Minister of Finance, agreed that funds for foreign propaganda had hitherto been insufficient, and he promised Goebbels financial backing as soon as his new organization was established. Hitler wound up the conference by pointing out that 'no amount was too high for a good working propaganda establishment'; he said that the Foreign Ministry would have to 'limit itself to its previous traditional activity', and that 'active propaganda abroad' would be taken over by Goebbels's Ministry.

The conference resulted in a compromise: the Foreign Ministry was not to lose much, and Goebbels was given a free hand to create his own organization. But it was not a compromise that could be expected to last. The new Ministry and its chief were more dynamic, and they were in a better position to expand than the long-established Foreign Ministry. Goebbels benefited by Hitler's decree of 30 June 1933,[6] which removed the control of news and information abroad, of art, art exhibitions, sports, and films for export from the Foreign Ministry, and handed it over to the Ministry of Propaganda. In Berlin, the Foreign Ministry's press conferences declined in importance as the interest of foreign correspondents shifted to those run by the Ministry of Propaganda. Goebbels successfully divested the Foreign Ministry of many of its functions; at the same time, the expenditure on the *Promi*—the affectionate Nazi abbreviation for the Ministry of Propaganda—was rising fast, while that on the Foreign Ministry remained practically static. Compared with other departments of state, the Foreign Ministry was the Nazis' Cinderella: by 1937, they were spending on diplomacy less than 0.3 per cent of total government expenditure. In 1934, the government spent 26.1 million marks on the Ministry of Propaganda and 42.8 million on Neurath's Ministry; in the following year, the difference narrowed considerably: 40.8 million and 46.8 million were spent respectively on propaganda and diplomacy. In 1937 Goebbels's Ministry shot ahead with an expenditure of 55.3 million, compared with 49.4 million spent by the Foreign Ministry.[7] Neurath offered, on the whole, little resistance to Goebbels; in a National Socialist government, his was not a wholly safe position.

Nevertheless, in 1938, the situation began to change in favour of the Foreign Ministry. Early that year, Ribbentrop replaced Neurath as the Minister. Although expenditure on diplomacy did not quite catch up with the amount of money that was lavished on propaganda in the last two years of peace, it rose sharply from 49.4 million marks in 1937 to an estimated sum of 80.8 million in 1939. Ribbentrop was a party member who, unlike Neurath, felt no distaste for propaganda. On the contrary: Ribbentrop's ambition was to prevent the Minister of Propaganda from practising his art abroad. At the time of the Sudetenland crisis, Ribbentrop began by restoring the decimated press division in his Ministry: by the summer of 1939, an open conflict raged between the two departments. It was so acute that on 8 September— eight days after the invasion of Poland—Hitler ordered the Ministers of Foreign Affairs and of Propaganda to agree on a working compromise: this order was in fact not acted on until October 1941, when Goebbels and Ribbentrop signed an agreement on co-operation.[8] By that time, the press division of the *Auswärtiges Amt* consisted of fourteen sections; it was in a position to co-operate or compete on an equal footing with the agencies of the Ministry of Propaganda.

But, apart from these two Ministries, there were other institutions interested in propaganda abroad. At the meeting on 24 May 1933 [9] Alfred Rosenberg was also present. He had risen to prominence under the patronage of Hitler; he became the editor of the *Völkischer Beobachter* in 1921 and he was still in the job twelve years later; he marched at his leader's side in Coburg in 1922 and then again to the Munich Feldherrenhalle on the day of the abortive *putsch* in November 1923.

Rosenberg was a Baltic German—he was born in Reval in Estonia— and was educated in Tsarist Russia; he was in Moscow at the time of the Bolshevik revolution. As Julius Streicher was the leading party antisemite, so Alfred Rosenberg was the extreme exponent of anti-Bolshevism among the Nazis.[10] They regarded him as an expert on foreign policy. Indeed, it was symptomatic of the dearth of informed opinion among the party leaders that Rosenberg was given an opportunity to put his views and interests into practice.

On 1 April 1933 he was appointed, by Hitler, the head of the newly created Foreign Political Office (*Aussenpolitisches Amt*) of the party: Rosenberg and other Nazi leaders expected a great deal of the new institution. Three days after Rosenberg's appointment, the *Völkischer Beobachter* explained its editor's new job: 'With the creation of the Foreign Political Office, the particular desires and the unique aspirations of National Socialism will find expression within the area of foreign policy.' At a press conference on the same day, Rosenberg told the assembled journalists that his agency would 'make the German people aware that foreign policy is not a matter for a small caste, but the concern of the entire nation';[11] he declared that the functions of his office would include the treatment of the questions of the eastern and Danubian areas, of German equality, and the training of 'young people who might one day be called upon to participate in the determination of Germany's destiny in foreign policy'. Rosenberg saw himself as the new Foreign Minister: rumours circulated in well-informed circles that the Foreign Political Office was to take over the functions of the Foreign Ministry, and that, anyway. Neurath was on the point of resigning.

The animosity between Rosenberg and Neurath and his Ministry was therefore to be expected. Rosenberg disliked the Foreign Ministry as much as Goebbels did. There was, however, no love lost between Rosenberg and the Minister of Propaganda either. The tough and incisive Goebbels thought Rosenberg woolly and ineffective; he was highly critical of the ideologist's ability as an administrator. Rosenberg, for his own part, resented the various propagandist 'excesses' committed by Goebbels and his Department; he often complained that they exercised a pernicious influence on public opinion abroad. Remembering his erstwhile party comrade, Rosenberg said of him that he was 'the Mephisto of our once so straightforward movement'.[12] Rosenberg, who never left the straight and narrow path of loyalty to Hitler, thought Goebbels an unreliable man, with a liking for conspiracy and intrigue. Indeed, the personal relations between the two men made co-operation between them and their agencies impossible.

The effectiveness of Rosenberg's apparatus has been seriously over-estimated;[13] Goebbels's view of Rosenberg's administrative abilities was right; in addition, the head of the Foreign Political Office expended a lot of energy on inter-departmental squabbles. In any case, Rosenberg jeopardized the future development of his agency soon after its foundation. In May, he left Berlin on an important mission to London—it was to secure the acquiescence of the English to the Nazi plans for expansion in the East—as Hitler's own emissary. The mission ended in disaster. At the Foreign Office, Rosenberg was coldly received by Sir Robert Vansittart; the swastika-decorated wreath Rosenberg had laid at the Cenotaph was removed by irate members of the British Legion; he received a very bad press, and his efforts to see the Prime Minister failed.[14]

After the fiasco in London, Rosenberg's standing in the party declined. Hitler himself became less readily available: in a covering letter to the Führer with a confidential report on the situation abroad written towards the end of the year, Rosenberg complained that the Chancellery made it impossible for him, on several occasions, to discuss his views with Hitler personally.[15] His position in regard to other agencies dealing with foreign policy, and the *Auswärtiges Amt* in particular, also deteriorated. The funds for the Foreign Political Office were drastically cut down: he could no longer be regarded as a serious rival of either the diplomats or the propagandists. The agency continued its existence in the shadow of its more powerful and experienced rivals. While Rosenberg kept on sending long reports to Hitler, his office organized beer parties for resident diplomats and for visiting dignitaries; it sponsored lectures, and its clerks justified their existence by accumulating a vast library of newspaper cuttings.

Apart from foreign governments and peoples, there existed another important target for National Socialist propaganda. Some 27,000,000 Germans lived outside the frontiers of their mother country. Aside from the solidly German Austria, there were substantial German settlements in Poland and Russia, in Czechoslovakia, Hungary, Rumania, and Yugoslavia. These Germans had a long tradition behind them of settlement in eastern and south-eastern Europe. More recently, the Germans had begun to emigrate to the United States: between 1809 and 1929 more than 6,000,000 German emigrants left for the New World. The diaspora had fascinated German scholars. Since the end of the eighteenth century men like Ernst Moritz Arndt, Friedrich Christoph, Ludwig Uhland, and Jacob Grimm had devoted their attention to German settlements abroad. Indeed, it was natural for scholars to turn to ethnography when the unification of their country was the order of the day. Since the new state was to be based on the nation, questions such as what the nation exactly was, and where it could be found, became urgent problems of academic research. Nevertheless, scholarly work was merely a prelude to political activities, and the dividing line between them was often very thin.

By the end of the nineteenth century there existed many societies of the educational or gymnastic kind, designed to sustain the national consciousness of the Germans living abroad. In 1908—at a time when central and east European nationalism was becoming more intense and when its organizations were being overhauled— the *Allgemeiner Deutscher Schulverein* (the General Union of German Schools) became the *Verein für das Deutschtum im Ausland* (*VDA*, the Union of Germans Abroad). The new organization continued to support German schools in 'endangered districts'; in 1908, the Hamburg branch of *VDA* rendered assistance to sixty-two schools in both North and South America. But at the same time, the society widened its scope; it granted a considerable financial subsidy, for instance, to the *Tiroler Volksbund*, an organization dedicated to countering the advance of the Italian irredentist movement in South Tyrol.[16] A few months before the outbreak of the war, an organization similar to *VDA*—the *Deutsches Schutzbund*—was established; during the war two additional institutes were set up in order to advance research in German minorities abroad: the *Institut für Auslandskunde, Grenz- und Auslandsdeutschtum* in Leipzig in 1914, and, three years later, the *Deutsches Auslandsinstitut* in Stuttgart.

The peace treaties of 1919 further stimulated the ethnographers interest: apart from the Germans lost to the Reich, a much larger number of them had been deprived of the protection of the Habsburg dynasty; many of these Germans passed under the control of the successor states. Thus millions of new recruits joined the category of *Auslandsdeutsche*, and the activities of the *VDA* had to be considerably expanded. This work was carried on in the Weimar Republic. In 1925 the number of the local groups of *VDA* reached 1,707; by 1931 it had risen to 3,286.[17]

The study of minorities became a respectable academic subject, taught at many German universities, and the science developed its own terminology. There were the *Grenzdeutsche*, who inhabited ethnically homogeneous areas alongside Germany's frontier; it was assumed that they lived in the states of Austria, Czechoslovakia, or Poland against their will. The *Binnendeutsche*, on the other hand, lived by their consent in countries bordering on Germany, such as Switzerland. The *Inseldeutsche* inhabited compact settlements, and the *Streudeutsche* were scattered farther afield, outside Central Europe. Finally, the Germans living overseas were described as *Überseedeutsche*.

There can be no doubt that the minorities abroad attrached the keen attention of the Reich Germans during the Weimar period. Indeed, it was said of the various societies concerned with the *Auslandsdeutsche* that they helped in 'paving the way for Hitlerian nationalism and the formation of a larger German Reich in central Europe'.[18] And more than that. Very often, the nationalism of the Germans abroad was more intense than that of the Germans at home. While the latter supported the former financially, they were rewarded by the gratifying spectacle of the pure flame of a faith even stronger than their own. The National Socialists of course soon appreciated the opportunities that situation offered them.

In this respect, Rudolf Hess, Hitler's deputy, worked harder than any other leading National Socialist. He also possessed the qualifications that seemed auspicious for a Nazi interested in foreign affairs. He was born, in Alexandria in 1896, the son of a German merchant, and educated in Germany and Switzerland. During the war he was wounded twice, while serving on the western front. In 1920, Hess went to the university of Munich to study history, economics, and the new subject of geopolitics. There he came under the influence of Karl Haushofer, an ex-army general and a geographer, the leading German exponent of the 'science' of geopolitics. At the same time, Hess joined the embryonic National Socialist party; he was attracted by this movement after hearing Hitler speak in one of the beer-cellars. In Haushofer's speculations the German minorities abroad played a rather prominent role: his dominant belief was that all the inhabited parts of the globe were governed by a kind of geopolitical law of the jungle. It appealed to the budding Nazi; Hess became Haushofer's friend and assistant. When Hess was arrested with his Führer, after the unsuccessful *putsch* in Munich in November 1923, Haushofer was a frequent visitor to the Landsberg prison.

Indeed, a few months after Hitler became the Chancellor, Rudolf Hess began to show a marked interest in German minorities abroad. He circulated a strictly confidential 'record of a decision by the Deputy of the Führer';[19] it was drafted in Munich on 27 October, and it consisted of four points:

1. All questions regarding the German element beyond the borders (*Grenzdeutsche* and *Austandsdeutsche*) and questions regarding the strengthening of the whole German community, as well as all related matters within the Reich, are subject to my jurisdiction and supervision.

2. As a deliberative and executive organ, I have called together the *Volksdeutsch* Council (*Volksdeutscher Rat*) which is headed by Dr. Haushofer, University Professor, Munich.

3. Dr. Steinacher, Berlin, has primary responsibility for representing the *Volksdeutsch* Council abroad.

4. The *Volksdeutsch* Council does not appear publicly.

RUDOLF HESS

On the surface, this document was just another piece of evidence of the scramble for power among the party leaders. But it was also the beginning of an attempt to subject all the Germans living abroad to control by the National Socialist party. They should be organized in exclusively Nazi societies; they should be a willing instrument of the policy—whatever it might be at any given moment—of the Nazi government. Hess's associates on the *Volksdeutscher Rat* had a considerable experience behind them of the German minorities abroad. Haushofer's experience had been largely academic; that of Dr. Hans Steinacher was more of a practical nature. He was the chief of the *VDA*, the principal organization of Germans abroad;

for several years after the war he had conducted propaganda on behalf of the Germans in several disputed territories of Austria: in Carinthia, in Tyrol, and in Ödenburg (Sopron), near the frontier between Austria and Hungary.

Again, Hess's peremptory 'record of a decision' became the centre of a dispute concerning departmental competence. And again—as in the case of Goebbels's earlier attempt to control the *Auswärtiges Amt*'s press section—the Foreign Ministry had to defend itself against encroachments on its own territory. Its cultural Policy Department (*Abteilung VI*) under Senior Counsellor Friedrich Stieve had a section which dealt with German national groups abroad; on 11 November it supplied von Neurath with a brief for his conversation with Hess.[20] By then, Hess had written to the Foreign Minister, and Steinacher had also requested a discussion. Although the Wilhelmstrasse officials were prepared to listen to the ideas of the representatives of the *Volksdeutscher Rat*, they advised their Minister that these discussions could be conducted only on the following basis: 'The *Volksdeutsch* work and the minorities question are very closely linked with Germany's foreign policy in general. The Ministries concerned[21] will be glad to receive from the *Volksdeutsch* Council and to examine any suggestion relating to the furtherance of German nationality work. But the utlimate decision in all *Volksdeutsch* and minorities questions must rest with the Reich government, and specifically with the Foreign Ministry which is responsible for foreign policy.'

The dispute was settled in the end on the lines suggested by the Foreign Ministry. After the conversation with Hess, Neurath was able to inform his officials as well as other Ministries—the Ministry of Propaganda among them—that 'full agreement was reached on the point that the Council shall act only as an advisory body, which has the task of assisting the policies of the responsible ministries in questions relating to the German national community and the minorities. The Government will be able to use the *Volksdeutsch* Council at its discretion'.[22]

Apart from the formation of the *Volksdeutscher Rat*, an institution that was to gather under its wing all the older societies that concerned themselves with Germans abroad, Hess struck out in a different direction. It is possible that, after his brushes with the *Auswärtiges Amt* over the question of the Council, he realized that he had adopted the wrong approach and that the party, rather than government agencies, would show more understanding for his ideas. After all, the party had had connexions abroad before it came to rule the Reich.

Among the earliest Nazi groups abroad were those formed by the German immigrants to the United States and Latin America. Many of the half a million people who emigrated to the United States after the war were young, and they had grown up in Germany in the same conditions as the Nazi movement; some of them had been *Freikorps* members. In Chicago, these right-wing immigrants set up an organization, the *Teutonia*, in 1924; its chairman, who was an ardent follower of Julius Streicher, joined the Nazi party two years later.[23]

In Latin America, the *NSDAP* was making some progress as well: in 1928, a dozen Germans founded a local organization (*Ortsgruppe*) in Paraguay. Although local party organizations were set up in a number of European countries as well as in the Americas, National Socialist ideas cannot be said to have made much impression among the Germans abroad before 1933. They of course ran their national organizations of various political complexions: the Nazi organizations were in a minority among them. But this was enough to arouse the interest of the party members in Germany. In 1930, an office was established in Hamburg by Willy Grothe, a party member who had spent some twenty years in Africa; the function of his office was to keep in touch with German Nazis abroad. In May 1931 it was officially recognized by the party leadership; when Hitler came to power, it had some 3,300 party members on its files.[24]

Soon after the official recognition of the 'foreign division'— *Auslandsabteilung der Reichsleitung der NSDAP*— the office advertised a job in its African department. Ernst-Wilhelm Bohle applied, and got it. Bohle was born in Bradford in 1903; three years later, his father left England for Cape Town to teach physics at the university, and Bohle was brought up and educated there. He was certainly given enough opportunities to become a German nationalist: the Bohle children were forbidden to speak English at home; during the

First World War, young Ernst was the only German boy at his Cape Town school. He studied economics in Germany after the war, and from 1924 he worked for a number of business firms.

The work for the party's foreign division suited him: he had personal experience of the life of the Germans abroad, and he had strong views on the question of whether or not they should preserve intact their national identity. He joined the party in March 1932; his devoted work attracted the attention of Rudolf Hess—Hitler's deputy came from a similar background—and Bohle became Hess's protégé. From now on, his rise to prominence was fast. On 8 May, he was put in charge of the foreign division of the party which, by an order of Hess of 17 February 1934, became the *Auslandsorganisation der NSDAP*, usually referred to as *AO*—the Foreign Organization. Bohle knew his was a strong position, and that it could be strengthened still further. Shortly before his official elevation in May 1933, he wrote to a party comrade that his organization controlled 160 groups abroad, that there existed 'great possibilities for its further extension', and that it could render great services to Rosenberg's newly founded *Aussenpolitisches Amt*, as well as to Goebbels's Ministry.[25]

Soon, however, Bohle's organization began to outstrip in importance Rosenberg's amateur foreign office. Bohle was not weighed down by personal animosities and past party feuds; he was an efficient administrator, with good connexions in high party circles. Nevertheless, as the *AO* grew in stature, it came into inevitable conflict with the Foreign Ministry. Friction between the *AO* agents and the diplomats and between Bohle and von Neurath developed. In his more expansive moments, Bohle regarded his province as a '*Gau* without limits'; in return, the Foreign Minister described Bohle as a 'scoundrel [*Gauner*] without limits'. The conflict did not disappear after December 1937, when the activities of Bohle's organization were officially sanctioned, and he became a Secretary of State in the Foreign Ministry; it continued even after Ribbentrop became Foreign Minister. In his memoirs, Ribbentrop recorded that 'Especially during my early years as Foreign Minister, the activities of the National Socialist Organization of Germans Abroad caused me acute embarrassment, in South America, for instance. There, as

elsewhere, such things as processions, uniforms, and rallies created
the impression that National Socialism was to be exported. Indeed,
however wrongly, the Organization was described as a 'Fifth
Column', and furnished President Roosevelt with the grotesque
propaganda argument that Germany was trying to establish a foothold in South America, which it would use as a base for action
against the U.S.A. In view of these and similar difficulties in many
other countries, I often pointed out that while the Organization's
aims of keeping Germans abroad together was certainly right, the
manner in which this was done entailed disproportionate disadvan-
tages. However, the Organization of Germans Abroad was the pet
child of Rudolf Hess, and a shadow was cast over our original friendship by this difference of opinion, and also by the fact that it was not
easy to work with Bohle. . . .'[26]

Despite the animosity of the two successive Foreign Ministers
and the diplomates, the *Auslandsorganisation* prospered. From
humble beginnings in Hamburg it came to administer, by 1934, some
350 groups abroad; three years later, its head office in Berlin employed 700 people, who looked after 28,000 party members abroad, plus
23,000 organized merchant seamen. In the same year, all members
of the diplomatic service were organized into an *Ortsgruppe*,
another move by the party to tighten its grip on the Foreign Ministry. Indeed, this last arrangement clearly shows the administrative
complexities of the Nazi state and, within it, the curious double
status of the *AO*. As a State Secretary in the Foreign Ministry, Bohle
was directly responsible to the Minister; at the same time, his activities as the leader of the party's Foreign Organization and his responsibility to Rudolf Hess, Hitlers' deputy, remained unchanged.[27]

Technically the *AO* remained a province—a *Gau*—of the *NSDAP*,
and as such it was divided, like the party itself, into an hierarchy of
regional sections. There were eight departments in the *AO* head
office; Department I dealt with north-eastern Europe; II with
western Europe apart from Great Britain and Ireland; Department
III covered Austria, south-eastern Europe and the Near East; IV—
Italy, Switzerland and Hungary; V—Africa; VI—North America;
VII—Latin America; VIII—Great Britain, Ireland, the Far East, and
Austrialia; a special department dealth with the sailors. There were

also departments for teachers, lawyers, government employers, and students abroad, and 'functional offices', such as of foreign trade, culture, a 'speakers' department' which organized festivities in German colonies abroad.[28] At Altona, near Hamburg, the AO ran a school, the purpose of which was to instruct Germans from abroad in National Socialist agitation.

There was, however, some confusion as to precisely what kind of Germans the activities of the AO aimed at. An official pamphlet, published in Berlin in 1937, flatly stated that the Foreign Organization was concerned exclusively with German citizens living abroad.[29] This was a concession to the growing concern over the activities of the Nazis in the neighbouring countries; there was a convenient ambiguity in modes of expression, and usually no distinction was made between the Germans living abroad and those who remained German citizens. In the Nazi eyes, the question of citizenship was of a purely formal nature; ties of blood and race were assumed to be much stronger.

The main function of Bohle's organization was to unite all Germans abroad under National Socialist leadership; the party had been pursuing the same aim inside Germany before and after 1933. In order to work successfully, the propaganda conducted by the AO among the Germans abroad had to be founded on certain basic assumptions. Of these, the most important was the systematic opposition to any form of assimilation. At the *Parteitag der Ehre* in September 1936, where he 'honoured' fortyeight flags of the AO's local groups, Rudolf Hess said: 'The Führer had come in order to hammer into all of us the fact that the German cannot and may not choose whether or not he will be German but that he was sent into this world by God as a German, and that God thereby had laid upon him, as a German, duties of which he cannot divest himself without committing treason to Providence. Therefore, we believe and we know that the German everywhere is a German—whether he lives in the Reich or in Japan, in France or in China, or anywhere else in the world. Not countries or continents, not climate or environment, but blood and race determine the world of ideas of the German.'[30]

It was assumed that the Germans would resist assimilation in

their adoptive countries; a politically divided German cummunity
was, however, also undesirable from the National Socialist point
of view, Bohle stated this view soon after he had taken the leader-
ships of the *AO*: 'Today our fighters are often defending desperate
posts. They know, however, that at home and abroad only National
Socialism can prepare the way for a cohesive Germandom. Only
National Socialists who are ideologically well grounded can unite
the German colonies, which outside the homeland are often still
divided, and create a unity in which the guarantee for support of the
homeland by foreign Germandom can be given.' [31]

Since an attempt had to be made to unite all Germans living
abroad in supporting Hitler's régime, much of the activity of the
Auslandsorganisation consisted of propaganda. We shall have an
opportunity to examine the techniques employed by the Nazis
abroad in greater detail in subsequent chapters; at this point, suf-
fice it to say that the *AO* faithfully reflected the modes of agitation
used inside Germany. And since the Nazis were often confronted
with hostile governments in foreign countries, their situation resembled that of the party inside Germany before 1933. To a certain
extent they continued to use the mixture of propaganda and violence: the *AO* had a special section working on *Gestapo* commis-
sions.[32] The Foreign Organization's agents kept a watchful eye
on the activities of the refugees from Nazi Germany; there were
many instances of their intimidation.

Indeed, the Germans abroad were regarded in Berlin as the best
target and, at the same time, a suitable vehicle for National Socialist
propaganda abroad. And Bohle was the right man to direct it.
Although he came into conflict with the Foreign Ministry, he was
too remote from the centre of power in the Nazi state to be suspected, by the Nazi leaders, of empire-building; under the patronage
of Hess, he was able to build up the *AO* undisturbed. Even Goebbels,
who rarely left an opportunity for criticism of the endeavours of
his colleagues unexplored, treated Bohle and his organization
kindly. Early in March 1943 he wrote in his diary: 'Bohle gave me a
memorandum on foreign propaganda. In it he is highly critical of
the so-called propaganda abroad of the Foreign Ministry. This is
incredibly bad. The diplomats are not suited to conduct foreign

V.   'Russia arms!. . . and Germany?' 1933

Sie kämpften und bluteten für Deutschlands Freiheit

VI.   'They fought and bled for Germany's freedom.' 1932

propaganda. I am certain that I could carry out together with the *AO* a wonderful system of propaganda abroad but our diplomats stand in my way.'[33]

While those state and party agencies that dealt in propaganda abroad rarely lived at peace with each other, a large variety of unofficial organizations pursued their activities comparatively undisturbed. They could push forward the more extremist lines of National Socialist propaganda without any regard to their repercussions in the sphere of foreign policy; they formed knots of agitation on the fringes of official propaganda. Some of these organizations had existed before Hitler came to power; none of them could, however, have continued their activities without at least a tacit approval by the Nazi government; many received official financial support. These organizations specialized largely in antisemitic, anti-Marxist, and anti-Soviet propaganda: their main interests corresponded to those of Streicher and Rosenberg, the leading party ideologists.

In Erfurt, Colonel Fleischhauer ran one of the most active of these private institutions. Before 1933 he had worked independently of the National Socialists; he entered into a close contact with them after Hitler came to power, and his antisemitic activities prospered. They centred on a bi-monthly newsletter, in three languages, the *Weltdienst*; its first number was published in December 1933. Less than a year later, Fleischhauer organized an antisemitic congress; he found it necessary to emphasize in his periodical [34] that Streicher had not summoned the congress, and that the 'pioneers' of antisemitism could not be regarded as 'Hitler agents'.

Fleischhauer's Pan-Aryans were non-denominational Christians, on their guard against the Jews and the Freemasons. But Fleischhauer was faced with stiff competition. There was Ernst Pistor in Berlin, who published the newspaper *Der Judenkenner*, and who founded the short-lived *Alliance Raciste Universelle*; the semi-official institute which dealt with eugenics (*Aufklärungsamt für Bevölkerungspolitik und Rassenpflege*) published its house-magazine in both German and English. The *Deutscher Fichte-Bund* was founded in 1914 to propagate German views and aims abroad; when Hitler came to power, the organization survived unharmed: it

adapted itself easily to the attitudes of the new masters of Germany
The activities of the Fichte League in the field of foreign propaganda were intensified in the last two years before the war, and they
were largely directed at the English-speaking countries.

There existed many other approved, but unofficial, organizations; many of them were rather elusive, because they frequently
changed their names, their leadership, and their address. They
once again set off the poverty of the Nazi — or nationalist — ideologies:
they dealt in negative doctrines of a limited, sectional appeal. However, an attempt to create a truly international organization was
made. In the spring of 1934 an enterprising German lawyer, Hans
Keller, founded a society called the 'International Union of Nationalists' (*Internationale Arbeitsgemeinschaft der Nationalisten*);
it was based on Zürich, where its expensively produced pamphlets
were published. Its first congress took place in Berlin in December;
the principal delegates were invited by Goebbels to attend the
annual meeting organized by the *Reichskulturkammer* in the
Berlin Sportpalast. The delegates came from Warsaw, Paris, Amsterdam, Rome, and elsewhere; most of them were university
professors. It was, on the whole, a respectable gathering: perhaps
the men who came to it had not realized what purposes they were
to be used for. There can be no doubt that Keller sympathized with
the Nazis, and that his friends were expected to contribute to making
Hitler's government acceptable in their own countries.

Keller regarded the delegates as more representative of their
peoples than their respective governments: to make such a distinction is, of course, one of the basic techniques of the propagandist.
For Keller it was the central point of his *Weltanschauung*. He maintained that in Europe there existed a 'state' nationalism quite
separately from '*völkisch*', or popular, nationalism, and that their
identification was the only certain road to national salvation.
According to Keller, Hitler had succeeded in healing the rift, and
he led the way where others must follow. Keller's 'Third Europe',
composed of such rejuvenated states, was clearly a concomitant
of Hitler's Third Reich.

But Keller was forced to admit that the 'conceptual instruments'
for the discussion of the 'new nationalism' were still lacking.[35] And

apart from the elements of the National Socialist doctrine, Keller had nothing to fall back on. He did not, however, have to do all the work himself. Louis Bertrand, for instance, at the time President of the *Académie Français*, wrote in a pamphlet published by Keller [36] that the 'Nationalist International is going to unite the peoples against the Communist International, which is their mortal enemy'.

Anti-Communism was, on the whole, a safer subject than anti-semitism. At the first congress of Keller's organization, de Pottere, one of Colonel Fleischhauer's associates from Erfurt (he was using the name of Farmer on this occasion, and he said he represented Hungary) was hard put to it to define the new nationalism in a manner acceptable to the assembled intellectuals. He revealed his true opinions only towards the end of his involved speech. He said then that race alone mattered, and that the Jews, although they could speak German, were not Aryans. [37] Nevertheless, Keller's 'international' did not last long. His attacks on the Italian fascists was perhaps his gravest tactical error: anyway, Keller was too ambitious. The men he tried to bring together may have had certain attitudes, but no real community of interests or ideology in common. He organized two more congresses: at the end of 1936 the last of his pretentious pamphlets was published.

Perhaps with one exception,[38] the private organizations that attempted to disseminate National Socialist propaganda abroad were not very effective. They never did more than fill in the details in the overall propaganda outline; they were usually patronized by either Rosenberg or Streicher, the ideological extremists, and they often appealed to the lunatic fringe of public opinion outside Germany. The main burden was carried by the state and party agencies; Goebbles continued to exercise the strongest influence of propaganda abroad. He could do so through the press, broadcasting, and films: his control over these media was undisputed. But he regarded foreign propaganda, to a high degree, as extension of the propaganda at home. He was perhaps too busy inside Germany: at any rate, he was unable to make the distinctions between different types of political environment that are so necessary for the successful conduct of foreign propaganda. There were other highly placed party members—Rudolf Hess or Alfred Rosenberg—who regarded themselves as better qualified for this task, and they built up party and state agencies that played an important role in propaganda abroad. The Foreign Ministry remained the propagandists' principal whipping boy; the enmity between Goebbels and the two successive Foreign Ministers jeopardized a close cooperation between the two government agencies. Hitler took little notice of such rivalries, and he usually let his underlings squabble in peace. Nevertheless, the organizational anarchy in the field of foreign propaganda often made it difficult to disentangle the respective contributions of the various organizations to any given incident or propaganda effect that took place outside Germany. And at the same time, their activities blurred the image abroad of the National Socialist regime: a phenomenon that cannot be said to have always worked out to the disadvantage of Germany's rulers.

IV
Propaganda Abroad: The Message

Outside Germany, Hitler faced a situation much more delicate and complex than at home. Yet, on the whole, the contents of National Socialist propaganda remained the same whether it was intended for foreign or domestic consumption. The lack of international appeal in Nazi ideology, the limiting nationalism and inexperience of the foreign scene of the National Socialist leaders, their distrust of traditional diplomacy and reliance on German minorities abroad, all contributed to that situation. And, as Hitler's government thought it necessary to make its foreign policy acceptable at home, an additional link was created between propaganda at home and abroad.

Indeed, in the political literature of National Socialism it is impossible to find a body of basic directives dealing with propaganda abroad even remotely resembling those contained in *Mein Kampf,* which concerned propaganda inside Germany. There exist only a few scattered references. In *Mein Kampf,* for instance, Hitler congratulated the Allies on their propaganda effort in the First World War: he was unaware, however, of the fact that the Allied propagandists had been equally impressed by Germany's efforts with regard to Russia.[1] Some time in 1933 Hitler intimated that he had learned from the Bolsheviks, alluding at the same time to Sir Roger Casement and to revolutions, and hoping that 'we shall have friends who will help us in all enemy countries'.[2] But he saw propaganda abroad primarily as an instrument for the achievement of power, just as he had seen propaganda at home before 1933. Discussing the nature of the future war, Hitler is reported to have said: 'The place of artillery preparation for frontal attack by the infantry in trench warfare will in future be taken by revolutionary propaganda, to break down the enemy psychologically before the armies begin to function at all.' And then he added: 'How to achieve the moral breakdown of the enemy before the war has started—that is the problem that interests me.'[3] Nevertheless, the 'moral breakdown of the enemy' was the remote, the ultimate object of propaganda: we shall see that it was achieved only in special political circumstances. For the more routine purposes—including 'projection' of the Nazi state and its ideology—the Ministry of Propaganda was in the main content to translate the key themes of home propaganda to the international plane.

Though antisemitism figured prominently in Nazi propaganda, it did not make a significant contribution to Nazi success, especially outside Germany. Its value lay mainly in the manner in which it was manipulated to satisfy the psychological needs of the Germans. The Jews could be used as scapegoats; antisemitism could be employed as a smoke-screen which served to divert public attention from genuine social and political problems.[4] Ultimately, it could be traced to the Führer's personal predilections: Hitler was an antisemite by conviction.

Although he could calculate and exploit the appeal of antisemitism in Germany, he miscalculated its value for propaganda abroad. He regarded it as a more than suitable article for export: indeed, he is reported to have said: 'Antisemitism is a useful revolutionary expedient. My Jews are a valuable hostage given to me by the democracies. Antisemitic propaganda in all countries is an almost indispensable medium for the extension of our political campaign. You will see how little time we shall need in order to upset the ideas and the criteria of the whole world, simply by attacking Judaism. It is beyond question the most important weapon in my propaganda arsenal, and almost of deadly efficiency.'[5]

Hitler's estimate of the value of antisemitic propaganda was mistaken. On balance, the Nazi antisemitic drives abroad had more often a repulsive than an attractive effect. Even in Fascist Italy, there existed little understanding of this special type of Nazi racialism, and still less a desire to emulate it. In a report on the propaganda situation in Italy from October 1933, Scheffer, the *WTB* agency representative in Rome, had to inform the Foreign Ministry that Mussolini had personally received the Chief Rabbi of Milan and that 'Jewish propaganda' was being made, backstage, in Italy: Jewish business circles were, for instance, showing themselves unwilling to buy German goods. Nevertheless, Scheffer had a ready explanation for this state of affairs, an explanation which his masters in Berlin would understand. The Italian, he wrote, 'in whose veins there circulate racially different types of blood, cannot understand the Jewish question in Germany'.[6]

In the National Socialist view of the foreign scene, the Italians, though they were ideologically sound, were racially unrelated to the Germans, and therefore no sanity of views could be expected from them in matters of race. The Nazi view of the British, on the other hand, was the reverse of their image of the Italians: 'Englishmen'— this term usually embraced all the inhabitants of Great Britain— were racially related, although ideologically quite unsound. Hitler did not find in Britain the response to antisemitism he had hoped for. The national newspapers had reported on antisemitic outrages committed by the Nazis even before Hitler came to power: after January 1933 the treatment of the Jews was widely regarded as the testing ground for the intentions of the new government in Germany. The question then asked in many editorials was whether, carrying the new responsibilities of the government, the Chancellor could afford to continue his former policies.

In the following years, even the dailies—such as *The Times*— which supported the policy of establishing an understanding with Hitler's régime, continued to report on the treatment of Jews in Germany. Indeed, the reports on the pogroms of November 1938 marked the beginning of a strong revulsion, in Britain, against Hitler's régime.[7] At the same time, direct antisemitic propaganda did not make an impact of any significance in Britain; it was, on occasions, harmful to the Nazi cause. Goebbels's Ministry never appeared much concerned with this aspect of antisemitic propaganda: the German diplomats in London, on the other hand, realized that it should not be given too much prominence. But they received no guidance from Berlin; they used their own discretion.

As late as 19 July 1939, Dirksen, the Ambassador to London, wrote: 'Having regard to the stolid, tolerant racial character of the British, every antisemitic impulse must be valued all the more highly, since opportunities for disseminating anti-Jewish ideas are very limited.'[8] Apart from Mosley's party, there existed only a few other, more or less antisemitic organizations: Dirksen referred to that of Captain Ramsay (the Tory M.P.), and Lady Hardinge's connexions with such societies. Antisemitic ideas were also expressed in certain right-wing periodicals: Dirksen singled out for mention the low-circulation weekly, *The New Pioneer*; a section of the Catholic press also attacked the Jews, but in an oblique way, in connexion with Bolshevism. Nevertheless, Dirksen wrote, 'antisemitic attitudes are revealed more clearly by conversations with the man in the street than by press-sources'. The rapid increase in Jewish immigration promoted, according to Dirksen, the spread of antisemitism: indeed, he went on to say that 'A further increase of anti-Jewish feeling in Britain can be expected'. Dirksen's advice to the propagandists was that now — less than two months before the outbreak of the war — was the time to begin exploiting antisemitic mood in Britain.

In Britain, antisemitic propaganda either had only a marginal appeal, or it was entirely cancelled out by reports on National Socialist measures against the Jews in Germany. Nevertheless, for a short time and in special circumstances, receptiveness to antisemitic propaganda accompanied, and aided, the breakdown of the political order in central and eastern Europe. That order had shallow roots: set up by the peace treaties after the power of both Germany and Russia had been destroyed, it had, in 1933, a brief and unsettled existence behind it. In this part of Europe National Socialist propaganda was at its most effective: indeed, it corroded the foundations of the post-war régimes to such an extent that military conquest later appeared either welcome or easy. We shall have occasion to note that National Socialist propaganda was mainly aimed at the Germans, the *Volksdeutsche*, in this area: Hitler knew that their co-operation was sufficient to severely impair the working of the order established and supported by the western powers.

In addition the Jewish problem in eastern Europe could be exploited for the purposes of a second line of attack. Indigenous antisemitism, both organized and spontaneous, existed in Rumania and Poland: these two countries contained numerous Jewish minorities.[9] Most of these Jews lived in isolated communities, the progress of their emancipation was slow, and they retained their characteristic features, from religion to dress and mannerisms. The compact Jewish communities both stimulated the pogroms and made them easy to carry out; on a higher social level, the distinction the Jews achieved in commerce, industry, and in the free professions, created resentment among their gentile compatriots. In the nineteenth century, the emergent east-European nationalisms had often contained an antisemitic charge.

Indeed, antisemitism in eastern Europe anticipated, in many respects, the National Socialist attitudes to the Jews; after 1933, under the impact of Nazi propaganda and precept, antisemitism came to play an increasingly important role in the politics of this part of Europe. Early in 1936, for instance, a Jewish newspaper was banned in Poland for publishing insulting references to a National Socialist Minister; in October 1937, Colonel Kowalewski, one of the leaders of the government party, told his interviewer from the *Völkischer Beobachter*, after mentioning the brotherly feelings between the Poles and the German minority: 'For us there exists only one difference in the evaluation of the people in Poland: Christian and non-Christian.'[10] From that year until the outbreak of the war, a number of anti-Jewish measures were taken by the government, and discussion of the Jewish problem was artificially stimulated.

In Rumania, the situation developed on similar lines. At the end of 1937, the short-lived government of Octavian Goga and Professor Cuza pursued a pro-German policy combined with ruthless antisemitic measures. It lifted the ban on the import of Nazi propaganda books; Professor Cuza, in an interview with Julius Streicher's *Fränkische Tageszeitung*, demanded a common front of all 'awakened' nations against the Jews and therefore a German-Rumanian *rapprochement*.[11] For some time after the fall of the Goga government, and after the prosecution for treason of Corneliu Codreanu—the leader of the Fascist Iron Guard—the relations between Rumania and Germany deteriorated, and the position of the Jews improved.

The antisemitic measures of the former government were not revoked; they remained, for the time being, unimplemented. Nevertheless, after the fall of France, Horia Sima—Codreanu's successor—summed up the situation in the following manner: 'Absolute adherence to the Axis Powers with no swerving from this fundamental principle even if the Axis should be unfair to Rumania, because the present war is really one between the two worlds of Aryans and of Jews.'[12]

Whereas in Poland and Rumania antisemitic propaganda found a ready and receptive audience, in Hungary and Czechoslovakia the situation was, from the National Socialist point of view, less favourable. Many of the 500,000 Hungarian Jews had achieved a high degree of emancipation before 1918; even the antisemitic restrictions imposed under the government of Gömbös, in the years 1933-36, made a clear distinction between the 'Hungarian' and the newly arrived Jews. Only after the autumn of 1938, when Hungary joined Germany in the assault on the territorial integrity of the Czechoslovak state, was a more ruthless antisemitic policy developed alongside Hungary's increasing dependence on Germany.

In Czechoslovakia, National Socialist antisemitic propaganda remained ineffective in the Czech areas until 1938. Here, the Jews were also better integrated than in Rumania or Poland; Masaryk, the first President, had fought incipient antisemitism under the Habsburg rule. The two Fascist groups—one of them was run by Gerneral Gajda, who had played an important but obscure role in the intervention against the Soviet government in 1918, and who declared himself, in March 1939, the Führer of the Czechs—commanded only a limited popular appeal. Even Konrad Henlein, the leader of the pro-Nazi Sudeten Germans in Czechoslovakia, thought it advisable to keep antisemitism out of his party programme as long as his connections with the Reich National Socialist movement were secret. After the Munich agreement in 1938, the growth of antisemitism accompanied, and contributed to, the general demoralization in public life. In Slovakia, there had existed antisemitic trends in Father Hlinka's party before Munich: it was intensely nationalist and anti-Czech; it became the government party in the independent Slovak state under Hitler's patronage.

Indeed, the exaggerated claim Hitler made for the propaganda value of antisemitism nearly held true in eastern Europe. Here, antisemitism proved a disintegrating and demoralizing force; it accompanied the corrosion of the political system that had been established by the peace treaties, and it accelerated this process. The politicians who were receptive to its appeal thought of antisemitism as of one of the cornerstones of a right-wing popular movement; they exploited its value as a diversion of public attention from genuine social problems. In Poland and in Rumania, especially, antisemitism remained— as it had been described in nineteenth century Russia— an 'idiot's socialism'. In addition, it appealed to those politicians who were dissatisfied with the post-war settlement and the stresses it had generated: this was particularly true of Slovakia. Antisemitic agitation was of course more effective when it had a corresponding antisemitic mood to exploit. In Hungary Nazi propaganda had to appeal to 'revisionism'— the dissatisfaction with the peace treaty— rather than to the underdeveloped local antisemitism. But whatever the degree of development and the reasons for local antisemitism may have been, it always went hand in hand with a policy of understanding with Hitler's Germany, a policy which presented an assault on the *status quo*.

Anti-Communism was the other article of home propaganda which was vigorously exported. In National Socialist ideology, there existed an organic connexion between the two themes; the conflict with Communism became the battle royal for the National Socialists. Their leaders often said that the movement had grown up in this struggle, in which they expected it to grow stronger and finally to triumph. Certainly, the Communists were, together with the Jews, the main target of Nazi violence and abuse: they had competed for the same audience as the Communists. But whatever the intensity of the actual political engagement may have been at any given time, the National Socialists came to look upon it as a propaganda gold mine. The campaign had a wide and varied target. It was aimed, in Nazi terminology, at *'Gesamtmarxismus,'* that embraced all Marxist phenomena, from, say, a Communist cell in a Berlin working-class suburb to the Soviet Union.

On his own evidence, Hitler learned to detest working-class

organizations in Vienna before the First World War. There exists
no ground for doubting it. He looked at the workers' lives and politics
from above: he was among them, but he never regarded himself as
one of them. Their organizations were run on Marxist—for Hitler,
this meant Jewish—lines; they professed to be international and they
showed the young man the way back to his nation.[13]

When Hitler went into politics, revolution and counter-revolution
were the order of the day. He looked on German Social Democracy,
another aspect of *Gesamtmarxismus*, as having collaborated in
bringing about the defeat and ignominy of the German nation; he
witnessed the Communist bid for power in Bavaria. This, and the
gradual establishment of Communist rule over Russia, broadened
the target without altering, for Hitler, its nature. And Hitler's own
views on the subject were doubtless buttressed by the influence of
men like Alfred Rosenberg and Max Scheubner-Richter, German
refugees from the Baltic provinces. By 1921, anti-Communism was
firmly established as one of the major themes of Nazi propaganda.[14]
In the summer of that year posters appeared in Munich inviting its
citizens to a public meeting:

'We German National Socialists demand that the Russian people
be given help, not by supporting its present government, but by the
elimination of its present corrupters. Those who today give for Russia
do not give for the Russian worker but for his exploiter, the Jewish
commissar. German fellow citizens, come on Thursday 4 August
1921, to the great public giant demonstration at the Zirkus Krone.
Speaker: Herr Adolf Hitler, on the Dying Soviet Russia.'[15] The
National Socialists were now ready to fight the 'Marxists': the rules
of the conflict and its peculiar characteristics were developed before
Hitler left Munich, at the end of 1923, to serve a term of imprisonment. In a clash of this kind, marked by physical violence from
beginning to end, the Nazis never concerned themselves too much
with the theories of Marxism. There is no reason to believe that either
Hitler or his leading anti-Communist expert, Rosenberg, ever read a
single book or article by Marx or Engles.

At first, the German Social Democracy occupied a leading position among the phenomena of *Gesamtmarxismus*: it was gradually
replaced by Bolshevism. In *Mein Kampf*, Hitler still treated them

as of approximately the same importance; Bolshevism, however, was quite clearly becoming the threat of the future. In it, Hitler wrote, 'we ought to recognize the kind of attempt which is being made by the Jew in the twentieth century to secure dominion over the world'.[16] To this menace, Russia had already succumbed; it was now 'hanging steadily over Germany'.[17] Otherwise, apart from expressing his disgust with the 'Bolshevization of art' ('If the creative spirit of the Periclean age be manifested in the Parthenon, then the Bolshevist era is manifested through its cubist grimace'),[18] Hitler did not have much to say on the subject.

His attitude towards the first victim of Bolshevism—Russia— was ambiguous. He wrote of 'a gang of Jewish literati and financial bandits' (i.e. the Bolsheviks) dominating 'a great people'.[19] But in another context, this great people was demoted to the status of an inferior race. Discussing Germany's eastern policy, Hitler wrote: '. . . . when we speak of a new territory in Europe today we must principally think of Russia and the border states subject to her. Destiny itself seems to wish to point out the way for us here. In delivering Russia over to Bolshevism, fate robbed the Russian people of that intellectual class which had once created the Russian State and was the guarantee of its existence. For the Russian State was not organized by the constructive political talent of the Slav element in Russia, but was more a marvellous exemplification of the capacity for State-building possessed by the Germanic element in a race of inferior worth. . . . For centuries Russia owed a source of its livelihood as a State to the Germanic nucleus of its governing class. But this nucleus is now almost wholly broken up and abolished. The Jew has taken its place.'[20]

Although Hitler's attitude towards Communism had set by the time of the 're-establishment' of the party in 1925, there still existed certain striking deviations inside the National Socialist organization. They usually occurred on the Strassers' side of the party: in this connexion, the development of Goebbels's ideas is of interest. While working for the Strassers, Goebbels was a socialist rather than a nationalist: he detested western capitalism more than Bolshevism. The Locarno pact was for him, a 'horrible blend of deceit, meanness, infamy and hypocrisy', which meant that the Germans would become 'the mercenaries against Russia on the battlefields of capitalism'; anyway, Goebbels went on, it was better to 'go down with Bolshevism than live in eternal capitalist servitude'.[21] As late as February 1926, Goebbels was put off by Hitler's views on Russia and Boshevism, and on private property; in short, by his leader's 'reactionary' attitudes.[22] At the same time Goebbels was fighting hard the 'red rabble' in the streets and at Nazi meetings: the fight, as well as Hitler's offer of a high party office in Berlin, combined to secure his orthodoxy. But he had learned a lot from his adversaries. The posters for his first meeting in Berlin could hardly be distinguished from similar Communist productions.

As the post-war revolutionary tide began to ebb in central Europe, Hitler's interest in fighting the 'Bolshevik threat' increased. In the last years of the decade Nazi agitation against *Gesamtmarxismus*, and Communism in particular, was intensified, until in 1932 it culminated in the creation of an anti-Communist psychosis in Germany. The *Reichspropagandaleitung* started running 'anti-Marxist courses' under the direction of its expert, Paul Meier-Benneckenstein, who later rose, partly because of the importance of his subject, to the Presidency of the *Deutsche Hochschule für Politik*. The courses aimed at the 'achievement of a militant and systematic agitation and propaganda against the *SPD* and the *KPD*'.[23] The 'attack on the Marxist front' was continued after January 1933. Before that date, it had camouflaged Hitler's real aim—the achievement of political power—as well as helped him to achieve it; after January, it facilitated Hitler's bid for absolute power. The campaign was highly rewarding: in 1933 some sections of the German body politic, the *Deutschnational* party, the industrialists, and the military, handed power over to Hitler because they believed that he would save the country from Communism.[24]

Of necessity, this agitation had to exaggerate the gravity of the Communist threat. The Nazi propagandists succeeded in creating a pseudo-situation, in which a Communist revolution was imminent. They could not afford to take any note of the facts. At no elections between 1930 and 1932 did the *KPD*—the Communist Party of Germany—gain more than 17.6 per cent of the total poll; the party was incapable of waging a conclusive fight with the National Socialists, or indeed with anyone else. Stalin was preoccupied with internal Russian problems; it is probable that he disliked the idea of a united left-wing front in Germany, and that he regarded a nationalist government that would first concentrate on breaking the peace treaties as more suitable for his own ends.[25]

There of course existed some legitimate grounds for a sharp animosity between the Nazis and the Communists. They had fought each other in the streets of Germany for many years; the National Socialists found themselves, during the years of the economic crisis, in direct competition with the Communists for the favours of the industrial workers, who were then deserting the *SPD*. By grossly exaggerating the Communist threat, the Nazi propagandists forged an effective political weapon. Hitler was described as the saviour of Germany from Communism; what he had done for Germany, he could easily do for Europe.

There was a connection between the campaign against Communism in Germany and abroad as in the case of the drive against the Jews; there existed the same disinterest among the National Socialist leaders as to its precise international implications. In April 1933 Hitler's government turned its attention to the foreign scene; a secret circular was sent out by the Foreign Ministry to all its missions abroad, enquiring into the local propaganda situation.[26] A detailed reply from Moscow arrived in Berlin in August:[27] the Ministry of Propaganda took no notice of it. The report dealt with the possibilities of propaganda to the Soviet Union, but this was of no interest to Goebbels. His main pursuit—at any rate until July 1941[28] was propaganda about the Soviet Union and about Communism for the benefit of third parties. For them, the Communist threat was publicized and inflated.

A few months after the destruction of the German Communist Party in the spring of 1933, the *Antikomintern*—the Union of German Anti-Communist Societies—was founded under the patronage of Goebbels. Its function was 'to combat the Communist International and its allies',[29] i.e. the Jews, and, as an afterthought, the Freemasons. It was a well-endowed society; soon after its foundation it acquired spacious headquarters in Berlin. It housed the Department Soviet Union—it was also referred to as the Institute for Scientific Research on the Soviet Union (*Institut zur wissenschaftlichen Erforschung der Sowjetunion*)—which was made up of specialists in Russian economy, history, etc., or on propaganda relating to Russia. The department also contained a well-stocked library, a press-cuttings section, and a service for monitoring Soviet broadcasts. In it, propaganda and research were inextricably mixed: but, most important, it was intended to generate propaganda about the Soviet Union, not *to* it. The *Antikomintern*'s second department—the press section—ran various publications, such as the news bulletin which appeared twice a month in German, English, and French, as well as the twice-weekly information sheet on the Soviet Union; the foreign department looked after connexions with similar organizations and private individuals abroad. And finally, there existed a large department for 'antisemitic action': anti-Communist propaganda was, for the National Socialists, unthinkable without its antisemitic concomitant.

Although Communism had been defeated in Germany, its usefulness as a traget for Nazi propaganda had by no means ended. From now on, the *Antikomintern* was to serve as 'the most advanced position of the international anti-Bolshevik movement'.[30] The work of the *Antikomintern* was of course firmly based on the official propaganda policy: the organization performed certain important auxiliary functions. It could supply details, whenever necessary, for the rough outlines sketched by the *Promi*; it could lend pseudo-scientific weight to the pronouncements of the propagandists; it could, if need be, appear to pursue a policy independent of the party line. During the twenty months after August 1939, for instance, when the Stalin-Hitler Pact was operative, the *Antikomintern* still carried on its activities, if in a more subdued and modified manner. In this respect, the organization's independence of action was severely limited. The changes in the name and sub-heading of its house-magazine faithfully reflected the changing predilections of the Ministry of Propaganda. Until August 1939 it was called *Contra Komintern*, the 'Organ of the Anti-Bolshevik World Movement';[31] in the following month it became *Die Aktion*, with an eccentric sub-heading a 'Newspaper against Plutocracy and National Incitement',[32] which was altered, in December of the following year to 'Newspaper for a New Europe'. In September 1941, after Hitler's invasion of Russia, the circle was completed when this newspaper appeared together with a supplement called *Contra Komintern, Kampforgan der antibolschewistischen Weltbewegung*.

Before the big anti-Communist campaign that was launched at the 1936 *Parteitag*, the newly founded society concerned itself mainly with publishing or sponsoring the publication of books. *Bewaffneter Aufstand!* (Armed Uprising!) was written by the *Antikomintern*'s, chairman, Dr. Adolf Ehrt. In 1933, it was the society's most highly prized propaganda asset: by the end of the year, the fourth edition of the book — the fourth set of 50,000 copies — had been published; in the following year, an additional 75,000 copies were printed in German, and 160,000 in English, French, Swedish, Dutch, and Spanish. The book's sub-title was 'Revelations about the Communist Attempt at a *Coup d'État* on the Eve of the National Revolution'; it was based on a passage from Hitler's proclamation on 1 September 1933: 'There were weeks, at the beginning of the year, when we passed by, within a hair's breadth, the abyss of Bolshevik revolution.' This form of National Socialist propaganda was more vicious and gruesome than any other. The enemy was contemptible, and it had to be battered to death by the blows of words; photographs of stores of weapons, of degutted houses, of dead stormtroopers were distributed throughout the book with morbid regularity. The second of the *Antikomintern*'s much advertised publications by Ehrt and Max Roden, entitled *'Terror—A bloody Chronicle of Marxism in Germany'* (Berlin 1934) sank even lower. It set a new standard in atrocities propaganda. Page after page of revolting, detailed photographs of the stormtroopers who perished in street-fights were printed to prove that Marxism is evil.

These publications were intended for export rather than for the home market; in the introduction to *Terror*, the joint authors expressed the opinion that 'The international view of the new Germany still suffers because of an unusual misunderstanding. Nourished from contaminated sources, even the well-disposed press of other nations is guilty of an enormous distortion of history, which is keenly supported by the enemies of National Socialism and by the opponents of national honour and freedom.' The historical error, it was said, consisted of regarding the period of the Weimar régime as a time of freedom, whereas the truth was now declared to be that, in these years, the Marxists conducted a campaign of 'uninterrupted bloody terror against the German nation'.

A few months before the launching of the international anti-Communist drive, the *Antikomintern*'s activities were intensified, and they began to receive more attention in the German press. The *Berliner Börsen-Zeitung*—the equivalent of the *Financial Times*—obviously commanded a readership susceptible to anti-Communist propaganda, and it usually brought the most detailed reports on the *Antikomintern*'s activities. On 10 November 1935, it published a characteristic declaration by the *Antikomintern*. Its opening paragraph read:

'On 7 November the Soviet state celebrated the eighteenth anniversary of the Bolshevik revolution. The cannon-fodder of the Communist world revolution were driven across the Red Square. Tanks and bomber-aircraft were paraded. The Internationale was sung. In a telegram to Stalin from the official opening meeting, the expansion of Communism over the whole world was again stated to be the target.' After the juxtaposition of the plight of the Russians under the Soviet system with the jubilant, healthy Nazi Germany, the declaration concluded: 'The Soviet propaganda everywhere is trying to undermine the foundations of states, and to gather strength for new advances by employing the united-front slogans. As before, world revolution is the target. Today, the knowledge has started to dawn everywhere that Bolshevism is not a "Russian" affair, but that—because of its international character—it is resolved to interfere with the life of every nation. And everywhere, the forces of defence against the imperialist claims to power of the Third International are rallying. The struggle against the Comintern as the Bolshevik centre of subversion and murder has to summon all the forces that do not want to see their nations and states sold out to Communist chaos. The aim is a broad front against international Communism.'

At the same time, the *Antikomintern* began to extend its activities to broadcasting. On 16 October 1935, one of its chief executives, a Dr. Klein, wrote to Dr. Scheiner at the *Reichssendeleitung*, informing him of the activities of his organization up to date,[33] and adding: 'It is therefore essential that, apart from the press, exhibitions, lecture tours etc., broadcasting should be, before everything else, put at the service of this work.' Klein indicated that the *Antikomintern* should have, in November, some thirty topics ready for radio talks and plays; they included a play about mass deportations in the Soviet Union, a talk on the 'Kaganovich dynasty', another on 'race-pollution as a principle', and one on 'Trotsky, the eternal Jew'.

The *Reichssendeleitung* took up Klein's suggestion: in the following years the *Antikomintern* became the main supplier of this type of material to the German broadcasting system. It was constructed on the same lines as the *Antikomintern* publications; although it was of necessity repetitive it added a certain amount of colour to Nazi broadcasting. '*Bolschewismus*' was publicized as the main enemy of the human race, and the depths it had reached were contrasted with the achievements of National Socialism. Perhaps the best example of this type of broadcast was transmitted in the networked 'report on the week' on 31 July 1937. It was entitled 'At First They Were Seven!' (*Erst waren es Sieben!*—it referred to No. 7 party card carried by Hitler), the fourth *Antikomintern* broadcast in connexion with an exhibition, then touring German towns, called 'Bolshevism'. This is the beginning of the script:

First voice	When you, dear listener, walk through the various rooms of '*Bolschewismus*'—
Second voice	—when you have seen the Italian section, and taken in the struggle of fascism against Bolshevism—
First	when in the Hungary room the rule of terror by one Bela Kun has come to life for you,
A female voice	when you have been through the days of horror of the Munich Soviet Republic—
First	... and the atrocity of the Spanish civil war...
Female	... and the abominable suffering of the Russian nation itself—
First	when you have seen all these horrors, this poverty, this frightful blood sacrifice of Bolshevik terror all over the world—
Second	...then you come to the end of your journey in a room that shows pictures of the Third Reich—
First	and the frightful nightmare lifts—as if you came out of a dark cellar again into the bright light and the sun—

Second   ... and then you go on and remain standing for a while
in front of a picture of the Führer—

In the following months, from the beginning of October 1937 until
the end of the year, the *Antikomintern* scriptwriters were busy. The
Deutschlandsender transmitted seven of their broadcasts; Breslau
and Königsberg five each, Berlin and Hamburg two each, and Leipzig,
Stuttgart, Munich and Cologne one each.[34]

Since the campaign against *Gesamtmarxismus* was never far
from the centre of Nazi propaganda—it was consistently used, inside
Germany, to reinforce the loyalty of the Germans to Hitler's régime—
the services of an organization like the *Antikomintern* were indispensable; there were, however, times when the campaign was given
a special prominence. The *Reichsparteitag* in September 1936 was
devoted to it. The National Socialist régime was more confident than
at any other point in its three years' existence: the demilitarized
zone in the Rhineland had been successfully occupied and a vote of
confidence in the Nazi government had been passed in the *Reichstag*
elections in March; the spectacle of the Olympic Games in Berlin had
been brought to its impressive conclusion. The hostilities in Spain
had just been opened; the anti-Bolshevik campaign was unfolded
against the background of the first moves in the civil war.

The campaign was launched a few days before the opening of the
party rally. On 4 September the *Völkischer Beobachter* printed a
front-page headline story, entitled: 'Soviet Officials as Railway
Robbers'. The story was even slighter than its title: the Russians had
placed the Japanese Olympic team, returning to Tokyo across
Siberia, under strict supervision, and they impounded a portrait of
Hitler and a *Hitlerjugend* dagger that had been presented, in Berlin,
to one of the team's leaders. From then on the number of news items
dealing with the Soviet Union increased; on 8 September, the first day
of the party rally, an exhibition on the theme 'World Enemy No. 1—
World Bolshevism' was opened in Nürnberg. In his address, the
Deputy *Reichspropagandaleiter* set the tone for the anti-Soviet
campaign: Today, Germany is the unshakable fortress of peace and
order against Moscow'.[35]

The civil war in Spain provided Hitler with the peg for the anti-
Communist campaign. In his proclamation—it was read to the rally,

as usual, by *Gauleiter* Adolf Wagner—he described a situation in Spain that bore only a remote relation to reality. Franco, he declared, had not attempted a Fascist *coup* against the legal government; the Soviet Union had invaded the country.

'We see around us the signs of evil times. What we have preached about the greatest world danger of this second millenium of our Christian history. . . is becoming a frightful reality. Everywhere, the undermining activities of the Bolshevik string-pullers are beginning to take effect. At a time when bourgeois statesmen talk of non-interference, an international Jewish revolutionary centre in Moscow is attempting, through broadcasts and thousands of financial and agitation means, to revolutionize this continent. Do not tell us that we, by continuously pointing out these facts, want to develop in Germany a psychosis of fear. Even today we are not afraid of a Bolshevik invasion of Germany, not because we do not believe in it, but because we are determined to make the nation so strong that it—as National Socialism has already done away with this world conspiracy internally—will defeat any attack from the outside with the most brutal determination.'[36]

In his speech on 10 September, Goebbels elaborated on Hitler's ideas in some detail. He laid special stress on the international aspects of the Bolshevik threat; its underlying thesis was that 'Bolshevism must be destroyed if Europe is to become sound again'.[37] He said at once that 'What we understand by ideals and *Weltanschauung* in general has nothing to do with what is usually referred to as Bolshevism. As far as that is concerned, it is a pathological, criminal nonsense, demonstrably thought up by the Jews and now, under Jewish leadership, it aims at the destruction of civilized European nations and the creation of an international Jewish world domination.'

Goebbels took pains to present Communist parties outside the Soviet Union as the 'foreign legions of the Comintern', and as the gravest threat to national life. They had—because Moscow was behind them—unlimited financial resources at their disposal; they used the same subtle propaganda techniques as Moscow. Indeed, countries that allowed strong Communist parties to operate on their territories were more or less 'under the dictate of Stalin'. The propaganda of these parties was international and aggressive; it was designed to mislead as to the true nature of Communism. It demanded 'maximal guarantees for peace' and yet, at the same time, the Soviet government indulged in an 'obviously imperialist arming'. It was impossible to come to an agreement with Bolshevism: although Goebbels said that National Socialism was not for export, only a country that adopted the 'social form of national organization' could fight Bolshevism successfully. Four days later, on 14 September, Hitler's concluding speech to the rally dealt with the Bolshevik threat again.

The powerful propaganda onslaught on the Soviet Union launched in 1936 was designed to create an anti-Communist psychosis in Europe in the same way as it had created one inside Germany in the years 1932 and 1933. It aimed to secure international support for Hitler, and it achieved some remarkable successes: it is likely that, without this preparatory move, the Nazi conquests of 1938 and 1939 would have been difficult, or perhaps impossible, to accomplish. Nevertheless, the close connexion of the anti-Soviet campaign with the civil war in Spain was perhaps its most serious flaw. The insinuation that the Soviet Union had somehow invaded Spain and that the Communists were trying to overthrow the established order did not sound very convincing to the supporters of the legal Spanish government. In any case, they were not the people most susceptible to anti-Communist propaganda.

The force of the campaign continued unabated throughout 1936: the German-Japanese Anti-Comintern Pact was presented as an instrument for combating world Communism. Although, in the following year, the colonial question started being given more prominence than before, it was complementary, from the propaganda point of view, to the anti-Communist drive. On the one hand the Nazi régime showed itself as reasonable, and prepared to negotiate, even though it regarded its demands as fully justified; on the other, it was presented as an uncompromising enemy of Bolshevism, the perpetrator of chaos and unreason. At one point, the two aspects of Nazi propaganda were brought together. In October 1937 the directives issued to speakers by the *Reichspropagandaleitung*[38] included one on the 'Bolshevization of the Colonial Empires'. It stated that Bolshevism, apart from aiming at independent countries, was hard at work for a break-through for its ideas in colonial territories. Under the slogan of the liberation of the natives from imperialist exploitation it had begun to revolutionize the natives of the colonial possessions. According to the directives for Nazi speakers, the dissembling promises and instigations of Communism fell, especially in these areas, on fertile soil.

In the years before the Hitler-Stalin Pact of 1939, the anti-Communist propaganda conducted by the National Socialists pushed the hard facts of the diplomatic relations between Germany and Russia into the background. Rather than attempting to explain foreign policy on its own merits, the Nazi propagandists adopted the technique of creating popular images of foreign countries: they were made additionally inflexible by the admixture of National Socialist ideology. The Soviet Union received a great part of the propagandists' attention. Although this technique had the advantage of being easily intelligible, it was found lacking when sudden switches of foreign policy had to be publicized.

In 1939, when the Nazi-Soviet Pact was negotiated, Germany's relations with the Soviet Union strained the ingenuity of the *Promi*. Propaganda about the Soviet Union could no longer be regarded as a substitute for diplomacy: it had to follow closely diplomatic manoeuvres. At the 18th Party Congress on 10 March 1939, Stalin made the first of the intricate moves that finally brought Germany and Russia together. Until late in May, Nazi propaganda with regard to the Soviet Union showed an unusual hesitation. On 12 May the *Reichspropagandaamt* asked the editors of German periodicals 'not to occupy themselves in any way—therefore not even in the form of quotations from the foreign press—with the foreign rumours of a *rapprochement* between Germany and Russia'.[39] Again, on 25 May, editors of German newspapers were advised that 'As long as the result of English-Russian negotiations is not known, a reserved attitude must prevail. Therefore no prophecies about their possible outcome! The press can, however, hint in the commentaries at the threat created by this alliance of England with Bolshevism'.[40] When Hitler welcomed the *Legion Condor* on its return to Germany from Spain, he made no mention of their fight against Communism: a notable omission.

By the end of May, the Germans appeared to be entirely exasperated with the Russians, and they made a determined effort to settle the issue one way or the other. They opened negotiations, with the Soviet Chargé d'Affaires in Berlin, on 30 May; at the same time, they instructed their agent in Moscow to resume discussions on economic matters.[41] On the same day, the *Reichspropagandaleitung* issued rather a pessimistic directive concerning the government's attitude towards the Soviet Union: 'For reasons already known the press controversy against the Soviet Union has recently been held back.' This reserve can be—as soon as the situation is cleared up after the inclusion of the Soviet Union in the system of encirclement—again given up. Our supposition, that the Soviet Union wanted to gain as much as it could by its policy of procrastination, has been proved right. This directive does not, however, mean that a new campaign against Bolshevism should start in the German press in, so to speak, an apoplectic manner; it should be regarded as a basis for our attitude towards Soviet policy in the near future.'[42]

On the following day—31 May—the favourable Soviet reaction to the diplomatic initiative from Berlin removed the hesitant note from German propaganda. Newspaper editors were informed: 'It has already been announced that at the moment the time is not ripe for an anti-Soviet campaign. The press is therefore asked that, in connexion with reports on the 'Condor Legion', animosity to Bolshevism, rather than to the Soviets, should be referred to: the ideological character of this fight should be stressed.'[43]

For more than ten weeks after the issue of this directive the Nazi propagandists had to maintain a reserved attitude towards the Soviet Union. In the meantime other pursuits began to occupy the propagandists. On 14 August, the first directive concerning German territorial demands on Poland was issued to the press. On the same day, negotiations were set in motion that finally led to the series of agreements concluded between Germany and Russia. In the evening of 23 August, the Non-Aggression Pact was signed in Moscow: the day before, the first of a number of detailed directives was released. Journalists were advised to comment on the significance of the Pact on the following lines: 'The news has acted like a bombshell all over the world. The decision represents a sensational turning point in the

VIIa. Respectable Hitler. Forty-four years old. Germany's Chancellor. 1933

VIIb. Austrian Nazis paint a *Hakenkreuz* on a rock face. 1934

VIIIa.   SA troopers and *Stürmer* posters. Party Rally, Nürnberg. 1935

VIIIb.   'Jews are not wanted here.' 1935

relations between the two countries, and it reaches back to the traditional community of German-Russian interests. The historical premises for such a formulation of policy have to be gone into deeply. . . .It can certainly be stressed that the announcement found a deep response in the nation. While the democracies talked, we and the Russians have acted.'[44] Further, the journalists were informed that the Pact was a natural outcome of the negotiations between the two countries on economic matters; while these were being discussed, the desire, on both sides, for an extension of the understanding to political affairs came to the foregound. The co-operation between the two states was also founded on their respective economic structures: agricultural Russia was complementary to the highly industrialized Germany. At this point, the journalists were reminded not to touch on the ideological differences between the two states. They were also forbidden to speculate on the changes in the international situation, or on the future of the Anglo-French military mission in Moscow. In the routine instructions on 24 August the editors were again reminded that any speculation on the effect of the Non-Aggression Pact on other countries and on the Anti-Comintern Pact were to be scrupulously avoided. No quotations on the subject from the foreign press were to be used; 'favourable comments from friendly and neutral countries, on the other hand, can be naturally passed on in detail'.[45] Approved pictures of Ribbentrop and Molotov were, at last, released.

In a more detailed set of instructions, issued on the same day by the *Reichspropagandaleitung*, the triumphant tone was kept up. The Non-Aggression Pact, it was said, would become the cornerstone of the relations between the two countries. The speed with which the negotiations were concluded was pointed at as having been especially impressive; it was also a proof of the earnestness and openness with which the contracting parties approached the various problems. There were to be no more diplomatic 'by-ways' for the two partners; their path lay straight and narrow before them. 'The hopes that were still nourished yesterday in the foreign press', the directive announced, 'that the German-Russian negotiations would be endlessly protracted, whereas the English-French-Russian military negotiations might achieve surprising conclusion, were completely destroyed by last night's events. At this point newspapers can certainly let a quiet malice [*Schadenfreude*] ring through, but it should not form the basis of the commentaries.' German newspapers were further to point out that consultations between the two partners were foreseen in the Pact, and they were to stress that the document was to remain valid for ten years in the first instance, becoming operative at once. It followed from the Pact, the directive pointed out rather ominously, that Germany and Russia would settle between them the outstanding problems in their spheres of influence in eastern Europe: the time was not, however, suitable for a deeper exploration, in the German press, of the various opportunities the situation offered. The deepening of the co-operation between Berlin and Moscow was to occasion an increasingly warmer tone in regard to the Soviet Union. The *DNB*—the official Nazi news agency—report that brought a quotation from *Pravda* concerning the ideological differences between the two régimes was not to be used by the journalists as the starting point for a polemic against the Russians.

A supplementary set of instructions filled in some interesting detail. Although the journalists were again strongly requested to make the tone of their observations on the improvement of German-Russian relations 'a degree warmer and more sympathetic'; they were advised, at the same time, to bear in mind the 'attitude of the German reading public up to date'. The public was bound to be puzzled by a flood of jubilant articles celebrating the newly-found friendship: this was why the theme should be entrusted only to the ablest members of the editorial staff. The 'warming up of the tone' had to be achieved delicately. The impression that the friedship between Germany and Russia was merely a tactical manoeuvre was to be avoided by every means; the survival of the idea of co-operation between the two countries over the past hundred years was to be regarded with satisfaction.

The campaign to make the Pact acceptable to the German public was regulated to the smallest detail. Photographs from Moscow had to be approved by the *Hauptreferat Bildpresse* of the Propaganda Ministry before they were used; pictures could be released more freely only when the public was 'psychologically prepared'. There had also been many enquiries, to the press department of the

Reichspropagandaamt, as to whether the new Russian policy meant that the publication of reminiscences of the battle of Tannenberg, on the occasion of its anniversary, were undesirable. The answer was that they could be published, as 'the treatment of the military and strategic achievement of the German military leadership and the soldierly qualities of the army can never spoil the relations between two brave nations'. There were therefore no objections to the publication of articles on the Tannenberg engagement: they had to be, however, tactful. No allusions were to be made to the basic causes of the conflict; terms like 'Cossack hordes' were entirely out of place.

The diplomatic negotiations with the Russians continued after the invasion of Poland by Germany. On 28 September a treaty of friendship was signed by Ribbentrop and Molotov, who announced, on the same day, that the definitive settlement of the Polish question had created the basis for a lasting peace in eastern Europe.

By then Nazi propaganda had, however, changed gear. A few days before the German invasion of Poland on 1 September, the topic of German-Russian understanding was dropped, and the second-string campaign — it was concerned with Poland, Danzig and other related topics — began, at the end of August, to move into its place. Parts of Hitler's speech to the *Reichstag* on 1 September were still inspired by the sentiments of the Russian-German friendship campaign of the previous week; nevertheless, both the National Socialist leaders and the German public found it difficult to keep up such sentiments. The twenty months of friendship between the two countries formed a propaganda interlude, without connecting links with the line before August 1939 or after June 1941. During this period the Russians annexed the Baltic States, marched into eastern Poland, and occupied Bessarabia and northern Bukovina: although they were acting in accordance with the agreements with Berlin, the public reactions in Germany to the Russian moves were highly unfavourable. Only the most careful direction of every means of political publicity kept these public attitudes under control.[46]

When this self-restraint was at last given up, a sigh of relief was clearly audible. It was sounded in the speech by Hitler on 22 June 1941, the day on which Germany invaded Russia; '. . .sentenced to a long silence lasting many months, the hour has at last come when

I can speak openly. . . . You have all felt that this step' (i.e. the invasion of Russia) 'was a bitter and difficult one for me to take. The German nation has never harboured inimical feelings towards the peoples of Russia. The Jewish—Bolshevik rulers alone have endeavoured, from Moscow during the past two decades, to set on fire not only Germany, but the whole of Europe.'[47]

The all-clear signal had been given: later on the same day, the press was instructed, rather breathlessly, that 'One should remind the reader that the Pact with Russia was never for us a question of ideology. We have never admired Soviet institutions, and there can be no question of some internal vacillation. National Socialism has grown up in the struggle against Bolshevism. The agitation was stopped only during the period of truce, and now we are returning to our original precepts. Plutocracy and Bolshevism have a common Jewish origin, their ideas and aims are the same. One can reach back to the old programme of the Comintern, its role in 1918, its activity in Spain, etc. The true feelings of the German nation—which it had formerly entertained towards Bolshevism—must be once again set free. The methods used by Bolshevism today are the same as those [employed] against us in the internal political struggle. We must prove that the mean game played by Bolshevism has never altered, in regard to other nations as well, over the past twenty years. Former-ly, we presented Bolshevism without its mask, and we can return to that [practice] today. Regardless of treachery, they wanted to deceive and betray us, there can be no doubt about that. Bolshevism has waited for its hour. We have proof that it would have stabbed us in the back.'[48]

Although no great enthusiasm for the war on Russia was evident— there existed a certain weariness and concern over the threat of war on two fronts—the hate campaign against the Soviet Union un-leashed immediately after the invasion of Russia was quite unneces-sary. The propaganda switch in the summer of 1941 was more acceptable to the German public than that performed some two years before.

The campaign against *Gesamtmarxismus* ran like a red thread through the texture of Nazi agitation. From humble beginnings—the back-street brawls in Munich in the early nineteen-twenties—it grew into the biggest operation mounted by the National Socialist propagandists. It became a drive mainly against Communism and the Soviet state; twice before the war it was given a special prominence: on both occasions, the magnitude of the threat to Germany and to Europe was grossly exaggerated. The anti-Communist campaign brought returns, for the Nazis, beyond the dreams of avarice. In 1932, it helped Hitler to achieve power in Germany, and in the following year to establish and consolidate a National Socialist dictatorship. The campaign that was anti-Communist in theory and as a propaganda effect became anti-liberal in political practice. In 1933 it became a witch-hunt that aided the suppression of every kind of opposition to Hitler's rule and the establishment of a one-party state. It was used for diversionary purposes in a similar way as was the antisemitic campaign.

Indeed, the two propaganda themes were intended to reinforce each other: Hitler knew that it was necessary to focus the attention of the nation on a single enemy; it is possible that he thought of both the themes as equally effective. In practice, however, they had to be treated separately: the intensity of the antisemitic campaign could remain more even because its target was less clearly defined. The anti-Communist campaign, on the other hand, had to be suspended or modified according to the demands of the diplomatic relations with the Soviet Union. Outside Germany, the antisemitic campaign appears to have been less effective than the anti-Communist drive. The National Socialist propagandists did not possess sufficiently reliable information on the effectiveness of their propaganda abroad; anyway, they did not seem greatly concerned. They were content to export the themes of home propaganda, and they expected them to be just as effective abroad.

On the whole, the antisemitic drive disappointed the high claims Hitler had made for it. It was effective—but only in combination with a variety of other factors—in eastern Europe; elsewhere, it repelled rather than attracted. The international anti-Communist campaign, on the other hand, was more rewarding. It convinced many Europeans that Hitler's dictatorship was more acceptable than Stalin's and that Germany—'the bulwark against Bolshevism'—should be allowed to grow from strength to strength. Indeed, many Europeans

came to see Continental politics exclusively in terms of a clash
between Communism and National Socialism. The Nazis never
bothered to understand either the intricacy or the appeal of Marxist
doctrine. They were quite unconcerned with the political differences
between Stalin and Trotsky, and the fact that Stalin had abandoned
world revolution in favour of the policy of socialism in one country.
Anti-Communist agitation in Germany was marked by abuse and
exaggeration and underscored with physical violence. It was brutal
and unsubtle, but it was never meant to be anything else.

V
An Appeal
to Compatriots:
Austria

In the National Socialist view, the Austrian nation did not exist as a separate entity; in terms of Nazi propaganda it was a 'halluci-nation'. Since February 1920 — when the party programme was published for the first and the last time — the *Anschluss* of Austria was regarded as a political and economic necessity; in 1928, the *NSDAP* leaders declared again that they were not prepared to neglect a single German in the 'colony of the League of Nations, Austria'.[1] Indeed, to try and create a distinct form of Austrian patriotism was, from the Nazi point of view, nothing but treason against the German *Volk*.

For this message, a potentially receptive audience existed in Austria. The Austrian problem was created in 1918, when the Habsburg Empire fell apart. From one of the dominant peoples of the Empire, the Germans of Austria became the citizens of a small, insignificant state. They tried hard to break out of the impasse. On 12 November 1918 the provisional National Assembly in Vienna declared Austria a part of the German Republic; the same programme was formulated by the Constituent Assembly on 12 March in the following year. The demand of course followed the spirit of President Wilson's principle of self-determination, but it threatened to upset the new order for Europe that was being planned, at the time, by the victorious Powers. Germany would have gained some six and a half million inhabitants and the new state of Czechoslovakia would have become largely encircled, The peace treaty signed by Germany on 28 June 1919 outlawed the *Anshluss*; it contained an article recognizing the independence of Austria, as well as binding Germany unconditionally to observe this provision.

There existed, in Austria, resentments similar to those in Germany, and they cut across the divisions between political parties. The grudge against the 'dictated' conditions of peace was reinforced by a feeling that the Western Allies had wilfully broken up the Habsburg Empire, and thus deprived the Austrian Germans of their former prominence. At the same time, some kind of Danubian federation was impracticable: the rift between those successor states of the Habsburg Empire that benefited by the outcome of the war— Czechoslovakia, Poland, Yugoslavia, Rumania—and those that suffered—Austria and Hungary—was too deep, and the way to restoring harmony would have been arduous and long. Nor was the creation of a genuine Austrian patriotism a task that could be accomplished swiftly and, anyway, it would have hardly done away with the reality and the feeling, among the Austrian Germans, of political impotence.

Apart from the ties of nationality, the similarity between the post-war political background in Austria and Germany, and the fact that Hitler himself was an Austrian, many of the roots of National Socialism itself could be traced to Austrian soil. Indeed, a professor at Vienna University remarked with a good deal of justification that 'National Socialism is that movement which puts the Prussians word at the disposal of Austrian lunacy.'[2]

An extreme form of nationalism developed in Austria-Hungary during the last three or four decades of the state's existence; its growth was expressed in the formation of political parties that recognized no loyalties other than the purely national. A few of them were named 'national-socialist': the first organization of that name was in fact founded in 1897, by the Czechs. It was intensely chauvinist; although it never developed racial or anti-parliamentary doctrines, its Panslav, pro-Russian policy was not entirely innocent of certain racialist features, and it implied approval of the Tsarist autocracy. It was founded with the explicit intention of counteracting Marxism among the working classes. Seven years later—in 1904—the Germans in Bohemia founded the *Deutsche Arbeiterpartei Österreichs* at Trutnov (Trautenau). Its leader, Walter Riehl, intended—like his Czech forerunners—that his party should attempt a conversion of the working class to nationalism; it exploited the economic and political animosities between the Czechs and the Germans in the ethnically mixed borderlands of Bohemia and Moravia. After the break-up of the Habsburg Empire the organization split into an Austrian and a Sudetenland branch: the Czechoslovak Republic, and not Austria, inherited the largest share of organised National Socialists from the defunct Empire. Of the four leading-figures of the old *Deutsche Arbeiterpartei*—Walter Riehl, Rudolf Jung, Hans Krebs, and Hans Knirsch—the last three men continued their political activities on the territory of the Czechoslovak Republic, while only Riehl carried on his work in Vienna. But even Riehl's political attitudes had been determined by his early experience of the national struggle in Liberec (Reichenberg).[3]

Riehl was one of the few men who was on intimate—*du* (thou) —terms with Hitler; their first meeting took place at the small inter-state party rally in August 1920 in Salzburg; a few weeks later—from 29 September until 11 October—Hitler travelled in Austria and, for the first time in his political career, he spoke at Innsbruck, Salzburg, St. Poelten, and Vienna. After the failure of the Munich *putsch*, several prominent Nazis—Hermann Göring among them—fled to Austria, where they were looked after by their party friends. The exiles laid the foundation for a closer co-operation between the Austrian and the German movements: in 1926 the Austrian party was reorganized under the name of *NSDAP Österreichs* (*Hitler-Bewegung*), and incorporated into the Reich organization; Austria became a *Gau* in the German party. In 1928 it began to receive financial subsidies from Munich; its membership then stood at 7,000 divided among 130 *Ortsgrupen*.[4]

Nevertheless, the National Socialists did not begin to make an impression on Austria's political life before the beginning of the subsequent decade. Until then, they had remained the minority party within the 'national' group which, in its turn, was uncomfortably wedged between the Christian-Socialist and the Social-Democrat movements. A negative attitude towards the state was deeply rooted in the programme of the national camp: under the Habsburgs, Schönerer's party looked towards Berlin, rather than Vienna, for support for the Austrian Germans; Schönerer's successors disapproved of the Austrian Republic more than he had done of the Habsburg Empire. In this respect, the National Socialists remained within the tradition of the national group of parties; they were, however, more extreme and vocal in their demands, and they had valuable connexions in Germany. Indeed, the successes of the Austrian Nazis followed closely those of their party comrades across the frontier.

In the Austrian parliamentary elections in November 1930, the National Socialists polled 110,000 votes without winning a single seat. But two years later, in 1932, the local elections in Vienna, Lower Austria, and Salzburg in April, the Vorarlberg elections in November, and the Innsbruck municipal ballot, brought considerable successes to the National Socialists. They were also helped by the economic crisis and the fast-rising numbers of the unemployed; the plan of the Austrian government for a customs union with Germany—it had to be abandoned by the Austrians in September 1931 because of international opposition—also contributed to the radicalization of the political life of the Republic.

At the same time—in the summer of 1931—the German National Socialist leadership began taking a keener interest in the political situation across the frontier. The leadership of the Austrian party was rather weak, and it doubtless needed an injection of outside talent; in the same way, a tighter control of the Austrian movement from Munich could be ensured. Theodor Habicht, a small businessman from Wiesbaden, who had at first worked as a rather undistinguished journalist and later as a provincial functionary for the party in the Rhineland, was sent over to supervise the activities of the Austrian organization. He chose Linz for his headquarters: although he arrived unburdened by any knowledge of the complexity of the local politics, he succeeded in strengthening and extending the party organization.

Habicht received every help from the Munich leadership. Financial subsidies began to arrive regularly from the Brown House, and the National Socialists were able to unfold a full-scale propaganda campaign. The lessons they had learned in Germany were applied in Austria. Nazi agitation was especially aimed at the unemployed: the first *SA* units were recruited from their ranks. (Rudimentary *SS* units had made their first appearance in Austria early 1930.) Towards the end of 1931, the National Socialists acquired a house in Hirschengasse in Vienna for 150,000 Austrian schillings, and it became the first permanent party headquarters.[5] New party offices and homes for the *SA* were opened in every Austrian province, and the various auxiliary organizations were set up on the Reich pattern: the *Hitlerjugend*, the students' union, the press club, the artists' club.

The summer of 1932 witnessed an intensified National Socialist propaganda campaign. First of all, the party became more militant: terror and intimidation were employed in Austria in the same way and for the same purpose as in Germany.[6] On 30 June the *SA* mounted its first major operation: they raided a country club in the Lainzer Zoo, and severely injured several guests. During the Austrian party rally in September fierce streets fights developed between the Nazis and the Social Democrats in Vienna; the first photographs of injured *SA* troopers were taken and published in the Nazi press. Shortly before the party rally, Goebbels himself arrived in Vienna, and spoke at a public meeting at the Sportplatz Engelmann. Judged by the standards of Nazi meetings in Germany, the stage management at the Viennese Sportplatz left a lot to be desired. Nevertheless, the slogan on the only banner displayed—'Citizens of Vienna awake! Give power to Hitler!'[7]—could leave no one in doubt as to the intentions of the Nazis.

As a sequel to the summer campaign, a 'two-months plan' for propaganda was put into operation in the autumn. Some 300 public meetings were organized; the antisemitic drive came to the foreground, and a number of raids on Jewish shops in Vienna and elsewhere took place. At the same time, and ever-growing number of party members from the Reich spoke or appeared at public meetings—Robert Ley, Erich Koch, Walter Spahn were among them—while others joined Habicht at his Linz headquarters.

All this work made possible the National Socialist successes in the local elections in 1932: the election landslide made a profound impression on Dollfuss and his cabinet. The opponents of National Socialism became concerned at the possibility that their adversaries might come to power by parliamentary means.

In October 1932, Dollfuss issued the first of his emergency laws. It broke up the structure of Austrian party organizations, and opened the road for a clerical fascist, and later for a National Socialist dictatorship. Although the Christian Socialists—Dollfuss's party—had suffered heavy losses, especially in Vienna, the Nazi election victories were achieved at the cost of other parties belonging to the 'national' camp: the *Grossdeutsche* party, the *Landbund*, and the national group inside the *Heimwehr*. Nevertheless, the core of the electors belonging to the two main political movements, the Christian Socialist peasantry and the Social Democrat workers, remained largely immune to the attractions of National Socialism.[8]

In the meantime, the official relations between Berlin and Vienna were friendly: after January 1933, the situation radically changed. Until that date none of the Austrian parties was averse to the idea of the *Anschluss*. But when it became the official—if undeclared—policy of the German government after January 1933, the leading parties in Austria came to delete the demand from their programmes. In March, both the Christian Socialists and the Social Democrats renounced incorporation into the Reich as a part of their programme.[9] At the same time, the government of Dollfuss began taking sharper measures against the National Socialist movement. On 4 March, the Chancellor suspended Austria's democratic constitution; on 15 May Hans Frank, the Nazi Minister of Justice, was expelled from the country; on 19 June the Austrian National Socialist party was banned.

The wisdom of forcing the National Socialist movement to operate underground was, of course, questionable: in this way, it acquired its martyrs as well as new adherents. Above all, it became more difficult to control. Documents, lists of members and a part of the finances of the Nazi organization were placed in the care of undercover party members; meetings took place in an inconspicuous manner at private houses, and news and orders were transmitted by word of mouth. The organization, run on the same principle as Communist party cells, was resilient enough to take the strain of illegal work. Eventually, lists of members were destroyed and replaced by code names; security precautions, especially where contacts with the Reich leadership were concerned, were stringent. Propaganda material continued to be produced: one cell in Vienna distributed some 50,000 leaflets in three months.[10] The aim of Nazi agitation was to undermine, by every means, confidence in the state. One of the techniques employed—it had been first used by the Russian Social Democrats during the 1905 revolution—consisted in urging the citizens to withdraw all their deposits from Austrian banks.

The National Socialists devoted particular care to the setting up of an intelligence network in Austria, which supplied the party headquarters in Munich with regular reports. Information gathered by the Nazis was evaluated in Munich by an intelligence centre especially instituted for this purpose and by the *Propagandaleitung*. Some of the information that was pouring out of Austria was then used for broadcasts on the Munich transmitter.

The para-military organizations—the *SA* and the *SS*—also remained active after the ban on the party. At first, their members continued to meet in the attics and cellars of private houses; after several police raids, this method was abandoned. Later, small meetings were organized in the streets, where the possibilities of fast dispersal were better. The troopers arrived at the appointed place singly or in pairs, to report and to obtain orders from their commander. Military training on a larger scale usually took place on Sunday outings. Illegal activity demanded a new division of the troopers: they were divided into specialized units for recruitment, propaganda, and terrorist purposes.

After the acts of terror in June that led to the ban on the party, the Nazi agitation continued unabated. The *Hakenkreuz* insignia were painted on houses, trees, and rock-faces; the appearance of Nazi leaflets was commonplace in Austrian towns. In October, the National Socialists went to much trouble to place their flags, rolled up, on public buildings; they were provided with a clockwork mechanism, that made them unfurl at a particualr time. But again, propaganda had to be reinforced by terror. At the beginning of October, the first tear-gas attacks occurred in cinemas, shops, and other public places: although they caused some confusion, they were not

effective enough. At the end of the month, the first 'paper bombs'—
forerunners of the *bombes plastiques*—were exploded. They were
made from a mixture of pasteboard and black gunpowder, with a
primitive ignition mechanism; they looked like litter, and could be
left lying about in the streets.

The Austrian police were soon able to collect enough evidence to
prove that a large part of the terrorist equipment came from Germany. The first transport of explosives and of printed propaganda
material was impounded on 19 October 1933 at the frontier near Salzburg; one of the largest consignments was confiscated on 24 December at Anthiesenhofen in Upper Austria.[11] A number of Austrian Nazi
party members were employed by the German frontier police; their
task was to run the underground connexions with Austria. In this way
the newspapers printed in Germany—*Der rote Adler*, *Die Alpenwa-
cht*, *Die Volkstimme*, and the *Mitteilungsblatt des Kampfringes der
Deutschösterreicher im Reich*—were made available to the Austrian
National Socialists. Apart from newspapers, leaflets and pamphlets,
copies of a forged declaration by the government in Vienna, inviting
the Austrians to support the *Winterhilfe*, the Nazi relief action for
the poor, were found among the contraband propaganda material.

After the ban on the party and the deportation of Habicht from
Austria (in May, Hitler's government had unsuccessfully attempted
to provide Habicht with diplomatic immunity by appointing him
Press Attaché at the Embassy in Vienna; on 12 June, Habicht and
several other Reich functionaries of the party were arrested and
expelled) the headquarters of the Austrian Nazis were transferred
to Germany. With the help of his Austrian party comrades—
Landesleiter Proksch, Biegler, the leader of the *SS*, and Reschny, the
leader of the *SA*, were among them—who fled the country when
Dollfuss began to take strong measures against the party, Habicht
built up a new leadership for Austria. The illegal organization
continued as an integral part of the *NSDAP*, and it was therefore
directly controlled by the party leadership, and ultimately by Hitler
himself.

While the exiled party leaders relied on the underground organization to generate a certain amount of indigenous agitation, most of the
propaganda activity against the Austrian government in fact

originated from Munich. Habicht was the official publisher and editor of the *Österreichische Pressedienst* which was printed by a Munich publisher; it was designed to supply the German and foreign press with news from Austria. And at the end of May 1933, Goebbels himself began to take an interest in the treatment of the Austrian question in the German press. Indeed, the campaign became a testcase of the direction of the German press by the *Promi*: newspapers were to be used, for the first time, to support a major propaganda drive.

In a sharp memorandum on 15 June, German journalists were reminded that Hitler's cabinet expected to receive every support from them, and that they must unconditionally toe the line.[12] A few weeks later Otto Dietrich, the head of the Press Department in the Ministry of Propaganda, summoned a special press conference; he told the journalists that their main task was to enlighten every German as to the reasons why the struggle for Austria had to be waged. For the first time, an 'atmosphere' had to be created: a topic was to be brought, and maintained, before the public; it was a trial run before the Saarland campaign.[13]

In the following months, the German press was ruthlessly exploited in the drive against Dollfuss's government. The press had to confine itself to discussion of the internal situation in the Republic: its foreign relations were hardly ever touched upon. When Dollfuss met Mussolini in August 1933, for instance, the journalists were advised to make no comment and to publish a few selected opinions of the foreign press.[14] This reserve was partly occasioned by the fact that Austria's foreign affairs—especially as far as her relations with Italy were concerned—were a highly sensitive topic; more important, however, was the endeavour of Hitler's government to keep its relations with Austria as a family affair, which admitted no outside interference.

Although the propaganda directives supplied the press with a consistent common denominator, and although all the German newspapers were committed to publicize basically the same ideas, there existed some variations in the forms they employed. On the whole, the official party newspapers enjoyed a greater freedom of expression than the rest of the German press.[15] They of course used this freedom only to handle the Austrian problem in a more aggressive manner than was officially required: their treatment of the subject simply intensified the party line. The official Nazi press, because of the connexions between its editors and the party leadership, was also used for the treatment of certain special questions, which fell outside the sphere of competence of the generally distributed directives.

Of the two editions of the *Völkischer Beobachter* published in Berlin and in Munich, the south-German edition devoted more space to the Austrian problem than that printed in Berlin; it went into greater detail and appeared to have entertained more caustic views on the subject. Before the July *putsch* in Vienna, both editions carried a situation report on Austria almost every day; the Munich edition stood, however, in a closer contact with the local *Reichspropagandaleitung* and with Habicht, whose articles it often printed. The attitude of the newspapers that were not run by the party was more restrained towards the friend—the Nazi movement in Austria—as well as towards the foe—the Austrian state. Indeed, before Goebbels achieved a complete centralization of the German press, there appeared some interesting deviations.

In this respect, the case of the *Deutsche Allgemeine Zeitung* and its editor, Fritz Klein, is the most illuminating. One of the most distinguished of the German dailies, Klein had run it, since 1925, on national, *grossdeutsch* lines. The Austrian question was of particular interest to the newspaper and its editor. Although Klein was a nationalist he was not a Nazi. For four months after Hitler came to power, Klein was highly critical of the National Socialist policy towards Austria. In a leader on 30 May, the editor of *DAZ* again demanded a 'sensible policy towards Austria', and he accused the members of Hitler's cabinet of lacking in 'civil courage'. All the copies of the newspaper were impounded that day, it was banned for three months, and Klein was forced to resign as its editor. When it reappeared, the *Deutsche Allgemeine Zeitung* followed the party line.

Although the offences committed by Klein did not appear particularly striking, they stand out against the background of uniformity of the German press. On superficial consideration, it might appear that the south-German newspapers took a more active part in the Austrian campaign than the press of north Germany—this was true for a short time of the two editions of the *Völkischer Beobachter*—but, in fact, the central direction of the non-party press was fast becoming more efficient, and the regional differences in their attitudes towards Austria soon disappeared. Yet the newspapers without any direct connexion with the party served an important purpose in selling the National Socialist attitude towards Austria to the German public.

Whereas the main task of the press was to creat a suitable climate of opinion inside Germany, broadcasting was employed to forge a link between the two countries. The National Socialist broadcasters were faced with a difficult task. They had to demonstrate, in the first place, that the views of the Nazi government and the German public on the Austrian problem were identical; they had to attack the Vienna government and prove that its very existence, rather than its policies, was contrary to the wishes of the Austrian public.

In March 1933 the Bavarian network, with its powerful Munich transmitter, began to be used for the purposes of the Austrian propaganda campaign. On 18 March Hans Frank, the Nazi Minister of Justice, addressed the 'oppressed party comrades in Austria' from the studios in Munich. The passage in Frank's speech in which he warned Dollfuss's government not to do anything that might force the German National Socialists to come to the rescue of their Austrian party comrades was especially offensive: the Austrian Minister in Berlin handed in the first of many official protests. The German reply promised to examine the text of the speech; when it was found that the text was not available, Hitler simply told the Austrian Minister that he was unable to 'run after every speaker'.[16]

Soon after his arrival in Munich in the summer of 1933, Habicht came to play the leading role in the Austrian broadcasting campaign. Of the eighty-four propaganda lectures on and for Austria, broadcast from Munich between July 1933 and February 1934, Habicht delivered twenty-one; they called for the end of Dollfuss's régime, they incited the population to resistance to the government, and they advised the Austrians to boycott the products of the state monopolies. The evening transmissions contained short situation reports on the poverty of the population and of the persecution of the National

Socialists. The suppression of most of the political parties in February 1934 gave a new impetus to Nazi propaganda: the government was presented as the enemy of political freedom. A large number of local reports from Austria—they were always related to the wider context of *Grossdeutsch* history—were transmitted, such as the programme on 'Graz, the Town of the German *Südmark*' on 10 January 1934; historical serials and plays also played down the differences between the Austrians and the Germans. Two radio plays—Alfons von Czibulka's *The Reich Saves Vienna* and Reimesch's *The Town in Arms*—dealt, in ridiculously imprecise terms, with the subject of the siege of Vienna by the Turks in 1683; they were transmitted by the majority of the German stations in August and September 1933. Within the framework of the 'Hour of the Nation' series, there was broadcast a play by A. Weinberger entitled *The Flight Home*, which described the flight of the persecuted National Socialists from Austria to Germany.[17]

Although the Vienna government repeatedly protested against the concentrated broadcasting onslaught, its representations produced no results. The Austrians had no effective means at their disposal for countering Nazi radio propaganda. The transmissions from Munich could be heard all over Austria, and in some regions better than the local stations; the technical broadcasting arrangements in Austria played into the hands of the Germans. The geographical shape of the Republic—its disproportionate length from the east to the west compared with its width, and the fact that Vienna, with its large concentration of population, lay in the easternmost part of the state—made a consistent radio coverage of the area difficult. The capital city alone disposed of a powerful transmitter; farther west, the stations at Linz, Innsbruck, and Salzburg were seriously under-powered.

The transmissions from Munich were keenly listened to in Austria, and their aggressive tone doubtless attracted new sympathizers for the Nazi cause. The deterioration of the political situation—the conflict between Dollfuss's government and the Social Democrats that culminated in the siege and shelling of the workers' quarters in Vienna in February 1934—contributed to the success of the Nazi broadcasting campaign. In its early stages, it was reinforced by the

IXa. Funeral orator. Dr Goebbels. 1936

IXb. Goebbels at the Exhibition, 'Ten Years' Fight for Berlin'. 1936

Xa.   Austrian plebiscite posters. 1938

Xb.   The first Nazi poster in Poland. 'England! This is your work!' 1939

leaflet-raids over the territory of the Republic by German planes: the leaflets contained information on the times and wavelengths of the Munich broadcasts. The first violation of Austria's air-space occurred on 14 July 1933: the raids were continued until August, when a protest by the Great Powers in Berlin was successful in putting a stop to them.

The agitation that radiated from Bavaria had to be, according to the basic precepts of Nazi propaganda, reinforced by a physical threat. This was done through the institution of the 'Austrian Legion'. It consisted of some 15,000 men, mostly refugee *SA* or *SS* troopers from Austria. They were trained by German Nazis, equipped with *Reichswehr* arms, and stationed at a number of camps in Bavaria. The government in Vienna was well informed about the Legion: from the middle of September 1933, it had at its disposal a large number of reports from 're-defectors'. Again, the Austrian representations were without avail: in a note of 21 September, the *Auswärtiges Amt* explained that Austrian refugees were assembled in labour camps 'in the interests of public order and on charitable grounds'.[18] Nevertheless, the existence of the Austrian Legion caused deep concern to successive governments in Vienna. A few months after its foundation, the *Kampfring der Österreicher*, its civilian sister organization, was set up in Germany. It embraced the Austrians living in the Reich, and it publicized among them Nazi views on the solution of the Austrian problem.

Finally on 12 July 1934, a directive to the press advised that the campaign should be somewhat cut back: at that time, the Nazi propagandists regarded public opinion in Germany as thoroughly prepared for the Austrian *putsch*. The tactics of the revolutionaries were partly moulded by the propaganda situation: the capture of the studios of the Vienna broadcasting station—the only serious adversary of Munich—was one of the main aims of the rebels. While a detachment of *SS* troops, wearing the grey uniforms of the Austrian Army, occupied the Chancellery and shot Dollfuss dead, another *SS* group forced their entry into the broadcasting studios, where they made the announcer read, at pistol point, the sentence: 'The Dollfuss government has resigned. Dr. Rintelen has taken over the business of government'.

The abortive *putsch* in Vienna marked the culmination and the end of the first phase of the Nazi propaganda campaign in Austria. The Austrian party leadership badly overestimated their resources and strength: they doubtless did so in order to keep their allies in the Reich interested. For a short time after the events of 25 July, Theo Habicht and his friends continued to feed the propaganda machinery in Germany with their own material. The first enthusiastic reports on the *putsch* that were supplied, on 25 July, by Habicht to *DNB*, the official news agency, had to be suppressed; two days later, Hitler's government officially regarded the events in Austria as a purely internal Austrian affair. Anyway, by 27 July, Habicht had been relieved of all his party functions.

The failure of the July plot taught the Nazi leaders a stark lesson. They would never again embark on an adventure abroad as ill-prepared as that in Austria. They had forgotten that they were no longer running a party without any responsibility; when confronted with the facts of the situation, they were not ready to commit the full resources of the state to the advancement of their movement. Although Hitler had made an attempt to enlist Mussolini's support for a change of the Austrian régime, he did not, however, make certain that the Duce would approve of the kind of change Habicht was planning.[19] Indeed, the Nazi leaders had no cause for surprise when, immediately after the *putsch,* Mussolini declared that he would protect Austria's independence. In the evening of 25 July, four Italian divisions began to move towards the Austrian frontier.

Hitler tried to deceive Mussolini when he said that the annexation of Austria was of no interest to him; he was, in turn, misled by Habicht as to the degree of support the National Socialists commanded in Austria.[20] The support Hitler had given Habicht was informed by emotion rather than by clear-sighted political calculation; the Austrian adventure resulted in a setback for the broader Nazi propaganda pursuit abroad—the attempt to inspire confidence in their régime. But even in a more technical sense, the efforts of Habicht's organization were not properly integrated into the National Socialist propaganda effort. When Habicht had interfered, for instance, in Austria's civil war in a broadcast from Munich on 19 February 1934, German newspapers received the following strictly confidential directive: 'Emphatic advice has come from a high official source [the Chancellery] that yesterday's radio talk by Habicht does not, as far as the German press is concerned, exist. In no circumstances should notice be taken of the broadcast. . . .'[21] Later, in the summer of 1934, it became clear that Habicht was entirely out of touch with Goebbels and the Ministry of Propaganda. The Ministry knew nothing of the *putsch* plans: the treatment of the revolt, and especially of its early stages, in the German press, was extremely uneven; a carefully prepared and centrally directed campaign was conspicuous by its absence.

For one day and two nights, the dilemma that the *putsch* had placed before Hitler's government remained unresolved. The *Reichsleitung* of the party in Munich was unable to disown the Austrian *Landesleitung*, its integral part, and the headquarters of the rebels. At 3 a.m. on 26 July, the Austrian frontier guards at Kollerschlag arrested a Reich German. He was carrying detailed instructions for the Austrian National Socialists on the measures to be taken after the demise of Dollfuss's government, as well as the key to the code that was to be used for the transmission of messages to Germany.[22] The Austrian Legion was drawn up alongside the frontier; during the two nights following the *putsch*, a number of illegal crossings from Germany into Austria took place. The *Kampfring der Österreicher* had been mobilized a few days before 25 July, and all its members able to perform military duty were alerted.

Habicht and his Austrian *Landesleitung* remained hopeful longer than the Nazi leaders in Berlin. On 26 July Hitler wrote to von Papen asking him to head a special mission to Vienna and to replace the German Minister, who had—in view of the failure of the revolt in the capital—acted unwisely. In the letter to von Papen, Hitler expounded the new party line in regard to Austria: 'The attack on the Austrian Federal Chancellor, which the Reich government most sharply condemn and regret, has aggravated, through no fault of ours, the already unstable situation in Europe. It is accordingly my wish to contribute to a relaxation of the tension in the general situation and particularly to see the relations with the German—Austrian State, which have long been troubled, led back once more into normal and friendly paths.'[23]

In the letter to von Papen, Hitler adopted the views of his Foreign Ministry. The diplomats had known even less about Habicht's activities than Goebbels, and they had advocated caution all along the line. In a communication to the Ministry of the Interior on 25 July, Bülow set out all the dangers connected with an aggressive Nazi action in Austria. He added that 'The latest attacks on Germany, however, which are growing steadily more severe and which, according to reports at hand, must be expected to be taken up by other foreign countries in the near future, make it urgently advisable for all authorities here to realize the increasing gravity of the situation and the international dangers arising from it.'[24]

The penalties of failure came down swiftly upon Habicht's head. The Austrian *Landesleitung* was disbanded, and Habicht was thrown out of the party. Two days after the *putsch*, the National Socialist leaders were united in condemnation of Habicht's work in Austria: even Steinacher, the head of the *Volksbund für das Deutschtum in Ausland*, chipped in with a sharp criticism of the manner in which the revolt had been conducted.[25] While the Munich headquarters of the Austrian Nazis fell into oblivion, the Ministry of Propaganda and the Foreign Ministry regained their rightful places in the Nazi counsels in regard to Austria. Indeed, the prompt diplomatic action and its backing by propaganda did away with much of the discredit Hitler's régime had incurred through its activities in Austria.

Goebbels's press directive on 27 July announced that 'Austrian questions should be treated with a cool reserve, and polemic or even invective should be avoided.'[26] The order concluded the militant campaign of the German press against the Austrian government, and it initiated the second phase that was to last for two years, and that was dominated by the attitude of 'cool reserve'. At the same time, the National Socialist leaders were obliged to tighten up the propaganda apparatus: they realized that extremist trends inside their own party could be as dangerous as opposition outside it. In order to avoid aberrations of the Habicht type in the future, Hitler informed Goebbels, Hess, von Papen, and the Office of the Secret State Police on 8 August that 'In order to ensure the uniform policy which I wish to see pursued in future, I hereby order that neither party authorities nor anyone else may discuss, either on the wireless or in the press, questions concerning German-Austrian policy, unless agreement has previously been reached between the Reich Propaganda Minister and the present Minister in Vienna, Herr von Papen. In particular I forbid party authorities to discuss such questions on the wireless on their own intitiative.'[27]

In the summer of 1934 the Austrian problem was demoted from the first rank of foreign propaganda: its place was taken by questions that appeared easier of solution: the Saarland, the Rhineland, and armament parity. This did not of course mean that Austria entirely disappeared from Nazi publicity. The intensive pre-25 July campaign had to be faded out slowly; from 17 August reporting on the subject was to be undertaken on the following lines: 'All reports have to be founded in the spirit of conciliation. News of abuses that have been recently perpetrated in Austria should be published only when they are absolutely reliable.'[28] Although the word 'conciliation' meant little more than the absence of virulent attacks on the Austrian government, the new party line was strictly enforced until the next major event in the relations between the two countries.

This was the German-Austrian treaty, signed on 11 July 1936. There was no need for special propaganda preparations for the treaty and, anyway, the negotiations for it had been conducted in secret. It is quite likely that Goebbels had known nothing about the negotiations. On the evening of 11 July Goebbels arranged a special press conference at his Ministry; he did not appear very enthusiastic about the agreement between Vienna and Berlin. He said that the task of the German press was to create the impression that the treaty would contribute to the pacification of Europe;[29] according to a reliable eye-witness he answered an enquiry as to what the pact was really about by saying that 'it is the prelude to an Austrian 30 January 1933'.[30]

Despite their diplomatic manoeuvres, the Nazis never gave up hope for the creation of a *Grossdeutsche* Reich, with Austria as its part. In diplomatic terms, their 'conciliatory' attitude meant that the international situation ruled out any other move in regard to Austria; in terms of propaganda it implied that the vitriolic tone, used from the spring of 1933 until July 1934, was no longer admissible.

Meanwhile, the Nazi party in Austria was going through a critical period of its illegal existence. From the end of July 1934 it was entirely on its own: all its relations with the Reich organization were broken off. The para-military organizations had suffered considerable losses: many party functionaries fled to Germany and some to Yugoslavia, while others were arrested and sentenced to death (thirteen capital sentences were pronounced by the Austrian courts after the July rising) or to long terms of imprisonment. For a short time, the party disappeared from Austria's political life.

It did not take long to recover. In the spring of 1936 another police action had to be taken against the Austrian National Socialists, and a new wave of arrests swept across the country. A comprehensive police report on the state of the Nazi movement, which was drafted on 4 April 1936, pointed out that 'despite three years' fight against it by the security authorities, the illegal apparatus still possesses a striking power that should not be underestimated'.[31] No significant changes had occurred, according to the report, in the social composition of the movement since 1933. The leadership still consisted largely of the unemployed intelligentsia; the para-military organizations still attracted the down-and-out ex-service men; the ideas of the movement were applauded by the lower-middle classes, the dispossessed bourgeoisie, and by Austrian youth. Although Nazi propaganda had made little impression on the working classes, it had achieved success, by 1936, among the peasants. Again, Nazi ideas fared better among the economically depressed sections of the peasantry in the frontier districts and especially in the mountains. Indeed many foreign visitors gained the impression that in Austria, 'the Third Reich begins at the height of 3,000 feet'. [32] There were illegal Nazi newspapers in circulation among the peasants, which described conditions in the Reich in a simple and laudatory manner; the peasants with Nazi sympathies were convinced that in the Reich, the National Socialist state imposed no taxes on the farmers.[33]

In 1936, Nazi pamphlets could still be found in Austria, *Haken-kreuz* flags were still being unfurled from public buildings, swastika signs were painted in conspicuous places. Although the Austrian Nazis continued to regard the Reich as their lodestar and though they continued to be impressed by the achievements of Hitler's régime, hints as to their connexions with the Reich movement disappeared from their propaganda. It concentrated on internal Austrian matters: the demand for elections and for economic improvement. The strained political relations with Germany were equated with the depressed state of Austria's economy; and the campaign was reinforced by intensive antisemitic agitation. The staple technique of Nazi propaganda — the identification of National Socialism with the nation — was exploited to the full. Every measure by the state against the National Socialists was treated as another move against the German nation.

Although terrorist activities were in abeyance at the time, the Austrian security authorities expected them to come into play again. Indeed, the Republic's high officials took a pessimistic view of the future. Apart from terrorism, they thought the Nazis might intensify their agitation among the workers; they knew that their own ranks were weakened by the presence of Nazi sympathizers. Although the view was put forward that Hitler's movement had to be combated in an uncompromising manner, nobody expected the effort to be rewarded by success. In the spring of 1936, Austrian officials were convinced that a strong National Socialist movement would exist in Austria as long as Hitler's régime remained in power in the Reich. They saw no immediate prospect of a political change in Germany.[34]

The situation remained unresolved until March 1938. The attempts of Schuschnigg's government in the previous year to gain support from the moderate wing of the Nazi movement came to nothing; early in 1938, the Austrian authorities discovered yet another Nazi plan for a *coup d'état*. Finally, on 12 February, a meeting took place between Hitler and Schuschnigg at Berchtesgaden. Here under massive threats of military intervention, Austria's Chancellor was forced to come to an agreement with Hitler that set off the events of the following weeks. Seyss-Inquart, the Viennese lawyer and a Nazi sympathizer, became the Minister for Security; the public activities of the Austrian National Socialists took place, from now on, undisturbed. On 9 March, Schuschnigg's government announced that a plebiscite would take place on 13 March; after two days of hectic plotting and counter-plotting, the Chancellor showed himself willing to rescind the order. But the German troops were already massed on the other side of the frontier; Schuschnigg resigned and, in the evening of the same day—11 March—a government under Seyss-Inquart was formed. On 13 March it issued a decree on the annexation of Austria to the Reich. On the following day, Hitler gave the 'grand account of things accomplished' on all German and Austrian transmitters. He said: 'As the Führer and Reich Chancellor of the German nation and of the Reich I report to history of the entry of my home country into the German Reich.'[35]

Against the background of fast-moving political developments, the effectiveness of Nazi propaganda depended on its flexibility. During the first stage of the preparations for the *Anschluss*, in the early weeks of 1938, it had to pursue two distinct and somewhat contradictory aims: it had to avoid giving the impression that the Reich Nazis had begun to interfere in Austria's internal affairs, while making it clear that the relations between the two countries could no longer be regulated by the treaty of July 1936. After the Berchtesgaden agreement of 12 February, Nazi publicity set out to prove that the Austrian problem could be solved only on National Socialist terms, that the agreement had left no margin for other solutions.[36]

Every reference to the fact that another *coup d'état* was being mounted in Austria was scrupulously avoided. When the government in Vienna released the news of the discovery of the plans for a Nazi *putsch*, the German press at first ignored the reports, and then a few newspapers simply denied their authenticity. No propaganda preparations were made before the Berchtesgaden meeting; immediately after its conclusion, the German press was advised that 'Only the *DNB* communiqué is to be printed about the talks between the Führer and Dr. Schuschnigg. No comments are to be made.'[37] The order for silence was lifted only four days later, on 16 February, when the German press received a detailed directive on the treatment of the Austrian situation.

The reorganization of Schuschnigg's cabinet and the political amnesty were to be regarded not as the final 'pacification' of Austria, but only as a basis for its achievement. People of National Socialist convictions were to be granted the same freedoms as members of the other movements: all this was to happen, however, within the framework of the Austrian constitution. The journalists were forbidden to quibble (no petty criticism), or to turn their minds to the past. The international angle on the situation was that Hitler was trying to do away with the causes of world tension, and that at Berchtesgaden he had achieved a remarkable success. It had to be acknowledged, however, that the Austrian statesmen met him half way. Quotations from the foreign press, including indications that the first steps towards the annexation of Austria had been taken, could be used; speculations on the *Anschluss* were, however, in no way to be emphasized. It would be quite wrong, the directive pointed out further, even to hint that Schuschnigg had given way under pressure.[38]

The Nazi publicity maintained the line given in this directive until two days before the *Anschluss*. The news of Schuschnigg's speech of 9 March on the plebiscite, for instance, was not published till some twenty-four hours later. Indeed, the arguments used shortly before and during the *Anschluss*—that the annexation was taking place on Austrian initiative—could have been employed only after a singularly restrained propaganda campaign in Germany. It entered its last phase on 11 March. At the morning press conference, editors of evening newspapers were invited to pay more attention to the events in Austria. Any semblance of uniformity was, however, to be avoided; tabloid newspapers were to use prominent headlines, while the more serious dailies were to devote two front-page columns to Austria. Later on, at night, additional directives were transmitted to the press. The allegations against Germany which Schuschnigg had made in his farewell speech were to be sharply denied. The ultimatum—the Chancellor's resignation or occupation of Austria by German troops—was to be presented as having come from Schuschnigg's colleagues, and not from Berlin. The Austrian side of the picture was to be filled in by reports on the unrest among workers that had broken out in several towns; the German attitude of noninterference underlined by stressing that Hitler had not demanded the reorganization of the Austrian government. At the same time, the contents of the declaration broadcast by Seyss-Inquart were released: the journalists were told that Seyss-Inquart, as the only Minister remaining in office, was acting in place of the government, and that he had sent a telegram asking the Reich cabinet for troops to restore order in Austria. Directives for various types of commentaries were also issued: the impression of spontaneity was to be achieved through careful management.[39]

Although one day before the *Anschluss* the aim of Nazi propa-

ganda was to create the appropriate 'annexation mood'— in this
sense it anticipated events—on 13 March it was toned down to
produce the right background for the fast-changing political situation. The 'liberation' and the 'return home' of Austria were celebrated; the development had to be presented, however, as having had
a 'peaceful character'. The reports suggesting that a panic situation
prevailed in Austria disappeared from the German press; the word
'war' had to be carefully avoided, and the process of annexation
described as completely orderly. At the same time, only 'positive'
foreign reports—especially English and Italian—were to be quoted;
two days later, newspaper editors were asked sharply to deny all
negative foreign opinions.[40] The annexation campaign was concluded on 16 March, the day of Hitler's arrival in Vienna. The event was
treated as the most important centre-piece of the day's news: Hitler
was hailed as the liberator of Austria.

Compared with the first groping steps in 1933 and 1934, the second
Austrian campaign was executed smoothly and efficiently. In 1938,
Goebbels conducted the propaganda orchestra with a supreme
mastery: there was no discordant note. First the simulated dissocia-
tion from the Austrian events, then a detached kind of interest, the
shifting emphasis in the treatment of news, the guidance as to comments and quotations, were all carefully calculated to produce the
desired effects. The 'annexation mood' in Germany, a seemingly
spontaneous phenomenon, was in fact carefully engineered. Above
all, the propagandists had accepted that they were part of the overall
state machinery. They had to follow the manoeuvres of the National
Socialist foreign policy: this time, the armed forces were fully
committed. Propaganda played only a supporting role.

In comparison, the abortive *putsch*, run for the party by Theo
Habicht, four years earlier, appears amateur and doomed to failure.
The National Socialists regarded Austria as a part of Germany: it was,
after all, another *Gau* in the party organization. And party attitudes
and arrangements blinded them to the international implications of
their actions. Until 1933, the overspill of the Nazi organization from
the Reich into Austria had been tiresome for the Austrian officials,
but it had not created an explosive international situation. The
National Socialists were slow to realize that their new responsibilities

committed them to a new kind of behaviour; that, in order to achieve their aims in Austria, they could no longer rely on the twin instruments of party organization and propaganda only: there was a big difference between supporting a sympathetic cause abroad and committing the full resources of the state to this support. In addition, Habicht made the customary mistake of conspirators with powerful outside supporters. He misled his allies in the Reich as to the strength of the Nazi movement in Austria: the failure of the *putsch* in July 1934 was his ultimate penalty. The Nazi leaders benefitted by the Austrian lesson, and they never made the same mistake. They never again regarded the state as a mere extension of the party: propaganda had to be guided by cool calculation rather than by emotion, and it had to fall into line with the foreign and military policy of the Reich.

VI

An Appeal to Foreigners: Britain

On their way to power, the National Socialists had seen Europe in terms of a hostile constellation of states that was preventing Germany from achieving her justified aims. After 1933, they had to withdraw this negative image from circulation: it stood in the way of achieving their main aim at the time. First of all, they had to try and make their régime acceptable abroad. Hitler's famous 'peace speech' on 17 May 1933 launched this campaign, and it set the pattern for many similar pronouncements that followed. For the first time, Hitler used the *Reichstag* as a platform for speeches that were brought to the attention of the whole world. He pointed out how faithfully Germany had fulfilled disarmament obligations imposed on her by the Versailles Treaty;[1] he intimated that Germany was prepared to co-operate with all European countries on the basis of trust and equal rights. The 'acceptance' theme kept recurring, in a number of variations, in propaganda designed for foreign consumption, until the last weeks before the outbreak of the war.

The Nazi propagandists never wearied of pointing out that a strong leadership was now making decisions in Berlin on behalf of Germany, that the country was no longer a burden to anyone else, and that other European governments should therefore be grateful to the National Socialists for taking over the responsibility. The argument that Hitler's party had defeated Communism in the heart of Europe was of course often used in the drive for acceptance; during the implementation of the four-year plan—announced at the party rally in 1936—the economic motif came to the foreground. It consisted of an account of Germany's achievements in that field, and it was often accompanied by offers of trade treaties, especially to the agrarian countries in south-eastern Europe.

Nevertheless, concurrently with the propaganda campaign for acceptance, the campaigns for the subversion of the established order in Europe were developed. On the surface, the two broad pursuits of National Socialist propaganda appeared incompatible; they were not so in fact. From the abortive *putsch* in Austria in the summer of 1934, to the occupation of post-Munich Czechoslovakia in March 1939, subversive propaganda campaigns were confined to Central Europe; the drive for acceptance was largely aimed at the European Powers that were seen as the main pillars of the *status quo*.

The secret circular sent out to all its missions abroad by the Foreign Ministry on 26 April 1933, and entitled 'Propaganda Against Germany and Counter-propaganda'[2] clearly regarded France as Germany's main adversary. In the field of international propaganda, the activities of the French were the most suspect; the Germans regarded them as the main architects of the post-war order in Europe; among all the Great Powers, France had the greatest interest in the preservation of the *status quo*. But in the National Socialist perspective, France was not a dangerous adversary at all. A long time before, Hitler had detected the trend that France was becoming 'more and more negroid',[3] and that its population was on the decline, an artificial decline at that. In the long-term Nazi view, the French were the extreme example of a 'dying nation': a charming, lovable, perhaps a fortunate people, but at the end of its political tether. Apart from its rather base political manoeuvres, it had no higher aims, and it was therefore without consequence. It had become, or was becoming, a small nation with a crushingly large spiritual heritage.[4]

Indeed, by the time Hitler came to power, Britain had taken over from France the political leadership of Europe: the situation remained unchanged until the outbreak of the war. A week after

Hitler's appointment as the Chancellor of the Republic, the German Ambassador reported from London that 'A comparison between the French hegemony under Laval in the autumn of 1931, with England in a state of almost total financial impotence and greatly impaired political activity, and the present situation, which shows England to be active and France in an increasingly defensive position, provides clear proof of the change-over that has taken place.'[5] It further stimulated the attention the new rulers of Germany lavished on Great Britain: when they made statements intended for general consumption abroad, they had London, rather than Paris, in their minds.

It was a recurrent theme in *Mein Kampf* that Great Britain was Germany's natural ally against Russia, and that without her backing Germany could make no move in the East; Hitler also believed that British and French diplomacy were bound to come into a sharp clash on the Continent, from which Germany could only benefit. The Nazi leaders spared no effort to make an impression in Great Britain: the effects they aimed to achieve ranged from persuading the British to accept the new order in Germany to influencing the decisions of their government. Although the *Promi* found it difficult to create a sharp image of Great Britain for the home market, the country always loomed large in the calculations of the National Socialist leaders. For them, Britain's friendship was indispensable for the achievement of their aims on the Continent, and especially in its eastern territories; in the two years before the war, British acquiescence became essential for the completion of Hitler's piecemeal conquest of central Europe.

In their relations with Great Britain, the National Socialist leaders usually lacked self-confidence, and they were highly sensitive to criticism. Soon after they assumed the responsibility of government, a striking example of the way in which they mismanaged this relationship became available. Alfred Rosenberg visited London early in May 1933; he said that his object in visiting England was to 'clear up certain misconceptions which existed abroad in regard to recent events in Germany'.[6] It is very likely that Rosenberg had consulted Hitler before he left for London, and that he went with the Führer's blessing. It was neither a secret diplomatic mission nor a propaganda trip. In both respects the journey was a dismal failure. The leading Nazi ideologist made a very bad impression in London. The reasons for his visit as well as his status were vague, and he arrived without any official credentials: a situation that would hardly recommend itself to the Foreign Office. It was not clear from his behaviour whether he was offering or expecting some kind of political advantage; he gave the impression of confusing propaganda with diplomacy, and of believing his own side's propaganda. Vansittart later described his visitor as a 'Balt who looked like a cold cod'.[7] When faced with the civil servants, Rosenberg tended to behave like an unscrupulous agitator; at his press conference, he gave the impression of distance and inscrutability. He got a very bad press: only the *Sunday Graphic* gave him an opportunity to enlighten its readers with an account of what the Nazis stood for. In the end, he wisely decided to cut his visit short and leave London as unobtrusively as he could.

The failure of Rosenberg's visit to London had far-reaching consequences. It resulted in a sharp decline of his prestige in the party, and it extinguished the hopes he had placed on his private foreign ministry.[8] More important, the Nazi leaders, in their attempts to influence the British, gave up the direct and personal approach: from now on they relied almost exclusively on their diplomatic representation.

Indeed, in regard to Great Britain, National Socialist propaganda commanded none of the advantages offered by the direct connexious of the party with the Germans in, say, Austria or Czechoslovakia. The Nazi leaders could afford to disregard the views of the German Minister to Vienna because they possessed alternative sources of information and other instruments for conducting their policy towards Austria. This was not the case in Britain. Here, the views of the diplomats carried weight.

In his detailed report on British—German relations, dispatched on 16 August 1933, Hoesch, the Ambassador to London, pointed out that the idea of a 'systematic and organized campaign of propaganda should from the start be discarded as erroneous'.[9] He went on to say that, since the end of the First World War, the British had lost their taste for propaganda because they 'were forced to experience too strongly the anguish of the modern art of propaganda, when it meant, at the time, bringing to boiling point and infecting with war mania a people who were in themselves entirely averse to the war, and in no way prepared for it. Neither a propaganda campaign in the press, however ingeniously prepared—if such a campaign could be carried out here at all—nor a swamping of England with pamphlets in which the German point of view is explained, nor finally the dispatching of more or less official publicity agents seem to me suitable means for the winning of public opinion here. Everything tempestuous, vehement, and blatant must be avoided, and it would be better to reckon with the possibility of only a slow change for the better than the possibility of failure through over-hasty attempts'.

Among the appropriate methods for influencing British public opinion, Hoesch listed trips by prominent Englishmen to Germany and, he wrote, 'gracious reception and attentive treatment of these travellers in Germany seem to me desirable'. The suggestion was taken up by Nazi authorities: in the six years of peace, thousands of officially sponsored visits to Germany took place. Some of them produced interesting results. In May 1934 Sir Arnold Wilson, a Tory M.P. and the editor of *The Nineteenth Century & After* was invited to visit Germany by a Nazi-sponsored organization. In that and in the following year he travelled in Italy, Belgium, and France as well as Germany. In May 1936, the first edition of his book, *Walks and Talks Abroad*, was published; the second edition followed in October, and the third in April 1939. Sir Arnold described his own political outlook as similar to that of Lord Milner—'national rather than international'[10]—he also detested the 'anti-Christian basis of Communism'. Although he abhorred the persecution of the Jews in Germany and the Nazi racial doctrines, he wrote that 'I cannot refuse to recognize that the Nazi government has in the past three years achieved much and secured and maintained, in face of great difficulties, a far more ample measure of public acceptance and approval than any of its predecessors. Judged by whatever internal standard—of national health, of employment, of public amenities, of internal development of the standard of living of the masses—the recovery of Germany has been without parallel in Europe, though at a heavy cost, not to be

XIa. 'Check to the King.' 1940

XIb. Churchill, a sniper. 1941

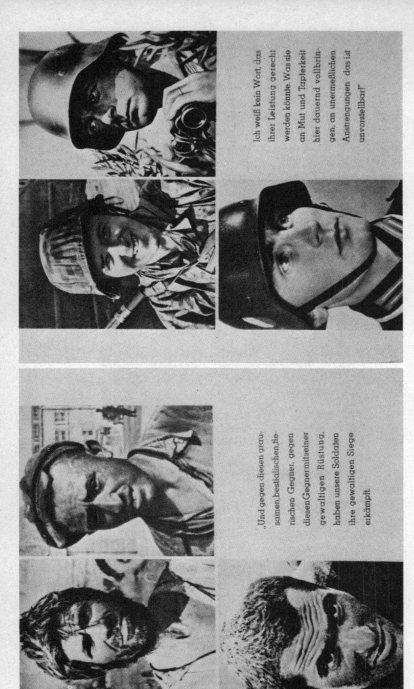

Ich weiß kein Wort, das ihrer Leistung gerecht werden könnte. Was sie an Mut und Tapferkeit hier dauernd vollbringen, an unermeßlichen Anstrengungen das ist unvorstellbar!"

„Und gegen diesen grausamen,bestialischen,tierischen Gegner, gegen diesen Gegnermitseiner gewaltigen Rüstung, haben unsere Soldaten ihre gewaltigen Siege erkämpft.

XII.   The Soviet *Untermenschen* contrasted with the defenders of European civilization. 1941 measured in cash'.[11] Although Germany's attitude towards the Jews, Sir Arnold wrote, increased the country's difficulties in many, but not all, foreign markets, he was confident that the present regime would survive; he believed that the structure of the Nazi state would grow in strength and would endure because it had 'the passionate support of many, and the assent of the great majority of Germans at home and abroad'.[12]

Sir Arnold was convinced that Britain could learn a lot from the totalitarian countries—Germany, Italy, and perhaps even Russia—how to look after her own citizens better, how to improve social services, even how to breed a better type of child. He quoted, with approval, Hegel's dictum about the state as being 'the product of reason, endowing every individual with new forms of liberty in return for the surrender of some selfish privileges'.[13] The enforced surrender of selfish privileges in concentration camps was also witnessed by Wilson on his travels; he went to see Dachau, and he reported that 'this is nothing new'.[14] He accepted the suppression of minority opinions as something inevitable. The views he faithfully reported were Nazi; when he described a situation as odious or unintelligible to the English mind, he usually produced the Nazi point of view in order to explain it to his fellow-countrymen. He was plainly impressed by Germany.

A variety of similar books appeared before and even after the outbreak of the war.[15] Some of their authors—notably Sir Arnold Wilson—later changed their views as to the nature of Hitler's régime. When they wrote their books, however, they all believed that they were making a contribution to the cause of understanding between Britain and Germany, which they regarded as essential for the preservation of peace in Europe. The books sympathetic to Hitler's Germany were, in comparison with the amount of anti-Nazi literature, in the minority: their authors were trying to present the views of the 'other side'. But in the process, they made use of Nazi propaganda material, and they contributed to the effort of making Hitler's régime acceptable to the British public. Their books were the outcome of the public relations work recommended by the German Ambassador to London. They were not dishonest insofar as their authors did not intentionally mislead their readers: they were misleading because they leaned over backwards to present the case for the 'other side'.

The German diplomats in London also made a determined effort to influence the British press. The Embassy became the fountainhead and controlling agency for these activities. From the spring of 1933 it had on its staff a young man called Sigismund-Sisso Fitz-Randolf, who ran its press department. He had had no diplomatic experience; he was responsible to the *Promi* direct rather than to the Foreign Ministry. In the spring of 1933, the Ministry approved of the principle that propaganda material should flow through British, rather than German, channels: the principle was formulated in connexion with an offer from a British journalist to put a newly-founded agency at the disposal of the German government.[16] But the offer was not taken up by Berlin, and the principle was abandoned.

FitzRandolf was assisted by a large contingent of 'correspondents': as the number of the newspapers published in Germany was decreasing, the number of the German correspondents in Britain grew. By the beginning of 1938 there were sixty of them in London, and a year later eighty. Most of them were engaged in propaganda and espionage activities. Their influence on the press was negligible; Nazi propaganda in Britain was vulnerable because it could easily be traced to its sources; it could be, in the last instance, curbed by administrative measures. The first German journalist in London to receive a deportation order, as early as November 1935, was Dr. Thost of the *Völkischer Beobachter;* in August 1937, the Home Office refused three journalists renewal of their permits to stay; more expulsions followed in 1939.

One of the most thorough attempts to influence the press in favour of Hitler was made, in the first half of July 1936, by Freiherr von Rheinbaben. He was a retired diplomat, who had served with the German delegation to Geneva in the years between 1926 and 1933; he had also held the post of Secretary of State in the Reich Chancellery. He was, at the time of his visit to London, an active and well-known publicist. He undertook the mission at the instigation of Dr. Johannsen, the head of the *Auflkärungsausschuss* in Hamburg, a propaganda organization closely connected with the

Foreign Ministry; its main purpose was to find out which newspapers would be prepared to print articles by Rheinbaben.[17]

As far as the national newspapers were concerned, Rheinbaben drew a blank; he was more successful in the field of the serious periodicals of opinion. Sir Arnold Wilson, the editor of *The Nineteenth Century and After,* promised to take an article of 4,000 words on a topic of foreign policy; Professor Gooch, the editor of the *Contemporary Review* undertook to publish 3,500 words by Rheinbaben on German foreign policy; Vernon Bartlett, the editor of the *World Review* was prepared to accept a longer article on Germany's attitude to the reform of the League of Nations. It was prominently featured in the September number, under the title 'German Views on League Reform'. The article called 'German Foreign Policy' appeared in the October issue of the *Contemporary Review:* it presented the well-worn themes of Nazi propaganda. Hitler's Germany was 'unthinkable without the peace treaty', the most deplorable agreement in the annals of European history; Nazi Germany was a powerful bulwark against the 'bolshevization' of Europe. The article concluded on an ominous, yet hopeful, note: 'To prevent war by a wise policy before it is too late is a thousand times better than to prepare for it and organize it by a hundred pacts'.

Although Rheinbaben was perhaps more effective than any other German in exerting direct influence on the British press, he was by no means optimistic about the Nazi effort in this field. Summing up his experiences after the trip to Britain, he wrote: 'it is a rare exception when the placing of whole German articles in the English press actually succeeds. I was told on two occasions that, on the whole, the material sent to Britain by the various organizations in Germany was not suitable for publication. The English press refuses everything that looks like "propaganda". Although there existed the wish, in this country, for 'some kind of understanding with Germany' it ran against the 'powerful forces that continually influence the public against Germany'. And Rheinbaben concluded: 'The forces working against us in England by the printed word must at least be "contained" by us in the same field, that is by the printed word'.

National Socialist propaganda was unsuccessful in achieving the objective set out by Rheinbaben at any point before the war. Most of

the papers that upheld the editorial policy of an understanding with
Germany after 1933— *The Times* was one of them— had done so before Hitler's coming to power. Although Barrington-Ward, a member of *The Times* editorial staff, maintained connexions with the German Embassy before and after 1933, *The Times* policy cannot be
said to have been directly influenced. Its sharply defined distinction
between news and comment made the printing of news unfavourable to Hitler's Germany possible. This confused the Nazi propagandists: they were quite unable to see the point.

Indeed, they were unsuccessful in making a lasting impression
on any of the available means of mass communication in Britain.
Reporting on Nazi Germany in the national press remained consistently hostile, even when the paper's editorial policy was based on
a desire for an understanding with Germany. According to Rheinbaben the BBC, in its choice of lectures, excerpts from the press,
etc., also had 'little understanding of Germany'.[18] Nazi propagandists had to be content when they succeeded in influencing media
with a much more confined reach, such as low-circulation books,
pamphlets, magazines, and the pro-German societies.

The organizations fostering Anglo-German friendship became,
from the point of view of Berlin, one of the most important instruments of Nazi propaganda to Britain. Early in 1935— when the way
for the naval agreement was being prepared— the initiative for the
foundation of a 'German institute' in London came from a Mr.
Kitson. He was a friend and collaborator of Colonel Fleischhauer,
the publisher of the antisemitic magazine the *Weltdienst*, and he
wrote to Fleischhauer about the project. Rosenberg was also
interested, and recommended it to Göring's attention.[19] A month
later, Prince Bismarck reported from London that the idea of a
German institute was by no means new. There already existed the
Deutsche Akademische Austauschdienst, the activities of which
could be broadened.[20] In the following years, this organization
came to be employed for the purposes of cultural propaganda; it
operated mainly in academic circles and organized exchange visits
for approved students and teachers, German language courses,
discussions and lectures.

On the British side, public opinion followed government action.

Three months after the conclusion of the Anglo-German naval agreement, in October 1935, a society called 'The Anglo-German Fellowship' was founded with the approval of the Foreign Office.[21] It was set up to 'promote good understanding between England and Germany'; it was non-political, and its membership 'does not necessarily imply approval of National Socialism'.[22] The Germans, for their own part, were not slow in reciprocating the interest the Fellowship showed in them. A sister organization—the *Deutsch-Englische Gesellschaft*—was established in Berlin; the Duke of Saxe-Coburg-Gotha became its President, and it was housed in an imposing building in Bendlerstrasse, between the Zoo and the American Embassy. It was formally opened in January 1936, and some twenty members of the Fellowship accepted the invitation to the opening in Berlin. In comparison with the official Nazi munificence showered upon the *Gesellschaft*, the Fellowship was seriously under-capitalized. It had received one donation of £500 from a British firm, and a number of smaller sums from business and private sources; its secretary, Elwin Wright, was to be found in rooms at the unprepossessing Hotel Metropole in Northumberland Avenue, London, W.C.2.

A similar organization called 'The Link' was established in July 1937. Two years after its foundation, the society was running some thirty-five active branches, the largest of which in Birmingham, had more than 4,000 members. Whereas the Fellowship specialized in improving understanding between the two countries through personal contacts, 'The Link' operated on a lower social level than the Fellowship; it organized lectures and meetings that were often addressed by German nationals; its functions were more blatantly propagandist.

A member of the council of 'The Link' was Mr. C.E. Carroll, who edited the *Anglo-German Review*. This was a monthly magazine that appeared for the first time in November 1936; it was expensively produced and sold at 1s until June 1937, when the price was halved because, it was said, of the great success it had scored. Early in 1939, the *Review* claimed a readership of 12,000. It is likely that the *Review* received subsidies from Berlin via 'The Link': although it had started as an independent magazine, it became closely associ-

ated with the pro-Nazi organization. 'The Link' was tainted by
Fascism more obviously than the Fellowship. In August 1940,
Charles Lines, the secretary of its Birmingham branch and a former
member of the British Union of Fascists, was detained under Section 18b of the Defence Regulations.

The German diplomats regarded the friendship societies as more
suitable, for propaganda purposes, than the political organization
of British Fascists. The societies had many well-meaning members
who were primarily interested in the cause of a better understanding between the two countries. A few of them were prominent
people, who were in a position to influence political attitudes at
every level of British society, and who were untainted by political
eccentricity. They may have regarded Fascist Germany as a lesser
threat to European stability than Communist Russia; their difficulties in grasping the dynamic and aggressive nature of Hitler's régime
was the price they paid for their political preferences.

The National Socialists did not attempt to organize, before the
war, a right-wing international movement on the lines of the Comintern. Apart from Nazi parties in German territories outside the
Reich, they neither trusted nor used any other national organizations. The British Fascists were rather neglected by Hitler's government. Laudatory articles on Sir Oswald Mosley and his movement
of course appeared in glossy propaganda publications such as
Europa will leben,[23] and large uniformed delegations of the British
Union of Fascists made inevitable appearances at party rallies in
Nürnberg. Symptomatically, there was no mention of the Union of
Fascists in the memorandum for Hitler that Rosenberg produced
some months after his ill-starred visit to London in 1933.[24] The
reports of the Embassy concerning the Fascist movement were
detailed and quite frequent: they were not, however, calculated to
arouse the interest of the leading Nazis.[25]

It is difficult to account for the powerful movement, in Britain,
working for an understanding with Hitler's Germany by the operation of Nazi propaganda. The men who upheld such a policy acted
largely for reasons of indigenous British origin, and many of them
carried on a policy that had been initiated before 1933. The desire
for an understanding was also strengthened by the anti-Communist

and anti-Soviet attitudes current among certain influential right-wing circles: such attitudes can usually be traced to Lord Milner and his kindergarten. Milner opposed the terms of the peace treaties while they were still in the making: for him, Germany was fast fading out as Britain's most dangerous adversary, and it was being replaced by the rising menace of Bolshevik Russia. Moscow Communism was seen, from London, as an article for export: it was easier to regard Hitler's regime as a system for running Germany. On the other hand, Nazi antisemitism struck no responsive chord in Britain; it repelled rather than attracted.[26]

Although the direct influence exercised by Nazi propaganda in Great Britain was only marginal, indirectly the National Socialists were more successful. In the course of Goebbels's foreign campaigns—in the Saarland and the Rhineland, in Austria and in Czechoslovakia—the reactions in London were of the greatest interest to Hitler's government, and they were closely followed. The impression they produced was, from the point of view of the *Promi*, quite satisfactory. The artificial nature of 'popular enthusiasm' among the Germans inside and outside of Germany remained hidden from the view of the British politicians: many of them saw German nationalism as a spontaneous force that had to be satisfied.

By the spring of 1938 the National Socialist propaganda machinery had reached its peak performance. It was a formidable instrument, impressive to observe in action. It was completely integrated into the diplomatic and military manoeuvres of the Reich government. The beginning of the last phase of the *Anschluss* campaign[27] coincided with the launching of the propaganda drive against Czechoslovakia. On 20 February 1938 Adolf Hitler spoke to the *Reichstag* deputies; the speech was transmitted by all the German and, for the first time, the Austrian and Czechoslovak broadcasting stations. (The Austrian broadcast was made possible by the agreement between the Führer and Schuschnigg at Berchtesgaden eight days before.) At the same time, Berlin cinemas showed a closed-circuit television transmission of Hitler's performance. He spoke of 'ten million Germans' isolated and suffering at the hands of two neighbouring states: he mentioned neither Czechoslovakia nor Austria and Poland by name. But in February 1938 all was still well in Danzig, as far as Hitler was concerned; the improvement of Germany's relations with Poland had been facilitated because the country was not run by 'western parliamentarianism, but a Polish Marshal'.[28] The 'ten million Germans' Hitler had in mind lived in Austria and Czechoslovakia.

The *volksdeutsch* revolution that had been inaugurated in central Europe in January 1933 was now being brought to its concluding stages. The subversion of the established order, Hitler knew, could be accomplished by the Germans living in this area. After Austria, Czechoslovakia became the main target of the *Promi*.

In the Czechoslovak Republic, Nazi propaganda successfully exacerbated relations between the Czechs and the Germans. We have noted (see above, page 112) that initially, National Socialism developed in the Czech lands of the Habsburg Empire, where the Czechs and the Germans competed for political advantages as well as jobs. But this extreme form of nationalism affected only a small part of the two peoples: neither the Czech nor the German National Socialists became, at any point before 1914, serious contenders for the power and the position of Social Democracy.

After 1918 and the break-up of the Habsburg Empire the Germans of Bohemia and Moravia played, for a short time, hard to get. They had lost their position of effortless supremacy, and they were not quite certain whether they wanted to, or indeed would have to, come to terms with the Czechoslovak state. [29] But in the political situation of post-war Central and Eastern Europe, their position was weak. For instance, Karl Renner, the Social Democrat Chancellor of the Austrian Republic, supported the incorporation of the Germans living in Czechoslovakia into Austria not because he thought the plan practicable, but merely because he wanted to strengthen their hand in regard to the new state.

Despite the fact that the German minority was not invited to participate in the making of the constitution and the basic laws of the Czechoslovak Republic, their provisions guaranteed the equality of citizens before the law. Later certain steps were taken to put constitutional theory into practice. There were German civil servants and schools in the areas inhabited by them; more than 90% of them were able to use their own language for official purposes, whenever they came in touch with the civil administration or the courts. Until the elections of 1935, those political parties which supported the programme of living peacefully together with the Czechoslovak state and its majority nation, represented between 75 and 80% of the German electorate.

As in any other ethnically mixed area, the Germans had, of course, genuine complaints against the state, but these could be settled, given time and patience; underneath the surface of politics, the situation was less hopeful. There was little non-political dialogue going on between the Czechs and the Germans. They tended to ignore each other. It took a long time for instance before the New German Theatre in Prague decided to put on plays and operas by Czech writers and composers. For their own part, the Czechs did no better. Paul Eisner, a Prague Jew who wrote prose in German and poetry in Czech, said in 1929 that 'the Czech cultural Germanophobia is slowly becoming something unique in Europe. . . . There are exceptions but they are unimportant for the overall situation, which is quite pathological.'[30] When Eisner addressed his audience the Czechs had not managed a single translation into their own language of either Kafka or Rilke, two Prague authors who happened to write in German. There was no contact between the Czech and the German universities in Prague, where the scholars pursued their disciplines and interests in isolation, behind the smoke screens of their respective languages and attitudes.

On a different level there was some inter-course between the two peoples. Intermarriage continued to be frequent after 1918. But once the couple married it had to opt for either the German or the Czech camp. The phenomenon of mixed marriages puzzled the Nazi propagandists. They would have it that the Czechs had to resort to miscegenation because they lacked certain important innate qualities; after November 1940 National Socialists were allowed to marry Czech girls only under a special party dispensation.[31] By then the Nazi view of the Czechs as the 'hereditary enemy' of the Germans had almost become true.

The campaign which led to the conclusion of the Munich agreement in September 1938 was conducted in a highly flexible manner, employing different permutations of the basic propaganda themes according to the needs of the day, even of the hour. There were no traces of such disastrous experiments as those that had confounded the initial onslaught against Austria. For the first time the Foreign Ministry—now under Ribbentrop's direction—came to play an important and integrated role in a subversive propaganda drive. It was at its most effective when supporting Henlein and his *Sudetendeutsch* party. This policy had been inaugurated as early as the spring of 1935, when Henlein received a subsidy of 331,711 marks for propaganda purposes during the campaign preceding the general elections in May.[32]

Apart from supporting the propaganda generated by the Sudeten German party, the Reich backing gave the Germans in Czechoslovakia the self-confidence they needed to challenge the authority of the government in Prague. They were never left for long to work independently of Berlin, even when the aim of Nazi propaganda was to create the impression that the conflict concerned exclusively the Czechs and the Germans of Czechoslovakia. As in the preceding foreign campaigns, the propagandists made a determined and successful effort to create a 'Sudeten atmosphere' in Germany herself. The link between the Sudeten Germans had to be forged, a 'spontaneous' mood had to be created. Finally, powerful offshoots of the Sudeten propaganda were intended to reach London and Paris.

Indeed, while the relentless war of nerves between Berlin and Prague was conducted, both parties closely followed the reactions in the western capitals. Hitler's aims were diametrically opposed to those of Beneš: the President of Czechoslovakia strove to draw the attention of the Western Powers to the threat to peace and the *status quo* in central Europe; Hitler, on the other hand, wanted to lull any suspicions that might have existed in these countries. The fact that their respective pursuits put the two men into false positions was of course exploited by the *Promi*. It was easy for the propagandists to present Beneš as an intransigent warmonger, and Hitler as the defender of peace.

The occupation of Prague marked the last stage of Hitler's easy, piecemeal conquests as well as of the smooth efficient operation of Nazi propaganda. In the Austrian and the Sudeten campaigns, the propagandists had played a prominent role. Although they kept a wary eye on the reactions abroad—a considerable part of their activities was directed at influencing foreign public opinion, and a special foreign press section was set up at the Ministry of Propaganda—they were pursuing limited objectives, where concentrated effort was both necessary and possible. The situation began to change in March 1939. The British guarantee to Poland was followed by minor and badly co-ordinated campaigns against the governments in London, Paris, and Washington; soon, there was the preliminary work to be done on behalf of the German-Soviet pact. [33] The preparatory work for the attack on Poland was therefore comparatively short, and it had to be fitted in among all the other pursuits of Nazi publicity.

Indeed, in the last months before the war, Nazi propaganda was skipping a good deal from one subject to another rather than developing one major theme gradually; from having been concentrated, it was becoming diffuse. Goebbels had not yet emerged from the crisis that occurred at the end of 1938, [34] at the same time, military problems were fast becoming the centre of Hitler's interests. In a way, when they launched their publicity campaign on behalf of the army, [35] the propagandists began to weaken their own position. There also exist numerous indications that, for reasons of security, officials of *Promi* and of allied agencies were now worse informed than before. Until 25 August 1939, for instance, the press was not allowed to report on the activities of the *Wehrmacht*, and it was officially told of the military preparations only the following day. [36] On a higher level, Fritzsche, a close collaborator of Goebbels and well-known broadcaster, was unaware of the true background to the alleged Polish attack on the Gleiwitz broadcasting station. [37] The sham attack on the *Gleiwitzsender* was in fact carried out by one of Himmler's *Einsatzgruppen*, commando units which were usually employed for secret acts of a provocative nature. They had been first employed in the Sudetenland, and they were now fast coming into their own. The former balance of propaganda and violence was being upset to the disadvantage of propaganda.

VII
The Decline
of Propaganda

No military engagement was considered by Hitler in connexion with the occupation of Austria. On 14 February 1938 he approved General Keitel's suggestion that neither the army nor the airforce were to make any preparations. Only 'false but credible information' was to be spread and manoeuvres near the frontier executed, creating the impression that military preparations against Austria were being undertaken.[1] On the day of Austria's occupation the War Ministry had no reports of military moves by other European states.[2]

In the course of the Sudeten propaganda campaign, however, the Führer was ready to consider the possibility of a cold war becoming a hot war. On 21 April 1938 at a meeting between Hitler and General Keitel, the basic directives for Operation Green—an armed assault on Czechoslovakia—were laid down.[3] The idea of an unprovoked attack 'out of the blue' and without any obvious justification was turned down, because of 'hostile world opinion which might lead to a serious situation'. Military action, the two men agreed, could be taken 'after a period of diplomatic discussion which would gradually lead to a crisis and to war'. A lightning action against Czechoslovkia could, however, be based on an incident, such as the murder of the German Minister in the course of an anti-German demonstration. After some detailed tactical instructions, a short section C of the memorandum was entitled 'Propaganda'.

It contained only two rough-and-ready directives: (1) Leaflets for the conduct of the Germans in 'Green' territory; (2) Leaflets with threats to intimidate 'Greens'.

The actual occupation of the Sudetenland in October 1938 was officially regarded as a military operation, and all reporting of it came under the censorship of the Supreme Command of the *Wehrmacht* (*OKW*). Although the *Promi* and the *OKW* were in constant touch during the campaign, and there was an army press officer attached to the Ministry, this meant a departure from the usual practices of Goebbels. He was inclined to rely on a tight control of the propaganda apparatus based on detailed directives, rather than on the censorship of independently produced material.[4] It was not until 10 p.m. on 15 October that the *Promi* resumed its former position as the sole controlling agency of the press.

But soon, the propagandists themselves were instructed to foster the prestige of the army. Four days after the co-operation between the *OKW* and the *Promi* was terminated, the *Reichs-propagandaamt* issued an order to the press on 'making the army popular'.[5] The German press was congratulated on the role it had played in the Sudeten crisis, and then requested to proceed to a no less important internal campaign. ' Through a longer and uninterrupted pressure by the German press, in word and in picture, in individual reports, in comments and in leading articles, the self-confidence of the German nation in its own strength and its military power should be reinforced.' It should be pointed out, the directive went on, that the great successes of Germany's foreign policy had been made possible by absolute military preparedness. In the last analysis— and this *motif* was to be stressed again and again— the whole German nation had been prepared to fight for the 'right to live' of its 3,500,000 Sudeten compatriots.

Goebbels disapproved of the war: he knew that it would affect his own and his Ministry's position. He remarked that Hitler would 'soon listen to his generals only, and it will be very difficult for me'.[6] Hitler of course saw the necessity of retaining the services of his leading propagandist and of the apparatus Goebbels had built up over the years. On 8 September 1939— a week after the invasion of Poland— the Führer dictated a 'command' concerning propaganda. [7]

It pointed out that 'Propaganda is an important instrument of the
Leadership for forwarding and strengthening the will to victory
and for destroying the enemies' morale and will to victory.' The
Promi remained the 'central agency for the practical application of
propaganda. Breaking it up during the war would be comparable to
breaking up certain components of the *Wehrmacht*'.

Nevertheless, Goebbels's fears were justified: from the first, the
war severely circumscribed the competence of his Ministry. From
the beginning of the war, directives for publicity came from three
different sources: the *Promi*, the Foreign Ministry, and the department of *Wehrmachtspropaganda* in the Supreme Command of the
Armed Forces (*OKW*). Goebbels was unsuccessful in establishing a
clear supremacy for his Ministry. The co-ordination of the directives
took place at daily meetings; from December 1940, the deputy
Reich press director Sündermann was in the chair, and the heads of
the press departments in the agencies concerned took part in the
meetings. At the same time, Otto Dietrich, the Reich press director
and Sündermann's immediate superior, was in the anomalous position of being, on the one hand, one of Hitler's most trusted collaborators and, on the other, an Under Secretary of State in the *Promi*.[8]
He spent most of his time in the Führer's personal entourage, and
his directives often came into conflict with those of the Minister
of Propaganda. The co-ordination of the directives to the press was
not very effective: often the contradictions had to be ultimately
resolved on the editorial desks.[9]

In addition, the key reports on the war situation were published
in the form of the communiqués of the Supreme Command of the
Wehrmacht. They were put together on the basis of information
which flowed from diverse sources and through a variety of controlling agencies—a process in which the Ministry of Propaganda
played only a small part. The original information came from one
of the three operational headquarters: the army, the navy and the
air-force dispatched their daily reports to the *Abteilung Wehrmachtpropaganda* at the Supreme Command. Here, the three reports were
collated and then passed on, as drafts of the '*Wehrmacht* sphere of
competence' (*Wehrmachtbereich*) to the Führer's Headquarters.
The draft reports concerning the 'home sphere of competence'

(*Heimatbereich*) — insofar as they did not relate to the air-force as a part of the armed forces — originated at the *Promi*: their importance increased later in the war, with the growing intensity of the Allied air raids. The two drafts were again collated at the Führer's HQ, and put before Hitler. Only after his approval, the *Promi* received the final communiqué for publication through the official news agency, the *DNB*, and through the broadcasting network.

Such a process was of course a long one, and it became longer as the war went on: on many later occasions the communiques were two days old before they reached the public. Nevertheless, the *Wehrmacht* enjoyed a good deal of prestige among the Germans, and the reports published under its auspices became the most important instrument of war-time publicity. They were generally regarded as more trustworthy than information derived from civilian sources.[10]

As the importance of the Ministry of Propaganda declined, and its work became technically simpler, the Minister's activities became more and more hectic. During the first, victorious phase of the war, Goebbels looked after everything. He toured armament factories in the Ruhr and the wharves in Hamburg; he was seen in the capitals of the occupied countries shortly after the arrival there of the military; he received Japanese youth leaders, Spanish publishers, Dutch poets. Everything interested him, from the price of potatoes to the sexual needs of the foreign workers in Germany. He planned a vast new building for his Ministry, which was to be erected soon after the fast-approaching end of the war and victory.[11] He also devoted a lot of care to keeping himself in the eyes of the German public: he wrote and broadcast more then ever before. He of course remained loyal to Hitler, and he helped where he could. The *Promi* produced anonymous letters for employment in France during the military attack; Goebbels instructed his assistants, Gutterer and Raskin, to publish a diary recording the pornographic experiences of a British soldier in Paris for distribution in France.[12] Churchill fast became the Minister's personal enemy, and Goebbels poured scorn and abuse upon his head. Apart from one exception, the Minister of Propaganda never ran out of commentary for important occasions during the war. After Hess's unexpected descent, by parachute, on Scotland, Goebbels disappeared from Berlin. When he was informed of the party line—it had been worked out by Dietrich and Bormann, and approved by Hitler—that Hess was 'mentally sick', he strongly disapproved.[13]

Nevertheless, the victories of the armed forces opened fresh vistas before the propagandists. The experience and technical knowledge they had gained in manipulating public opinion in Germany could now be put to use in the occupied as well as the 'allied' countries. Under the guidance of *Promi*, the *Gleichschltung* of the means of mass communication was swiftly carried out. New Nazi newspapers began to appear; new controllers were installed at the broadcasting stations: occupied Europe became a monopoly market for Goebbels's films and travelling exhibitions. At the same time, an attempt was made to work out and publicize a plan for the reorganization of Europe. As the Hitler-Stalin pact was still operative, it was impossible for National Socialist propaganda to stake any claims to defending Europe from Bolshevism. For the time being, the Reich and the European themes had to be employed: in this respect, there existed some tenuous connexions with pre-war propaganda.

At the party rally in 1938, a new ideological opening had been tentatively explored: ideas connected with the Holy Roman Empire were briefly paraded before the party members. Seyss-Inquart had brought with him the Imperial insignia from Vienna, and they were ceremonially handed over to the Mayor of Nürnberg. Germany was presented as the leading power in central and eastern Europe, an area to which Britain and France were 'alien', and as a power which was able to impose here a *Pax Germanica*. Hitler's first aggressive moves had taken place under the slogan *Ein Volk, ein Reich, ein Führer*; in March 1939, the Czechs were taken 'under the protection of the Reich' at their own request.

As the offensive against France was drawing to its close, the first number of the weekly *Das Reich* appeared in Berlin on 26 May 1940. Under Goebbels's sponsorship, the newspaper became the most representative example of Nazi war-time journalism or, more precisely, of the first phase of the military engagement. The ideas published in *Das Reich* were firmly based in the sense of Germany's military supremacy. The concept of the 'Reich' took precedence over that of '*Europa*'; although the Empire was not proclaimed 'holy', it was to be 'eternal'. It was unique and German, indisputably at the head of the non-German states. It was a vague concept, containing the racial, authoritarian, and hieratic ideas of the Nazis, as well as embracing a variety of historical notions. The Germanic Empire was to hold sway in northern Europe; in the south, an acommodation had to be made for the Roman Empire of Mussolini. The geographical extent of the 'new order' was left undefined; political commitments were also usually avoided. It was assumed that political reconstruction would be carried out on the basis of the National Socialist pattern. Europe was to be built up as a self-contained economic unit, capable of resisting blockade and of breaking the international economic supremacy of Great Britain.[14]

Although a broadly-based plan for Europe was bound to remain incomplete without France, the National Socialists found it by no means easy to assimilate her into their schemes. Quite apart from concrete political difficulties, the work of conciliation was retarded by various ideological predilections on the part of the National Socialists. The victory over France represented for them a victory over the 'worn-out' ideals of the French revolution. Germany's military triumph was seen as the utlimate proof of the superiority of Nazi ideals, which were diametrically opposed to those of 1789. The National Socialist leaders were never quite able to take seriously the attempts to carry out a 'national revolution' in Vichy France. In addition, Nazi publicity tended to regard the victory over France as the defeat of the Versailles 'system'. British and French supremacy which had lasted for two decades disappeared without a trace, as did all the parliamentary systems and some of the small states established by the peace treaties.[15]

Against the background of distrust of the Vichy régime as well as the feeling of superiority on the part of the National Socialists, the 'soft-sell' propaganda which was employed in regard to France often lacked convicition. During the military assault, the small secret transmitter *Humanité* had been run on superpatriotic lines: after the conclusion of the treaty of armistice, appeals to French patriotism and self-interest continued to be made. Every sign of successful political co-operation with Pétain and Laval was accompanied by

an effusion of propaganda of good will. It aimed at antagonizing
the French public against the politicians who had driven the country
into the war on Germany; it pointed to Berlin's magnanimous treatment of defeated France. She was allowed to keep her fleet and
sovereignty in her colonial Empire; many of the prisoners-of-war
were set free; permission was even granted to France to build a new
army. It was a pity, the agitation was later continued, that the agreement of Montoire of October 1940 had been sabotaged, that the
French officers had broken their word, and that the Toulon mutiny
had forced the Reich to employ severe repressive measures. Most
of these arguments were restated, with some bitterness occasioned
by retrospection, in Hitler's letter to Pétain of 27 November 1942.[16]

Until the summer of 1941, the National Socialist publicity pursued
an elusive ideal in regard to Europe. Hostility to Britain and her ex-
clusion from the affairs of the Continent were the only constant
points of Nazi propaganda at the time. But the divided, suspicious
attitude of the Nazis towards Britain was reflected in Nazi wartime
propaganda. Goebbels closely followed the British propaganda
moves, and too often confined himself to replying to the points
which had been made in London. Later in the war he paid a compliment to Churchill by imitating, in his 'total war' speech, the Prime
Minister's 'blood, sweat, and tears' address of 1940. We know that
Hitler had been much impressed by the Allied, especially the English, propaganda in the First World War. After 1939 a large number
of Nazi posters was based on the directness of the 'Your country
needs you!' type of appeal.

A variety of plans for the partitioning of France were publicized
and dropped; the *Grossraum* projects concerning the Mediterranean and Africa got bogged down in the uncertainties in south
Europe: France was unreliable, and Spain remained neutral. At the
same time, Hitler remained immersed in military problems, and he
would enter into no commitments which might restrict his freedom
of action in the military field. Although some striking technical
successes were achieved in the field of *Gleichschaltung* of the means
of mass communication in occupied and 'allied' Europe, the construction of *Festung Europa* was far from complete at the time of the
attack on the Soviet Union.

The German Army crossed the frontier of the Soviet Union at 3 a.m. on 22 June 1941. Hitler now embarked on, in his view, the decisive stage of the war. In contrast with the detailed military planning of the 'Barbarossa' operation, very little propaganda preparation had been made. The demands of military secrecy ruled out, of course, a propaganda drive on the pre-war pattern; the Nazi-Soviet pact was still in force, and anyway, the campaign was expected to be one of short duration. At first, the propagandists themselves appeared to have been taken by surprise: they confined themselves to reiterating Hitler's arguments concerning the absolute necessity of the action against the Soviet Union. The decision of the Führer, it was explained, had been occasioned by a British-Bolshevik conspiracy against Germany.[17] The first instruction to the newspaper editors issued on 22 June were unusually hesitant: 'Unfortunately we had been unable to prepare the German nation, as on previous occasions, for the forthcoming decisions; this must now be done by the press. It must provide intelligible reasons, because it is politically educated, and the nation is not. We must make it clear that this [i.e. the attack on Russia] does not represent a change. Reporting on Russia was banned for months, so that the press should be spared difficulties during the necessary switch [of policy]. Now at last we can speak freely of the hypocrisy, by which the Soviets tried to deceive us for many years. The true feelings which the German nation instinctively entertains towards Bolshevism must be freed again. Bolshevism has waited for its hour We have proofs that it would have stabbed us in the back at a suitable moment.'[18]

But soon the campaign in the east, as well as broad European perspectives, were brought into a sharper focus. A week later the German press was instructed that 'Reports from the whole world make it apparent that a rising of the whole of Europe against Bolshevism can be noted, as it could not have been observed until now. Europe marches against the common enemy in a unique solidarity, and it rises, as it were, against the oppressor of all human culture and civilization. This hour of birth of the new Europe is being accomplished without any demand or pressure from the German side. On the contrary, it is clear that even the small and the smallest states have understood the common European task, since they have called up their sons to make a blood sacrifice for the common idea. For this reason we do not want to speak of a crusade. Newspapers are faced here with the immense task, as it is essential, especially in regard to America, that the unity of Europe in the fight against Bolshevism is made clear to the new world as well. The great hour has also come for the settling of accounts with the English phrases and thesis that Adolf Hitler is a dictator, who rushes restlessly from country to country like a modern Genghis Khan, because one aggression force him to other, further, and new [aggressions]. Adolf Hitler has proved himself to be the military leader of Europe on behalf of the common culture and civilization, and is recognized as such by the whole European world.'[19]

Almost all European nations took some military part in the Russian campaign: Finnish, Hungarian, Slovak, Italian, and Rumanian units were later joined by volunteers from Spain, Belgium, France, Holland, and Norway. However insignificant the participation of these allies was in fact, the whole of Europe could now be presented as defending itself against the threat of *Judeo-Bolschewismus* (the Jews were, incidentally, later described as the 'cement of the alliance between Soviet Russia and the Western Powers'), a threat which was compared with the earlier 'perils from the east'—Hun, Mongol, but not Turk—and the whole of Europe was to benefit from Germany's victory. Hitler himself took up the theme: on 11 December 1941 he asked the *Reichstag*: 'What then, my deputies, is Europe? There exists no geographic definition of our Continent, but only an ethnic and cultural one. The Urals are not the border of this Continent, but [the border has been] always the line which divides the Western from the eastern way of life [*Lebensbild*][20] In private, Hitler was more explicit: discussing the frontiers between Europe and Asia he said that: 'The real frontier is the one that separates the Germanic world from the Slav world'; the Slavs were peoples who 'are not destined to live a cleanly life. They know it, and we would be wrong to persuade them to the contrary. . . . It's better not to teach them to read. They won't love us for tormenting them with schools. Even to give them a locomotive to drive would be a mistake . . .'[21] Indeed, the campaign in the east added a new dimension to the Nazi European propaganda drive. It implied that there existed two sharply

defined civilizations in Europe, one of which was vastly superior; it
foreshadowed not only the widely divergent treatment of the inhabitants of the occupied territories in the west and in the east of Europe,
but also the *Untermensch* propaganda against the Slavs, the robot-
like sub-human creatures from the east.[22]

Nevertheless, the National Socialist propagandists faced, in the
summer of 1941, completely new tasks. Although a good deal of
their activities before the summer of 1939 had concerned the Soviet
Union, they had no experience of propaganda to the Soviets.[23] In
this respect there lay two broad choices before them. They could
identify the Soviet régime with the peoples over which it ruled, and
declare a ruthless fight on them. They could work, on the other
hand, for the creation of a system of selective alliances with certain
social groups and nationalities, and devote their energies to driving
a wedge between Stalin's régime and the people of Russia.

A month after the invasion of the Soviet Union, Goebbels set up
a secret station that specialized in broadcasting to Russia. It was run
by Albrecht, a Russian of German extraction who was the Soviet
Vice-Commissar for Forestry before fleeing to Germany during the
Moscow purges in 1936. The station ran three political subdivisions:
one of them was based on a general opposition programme, another
expounded a Trotskyist line, and another, possibly the most important of the three, conducted a 'national Bolshevik' policy. It maintained that 'Stalin, the slave of the capitalists, had sold the socialist
fatherland to the plutocrats'.[24]

There also exists evidence that the *Abteilung Wehrmachtpropaganda* was prepared to use the technique of antagonising the
inhabitants of the occupied territories of the Soviet Union from
Stalin's régime. A circular from the *OKW* to the armed forces
stated that: 'The enemies of Germany are not the peoples of the
Soviet Union, but exclusively the Jewish-Bolshevik Soviet government with its functionaries and the Communist Party, which is
working for a world revolution.' The German army did not come as
an enemy of the local population, it came to free it from the 'tyranny
of the Soviets'. Although hints that the Soviet Union would break
up into a number of individual states were to be avoided, German
propaganda was to employ the appropriate languages in the occu-

pied territories. Expressions like 'Russia', the 'Russians' and the 'Russian army' were to be discarded, and replaced by 'Soviet Union', the 'nations of the Soviet Union', and the 'Red Army'.[25] In practice, however, the army propagandists had to proceed with caution. In their leaflets to the Red Army—some 400 million of them were dropped over the Russian lines before the end of 1941—the Germans were simply described as liberators and the Soviet troops were invited to surrender. Yet, in spite of suggestions from the field and from the army propaganda experts that more positive slogans on such topics as self-government or private ownership of the land should be employed, no changes were allowed.[26]

Until the end of September 1941 the official statements on Germany's military achievements had been rather factual and guarded. But Hitler's estimate of Germany's military superiority at that stage of the war, and his stance as the conqueror of the east, profoundly affected the tone of Nazi propaganda. On 3 October, caution was abandoned and a high note of triumph was sounded. Hitler, who had made no public speech for five months, said on that day: 'I am saying this today for the first time, because I can say it today, that this enemy [in the east] has been struck down and will never rise again.'[27] Six days later, Dietrich released a special announcement to the press and the broadcasting system to the effect that 'with the formations already encircled, Timoshenko has sacrificed the last remaining armies of full fighting strength of the total Soviet front.' On the same day, in a broadcast on the *Deutschlandsender*, Hans Fritzsche said 'It is certainly possible that a régime of criminals with nothing else to lose will continue to drive their people to resist the advancing German front: that the seed of hatred of Germany and the fear of Bolshevik commissars will provoke further acts of senseless resistance.' But, Fritzsche claimed, further Russian resistance was futile.[28] Goebbels regarded such announcements as the biggest propaganda blunder of the war. They were, in his view, entirely irresponsible;[29] they certainly encouraged dangerous illusions.

In Hitler's opinion the military superiority of Germany had been proved, and the foundations of an eastern Empire had been laid. The Germans were now in a position to rule in the east, and they could do so without the aid of a calculated appeal to the Soviet peoples. Indeed, from the beginning of October, all discussion of the future of the occupied territories in the east was to be kept out of propaganda to the Soviets; no political commitments in regard to the local population were to be made.[30] Such confidence resulted in a ruthless attitude. In his 'order of the day' on 2 October Hitler said that 'this enemy does not consist of soldiers but to a large degree only of beasts'.[31] The theme concerning the subhumanity of the enemy—of the Slav *Untermensch*—thus received an official sanction from the highest place. Photographs of Red Army prisoners-of-war began to appear in German newspapers in ever-increasing numbers. These men were described as culturally and spiritually inferior; they were, in terms of Nazi propaganda, a mixture of the low and lowest humanity, truly subhuman. It was a theme which suitably complemented the 'European' campaign: the threat to Europe was depicted in the darkest colours.

The *Untermensch* propaganda was especially directed to the *Waffen SS*: in 1943 the SS published a pamphlet under that name. It was bound to affect the treatment of the population in the eastern territories, of the prisoners-of-war, and of the labour imported to Germany.[32] It could be ultimately traced to Hitler's overall view of the eastern policy of Germany. There had existed an ambiguity in his view of Russia long before the war: when he thought of the 'Jewish-Bolshevik ruling clique' he was quite prepared to make a distinction between it and the 'Russian people'; when he turned, however, to the plans for Germany's expansion in the east, the distinction disappeared, and its place was taken by contempt for the people who lived there.[33] And in 1941 Hitler did not set out to destroy Bolshevism in Russia, but to build up a German Empire in the east.

Alfred Rosenberg, the leading Nazi expert on the east, did not subscribe to this policy. The Great Russians were his main enemy: the peoples of the Ukraine and White Russia, of the Baltic states and of the Caucasus could be, in his view, set up in states dependent on the Reich, but enjoying a certain degree of autonomy. As the Minister responsible for civil administration in the occupied territories in the east—he was appointed to the newly-established *Ostministerium* in the middle of July—Rosenberg attempted to put his ideas into practice. He received little help from the Ministry of Propaganda. After a brief flirtation with the *Untermensch* line at the height of Germany's military triumph, Goebbels appeared ready, by the end of 1941, to return to more flexible methods of political warfare: although there existed, in this respect, no fundamental political differences between Rosenberg and Goebbels, their conflict developed into one of the bitterest inter-departmental rows of the war. Co-operation between the two Ministries, even of the most technical nature, proved impossible. Rosenberg jealously guarded the jurisdiction of his Ministry in propaganda matters: it possessed neither the experience and personnel, nor the equipment. When the *Promi*, for instance, offered Rosenberg broadcasting equipment, and although it declared itself ready to let the *Ostministerium* control the actual contents of the broadcasts, Rosenberg repeatedly turned the offers down. Attempts to produce anti-partisan propaganda films also failed; the cinemas in the occupied territories suffered seriously from shortage of material. Hundreds of older German films could not be shown because they contained an actor, even an extra, who was a Jew.[34] Although Goebbels tried hard to establish a foothold in the territories adminstered by the *Ostministerium*, the eastern section of the *Promi* at first operated only among the prisoners-of-war and the imported labour in the Reich. Goebbels finally made a break-through in August 1943, when his Ministry was authorized to set up shop in the east. Rosenberg retained only the control of the press; broadcasting and film passed under the control of the Ministry of Propaganda.

Apart from Goebbels, Rosenberg was faced with a formidable opposition. Most of the Nazi leaders—Himmler, Göring, and Ribbentrop—acquired an interest in the 'eastern problem', and pursued their own, often contradictory, eastern policies. In addition to being responsible for special tasks, such as liquidation and segregation of the prisoners-of-war, Himmler and the *SS* took care of police and security matters in the territories administered by the *Ostministerium*, and Himmler was empowered to direct Rosenberg's subordinates in matters of security. Rosenberg, an incompetent administrator, made a number of inept choices when selecting top personnel for his Ministry. Some officials were also forced on him; others, whose services

Rosenberg wanted to secure, would not leave the army or the Foreign Ministry. The *Ostministerium* was staffed by time-servers and men who were unemployable elsewhere: they cared little for Rosenberg's plans for the east. Finally, when the Ministry was reorganized in 1943, the influence of the *SS* within it considerably increased.[35]

Alfred Rosenberg's views on Russia received comparatively little publicity either in Germany or in the eastern territories. It was impossible to develop a unitary propaganda in the east against the background of administrative anarchy and incompetence, and continual inter-departmental squabbles that were caused more often by personal than by political differences. In face of the breakdown of indigenous administration, the formulation of a consistent policy and of a suitable propaganda to support it should have appeared a task of first-rate importance. It was not seen as such by Hitler. Ultimately, the exploitation of the economic and human resources in the occupied territories overrode all other considerations, and there was always the 'tough' line, for the soldiers and administrators alike, to fall back on. Only Himmler's *SS* units appear to have been consistent throughout. They had little use for propaganda, and their actions were enough to cancel any amount of mellifluous agitation generated from diverse quarters.

At the end of 1941 the end of the war in the east was nowhere in sight. The Nazi leaders had failed to develop a consistent programme for the future of the occupied territories. At first, there seemed no need for a determined effort to influence the Soviet peoples in Germany's favour. Indeed, in the first phase of the war, the swift succession of military victories was Hitler's best propaganda. But this phase was fast approaching its end. Early in December, the Red Army counter-attack halted the German advance in the suburbs of Moscow; a few days later, Germany and Italy declared war on the United States. The Anglo-Soviet-American partnership was then consolidated by the Washington and London treaties in February and May of the following year. At the beginning of 1942, Goebbels acquired an interest in defeatism in high military places: Hitler apparently had asked him to write a report on the subject.[36] It seemed as if Goebbels had sensed that he, and the instrument he represented, would again come into their own when the generals proved themselves inadequate to their task.

On 27 April 1942 Hitler spoke to the *Reichstag*; out of concern
for the Führer's health, Goebbels had no spotlights installed in the
chamber. After Hitler's speech. Göring introduced a new bill giving
the Führer plenary executive, legislative, and judiciary powers: it
was passed unanimously. Although Goebbels was at first quite
pleased with the speech, reports on the reactions of the public which
were passed on to the *Promi* were not favourable. The Germans were
asking why the Fuhrer had been given plenary powers, and why he
had criticized conditions at home so sharply; there was also concern
with the military situation. Hitler had spoken of a second winter
campaign: there were no more promises of a speedy conclusion of
the Russian war during the coming summer.[37]

Was it possible that Hitler was losing his touch as a speaker? After
a cautious start, he had allowed the hopes of the nation to be driven
sky-high in October 1941; after the first winter in Russia, the inevitable disappointment was setting in. The public image of the Führer
had been that of a harbinger of success and of military glory. When
there were no victories to announce, his powers as a speaker began to
fail him. Unable to confine himself to factual statement, however
unpalatable, the flights of his imagination and of his megalomania
were deprived of their foundations. He turned to criticism of the
conditions in Germany, which neither convinced nor attracted; he
may have been seeking a scapegoat and chose the wrong one.
Goebbels must have felt some disillusionment when he wrote in his
diary on 28 April 1942 that 'the Führer's speech represents, as it were,
the cry of a drowning man'. And Hitler himself may have sensed the
chill of approaching disaster. After a long silence, he made a determined effort at a come-back as a speaker on 30 September at the
Sportpalast, and then again on 8 November in the Hofbraukeller in
Munich. But the spell had been broken: in the future, his public
appearances would be very rare indeed.

Hitler's decline as the leading speaker of the party created a gap
which Goebbels did his best to fill. He chose a technique different
from that of the Führer. From the end of 1942, Goebbels began to conduct a propaganda of pessimism—it was modelled on Churchill's
example-that could serve as the driving force behind the total mobi-

lization of Germany's resources. At a conference of the departmental heads of his Ministry on 4 January 1943, he said: 'I myself want to see disappear from my mind and from the mind of the Ministry the idea that we cannot lose the war. Of course we can lose the war. The war can be lost by people who,will not exert themselves; it will be won by those who try hardest. We must not believe fatalistically in certain victory; we must take a positive view.'38 And total war required a total exploitation of his audience. He switched over to a tone of 'steely factuality', but above that, he appealed to the deepest defensive instincts of the nation: to hate and fear, to the need for self-assertion. On 18 November 1942 he declared, for instance, that: 'We want our nation to be filled not only with a deep love for its community, but also with an infernal hate of all the men and of all the forces who attack this community and who want to destroy it. When somebody objects that this is un-German, then I have to say: an exaggerated objectivity is a fault of the German character.' 39

Hitler went on giving most of his attention to the eastern front, where, at the end of the summer, the struggle for Stalingrad entered its opening stage. The propagandists were to make yet another fatal blunder in regard to the eastern front. On 24 August 1942, the Supreme Command of the *Wehrmacht* made an urgent request to the press not to write about the forthcoming fall of Stalingrad, but simply about the beginning of the battle. On 3 September, newspaper editors were asked to prepare material about the enormous importance of this fortress of Communism and industrial centre; on 17 September, the newspapers were informed that the struggle for Stalingrad was nearing its victorious conclusion, and that a special report was to be expected within forty-eight hours. But five days later, on 22 September, an *OKW* spokesman told the journalists that their presentation of the Stalingrad battle had created an impression—against the wishes of the Supreme Command—that the capture of the town was imminent. Finally, the directive for the press for 16 October read: 'The important military successes in the northern part of Stalingrad take the first place in today's newspapers. Caution in make-up and comment is recommended, so that the reader may not gain the impression that an event, which he had awaited for weeks, was about to occur.'40

Stalingrad did not provide the propagandists with the victory they needed so badly. The hopes they had raised during the first phase of the campaign were dashed to the ground, and a psychological crisis accompained the military defeat. In the last instance, the disaster had to be used for exhortations, to the nation, to a still greater war effort. Although the Stalingrad battle was held in the centre of public attention for many weeks, there were other disasters to be reported at the same time. At the end of October, Montgomery's Eighth Army broke through the German lines at El Alamein; on 8 November, Allied troops landed in North Africa; the intensity of the air-raids on the German towns was growing. But other, less tangible signs pointed to the fact that the Nazi domination of the air-space over Europe was highly vulnerable. The absolute monopoly of information the *Promi* strove for in Europe proved easy to break from the outside. The broadcasting war was also reaching the point from where the effectiveness of Nazi propaganda would begin to decline.

In the autumn of 1942, Nazi broadcasting policies had to be reviewed in accordance with Goebbels's drive for a total war effort. Early in November, the Minister of Propaganda appointed Hans Fritzsche to a new job. He became the political controller of German broadcasting, and also replaced Wolfgang Diewerge as the director of the broadcasting department in the *Promi*. In Fritzsche's view— and it can be assumed to have coincided with that of Goebbels—the main task of German wireless in the fourth year of the war was to create a bridge between the front and the hinterland. Broadcasting had to be made the most popular means of mass communication: 'it must speak to all, or it will reach none'.[41] Fritzsche also promised a better news service, brief, clear, and to the point. In addition, general military and political talks were to be broadcast more frequently and regularly during the peak hour, between 7.45 and 8 p.m. The speakers—soldiers and journalists, scientists and politicians—were to appear regularly, so that they would have an 'opportunity of establishing close contact with the listeners'. They were to use the method of 'candour towards the present, which distinguishes so conspicuously the articles published by Dr. Goebbels in *Das Reich*'. At the same time, these talks were to be modelled on the principle of an 'intellectual convoy'. This meant, Fritzsche explained, that just as in a convoy the speed of all ships was determined by that of the slowest vessel, such talks, addressed to the people, had to be based on the capacity of the masses.

Especially in regard to his news policy, Fritzsche had obviously learned a lot from the BBC; from now on, broadcasting was to be more tightly controlled, on the lines laid down by Goebbels. Certain technical deficiencies were also becoming visible: spare parts for wireless receivers were hard to come by; families who had lost their sets in air-raids were to be issued with special vouchers. But, most important, broadcasting was to bind together the nation, which had become dispersed by the war. There had occurred a German diaspora—troops, civil administrators, members of the security and of the technical services, were working in the Balkans, in the Caucasus, in France, and in Norway. They came in contact with a variety of new impressions and influences; they were exposed to enemy propaganda. They had in fact broken out of the ring where monopoly of information was highly organized; they were moving on its periphery. Broadcasting was regarded, by the *Promi*, as the most suitable means for remedying the situation. But, even on the home front, there existed grounds for concern. Since the spring of 1942 Goebbels was apprehensive lest enemy propaganda succeeded in dividing the Nazi leadership from the nation. On 8 April the press was instructed to take absolutely no notice of the American argument that the war was conducted not against the German nation but against the National Socialists.[42]

The Nazi monopoly of information was now in danger and the threat came from enemy broadcasting. Even some time before the war, the *Volksempfänger*, the cheap popular wireless set[43] had been constructed in a manner that made the reception of foreign broadcasts difficult. After the outbreak of the war, listening to all stations not under German control was forbidden by a special law.[44] The ban included broadcasting from allied and neutral countries, and every part of their programmes, including music and entertainment. In addition, the rumour was spread that it was technically feasible to establish, by the use of a special detection equipment, the wavelengths to which private sets were tuned in at any given time. Goeb-

bels argued that listening to foreign broadcasts was the spiritual
equivalent of a physical self-mutilation by a soldier. It was known
in Germany that no such ban on listening to foreign broadcasts
existed in Britain: to this, Goebbels replied that 'first of all we do
not cheat as much as the English, and secondly, we want to win the
war'.[45] Special permits for the monitoring of foreign broadcasts
were at first available to all the Ministries and other high party and
state offices: Goebbels soon had many of them cancelled. It was
explained, for instance, to Bernard Rust's Ministry of Science and
Education that listening to foreign broadcasts was an unhealthy
occupation, and that there had been a number of cases of nervous
breakdown in the monitoring section of the *Promi*.[46] Although
Goebbels was convinced that it did untold harm in spreading defeatism in high official quarters, he could do nothing about the Foreign
Ministry's monitoring service, which distributed a daily newsletter.[47]

The achievements of the army had in a way protected the monopoly position of the Nazi propaganda in the first phase of the war.
But as soon as the flow of announcements of military victories abated,
and when the first reversals were cautiously announced, growing
numbers of listeners began to turn to foreign broadcasts. Not only
were there individual 'black listeners' (*Schwarzhörer*), but there
existed whole groups, especially in the armed forces. The armed
forces possessed the necessary technical equipment, and listening
to foreign broadcasts became an accepted habit.[48] The legal and
technical counter-measures proved ineffectual. They ranged from
withdrawing permits from high officials to run their own monitoring
services, to death sentences in occupied Europe; from the construction of the *Volksempfänger* to the confiscation of private wireless
sets or at least of their short-wave bands. The confiscation of all
private wireless sets was contemplated on several occasions with
regard to a number of occupied countries and then, except in Holland
in May 1943, decided against, on the grounds that it would have
severely circumscribed the reach of Nazi propaganda itself. In
addition, the *Promi* did not command sufficient technical resources
to instal a satisfactory network of public loudspeakers, on the
Soviet pattern, either in the Reich or in the occupied territories. By

the spring of 1943, Goebbels was well aware that the Nazi monopoly of information was seriously threatened. On 25 May he recorded in his diary: 'There are reports . . . that many people are again listening to foreign radio stations. The reason for this, of course, is our completely obscure news policy which no longer gives people any insight into the war situation. Also, our reticence regarding Stalingrad and the fate of our missing soldiers there naturally leads the families to listen to Bolshevik radio stations, as these always broadcast the names of German soldiers reported as prisoners.'

As the war situation began to take an adverse turn for the National Socialists, there appeared signs of the need for a discussion of first principles of National Socialism. And in such a discussion, propaganda was certain to occupy a central place. Some time in 1943, a detailed memorandum concerning the party and the state was circulated among the high Nazi leadership; although it was unsigned, Martin Bormann, the last man to have arrived at a position of power by making himself indispensable to the Führer, was very likely its author.[49]

Propaganda was, it was argued in the memorandum, the original function of the party: 'from the beginnings of the movement, propaganda was linked with it most closely'. Its direction should, therefore, return to the party; the author of the memorandum was frankly amazed at the manner in which propaganda had been allowed to pass under the control of the state. The memorandum was largely retrospective, it concerned itself with administrative detail, and it was an undisguised attack on Goebbels. Nevertheless, the basic principles of propaganda, its effectiveness, its content, remained unquestioned. If the leading Nazis had doubts on any of these points — there is no evidence that they did — they certainly never expressed them, even among themselves. The author of the memorandum was simply moved by a sentimental hankering for the heroic age of the Nazi movement. Propaganda was to become again what it used to be in the *Kampfzeit*. In a way it did. Faced with a hostile world, Nazi propaganda had to abandon its former megalomania and address its audience in sober realistic terms. It had to compensate for the failure of the military to win the war.

The roar of the guns and tanks, the screech of the *Stuka* dive-bombers, had silenced the arts of Goebbels. Early in the war, we have noted, the Minister of Propaganda was being all things to all men, looking out for tasks which could satisfy his restless energy. Despite the fact that the *Führer*, once he had brought the army under his control early in 1938, acquired new interests, Goebbels's devotion to his master remained unimpaired. The image of the leader was there to be preserved and, again, modified. The friend of the people, who had frustrated the vile plots of the enemy, emerged as a military genius. In the euphoric stage of the war, when accounts of military victories filled the news bulletins of the *OKW*, Hitler was presented as a person who 'gives us as a people and as a nation that immense strength which foreign nations call and probably feel to be the German miracle'.[50] Hitler was more than equal to the task of construction of a new Europe.

But from the end of the year 1942, a more sober picture of Hitler began to emerge. The *Führer* was paraded before the Germans as a historical figure, 'utterly great and utterly lonely.' On his 54th birthday in April 1943 "indelible furrows on his face" had been written by endless days of work and endless nights without sleep. And when Hitler started retreating into his private lunacy, unable to face his public, Goebbels worked harder than ever. Between the Stalingrad defeat in January 1943 and the end of the war Hitler gave two public speeches and two funeral orations. Goebbels made virtue out of necessity: 'the *Führer* has almost completely disappeared behind his work.' In 1944— the attempt on his life had taken place in July that year— Hitler did not address, for the first time in the eleven-year history of the Third Reich, the customary assembly of the old Nazi guard in Munich on 8 November. Instead, Himmler read a proclamation by the leader announcing the formation of the *Volkssturm*, the people's militia, the last-ditch defence force against the closing forces of the enemy. At that time Goebbels concentrated on proving to the Germans that Hitler was alive and well—'if his head is slightly bowed, this is the result of his continuous study of maps'.[51]

Indeed, in the middle of military disaster, Goebbels achieved a striking personal victory. The man who had faced political ruin before the war, and the instrument of propaganda which had been pushed aside by Hitler, started moving back into their former place of prominence. As the blows of the Allied war effort fell more and more heavily upon the Reich, Goebbels, an exception among the Nazi leaders, showed himself to be tough enough to stand up to them. He was rewarded for his exertions. After the attempt on Hitler's life he became the Reich Trustee for Total War; in April 1945 Hitler appointed him the Reich Chancellor. Goebbels remained with his *Führer* till the bitter end.

The second rise of Goebbels coincided with the fall of the Third Reich. He had laid the foundations for his short-lived good fortune by his 'total war' speech, delivered in the Berlin Sportpalast in Berlin on 18 February 1943.[52] Goebbels said that the situation reminded him of the *Kampfzeit*, the period of struggle before 1933. Again, the German people were hard pressed; again, there were wounded men, the evidence of a hard struggle, in the hall. 'Before me sit rows of German wounded from the eastern front who had their arms and legs amputated, men with shattered limbs, men blinded in the war, who had been brought here by their Red Cross nurses, men in the best years of their lives. . . .' In a Berlin suburb in February 1927, Goebbels had spoken against the background of the stretcher cases which had resulted from the beer-hall fight. Sixteen years later, the victims of a larger violence, organised and sanctioned by Hitler's state, sat in neat rows in front of Goebbels. He made no comment on either the striking differences, nor the similarities, between the two occasions.

The Minister of Propaganda demanded even more effort and sacrifices from the Germans for the sake of the war. Though he thought it necessary to counter English propaganda—'the English assert that the Germans have lost their faith in victory'—his speech in the main part dealt with the threat, to his country and to the whole of Europe, from the east.

The German people, Goebbels said, educated by National Socialism, 'can take the whole truth'. And the truth was that Stalingrad had fallen, and that the Red Army had gone over into an offensive. 'The onslaught from the steppe on our venerable continent this winter had been loosened with a fury which surpasses human and historical imagination.' Goebbels did not bother any

longer to differentiate between the Russian people and the system
they lived under; it would have weakened the impact of his speech.
This was no time for making subtle distinctions: 'The masses of tanks
which are attacking our eastern front are the result of twenty-
five years of social misfortune of the *Bolshevik nation*.' (The author's
italics) He tried to make capital out of the Bolshevik threat: 'Behind
the attacking Bolshevik divisions we already see the Jewish extermination commandos'. Against the 'mechanised robots' only Germany
and her allies could afford Europe protection.

A Spartan way of life and total war effort was Goebbels's offer
to the Germans in the winter of 1943. The war potential not only of
Germany but of the whole of Europe would have to be mobilized;
the Germans did not mind doing the fighting, Goebbels implied,
while the rest of Europe worked for them. No one, especially women,
could go on thinking of their 'egoistic private needs': Goebbels
countered the suggestion that the practical measures for the conduct of total war would lead to the destruction of the German middle
class by saying that, after the war, it would be 'reconstituted, socially
and economically, in full measure'. 'We have to take off the kid
gloves and start bandaging our fists,' Goebbels stated, and referred
to the steps which had been taken in the new phase of the war. Bars,
nightclubs, luxury restaurants had been closed down: 'After the
war we shall gladly return to the principle live and let live; during
the war the principle obtains: fight and let fight.' In the last sentence
of his speech, Goebbels put forward the slogan of the moment:
'People, get up, and the storm breaks out!'

The storm broke and swept away Hitler's Germany. Military
success is the best propaganda in a war: in the last months of the
struggle for Europe the failure of the German arms was too apparent
to be obliterated by propaganda. Goebbels tried hard to divide the
allies by intensifying the anti-Bolshevik campaign, his old standby.
More and more often he referred to historical parallels and dedicated
his skills to promoting the careworn Hitler image.

On 17 April 1945 Goebbels talked to his colleagues about the
last of the Nazi historical films in colour, *Kolberg*, which illustrated
the resistance of the besieged fortress against the forces of Napoleon. On that occasion the tragic triteness of the showman down

on his luck was woven into his sentences: ' . . . in a hundred years' time they will be showing another fine colour film describing the terrible days we are living through. Don't you want to play a part in this film, to be brought back to life in a hundred years' time. Everybody now has the chance to choose the part which he will play in the film a hundred years hence. I can assure you that it will be a fine and elevating picture. And for the sake of this prospect it is worth standing fast. Hold out now, so that a hundred years hence the audience does not hoot and whistle when you appear on the screen.'[53]

VIII
Epilogue

The last conference of the Ministry of Propaganda took place on the morning of 21 April 1945. Twenty to thirty men, their faces haggard with lack of sleep, assembled in the film room of Goebbels's house in the Hermann Göring Strasse. It was dusty and dark there; the window-panes had long before been replaced by planks of wood; a few candles gave a sparse light. As always, Goebbels was slightly late; as always, he was dapper, elegantly dressed in a dark suit, his hair neatly plastered down to his skull. He began speaking before he sat down. He talked to the small, ghostly assembly as if he was addressing a monster-meeting at the Sportpalast: his theme was the treason committed by the old officers' clique against Hitler's Germany.[1] It is immaterial what was said at the conference. The means of communication had broken down in the beleaguered city; even if decisions had been taken, there existed no way of transmitting them to the few newspaper editors and broadcasters who were still carrying out their duties. Indeed, at the end of April 1945, the horizons of the Minister of Propaganda narrowed to the confines of the city of Berlin. Goebbels, who liked regarding himself as the man who won the capital of Germany from the Communists, was now defending it against the Red Army. There was an ironic continuity in his actions.

It was, however, too late in the day when Goebbels, and the skills he represented, began their return to favour. Total war and the fanatic defence of Hitler's Germany doubtless bore witness to the power Nazi propaganda exercised, in the concluding stages of the hostilities, on members of the Hitler Youth or on the aged veterans who were not fit to wage another war. The fact that these wretches were made to go on fighting for a worthless, lost cause, in which Hitler himself no longer believed, was the last achievement of Nazi propaganda. At this time, when the distance between reality and propaganda (the National Socialists had always been rather careless about that) widened into a gaping abyss, Goebbels, alone among the Nazi leaders, grimly carried on his duties. The process that Hitler had set into motion could not be reversed. The decline of the material and military power of Germany could not be arrested by propaganda, however skilful. The wish that propaganda should become again what it had been in the 'period of struggle' could have been inspired only by sentiment, or by a complete failure to grasp the changing place of propaganda in the Nazi scheme of things. In National Socialist theory, its place never changed: in fact it went through three distinct phases.

In the *Kampfzeit*—until 1933—its task was to create a situation in which Hitler could, by capturing the 'masses', make a bid for power in the state. He was not compelled to use the technique of conspiracy; Nazi agitation took place in full view of the public. The National Socialists ran a *Sammelpartei*, a party of national integration, which drew on the whole community—with the exception, of course, of the Jews—regardless of class, occupation, or sex. It was a nationalist much more than a socialist party, and its nationalism was of a particular kind. It was the vicious and intolerant kind that had begun to develop, at the turn of the century, alongside the ethnic frontiers between the Germans and Czechs in the Habsburg monarchy. To this tradition of nationalism Hitler was the proper heir: his supreme vice as a politician was that he thought in its terms, and that he wished it upon the rest of the German nation.

At first, however, the technical equipment at the disposal of the Nazis was slight: the totalitarian parties, the Bolsheviks and the National Socialists alike, achieved power mostly unaided by the means of mass communication available at the time. Regarded from this point of view, Hitler travelled light: he was an effective public speaker, but he had to rely, for many years, on the carrying power of his voice alone; throughout the nineteen-twenties, the party press could lay no claim to mass-circulation figures. In addition, the full flavour of Nazi propaganda translated badly into the terms of the printed word: much of its emotive quality was lost in the process. Public meetings, party rallies, and all the other activities generated by the party and its manifold offshoots, were regarded as more suitable vehicles for agitation than the press; physical violence was used with icy deliberation, as a propaganda asset.

Despite the effort they spent on propaganda, the Nazis did not create, unaided, the situation in which Hitler could grasp for power in the state. Their opportunity came with the slump in 1929. They had appealed to the discontented sections of the population, and they had cast the net of their organization over Germany: now they benefited hugely from the deepening economic crisis.

At this time, the National Socialist agitation proved especially aggressive: the physical struggle against the 'Marxists', accompanied by the generation of anti-Communist psychosis by Nazi propaganda, considerably sharpened political differences in the Weimar Republic. The National Socialist party proved more attractive to the unemployed than it had done to the employed workers; the anti-Communist drive appealed to the employers. At the time when there existed large numbers of potential recruits for the movement, its leaders were in a position to improve the methods of recruitment. They had their first taste of the new means of mass communication during Hitler's brief alliance with Hugenberg: nevertheless, after its break-up, the industrialists made it financially possible for the NSDAP to conduct propaganda on a massive scale. By the end of 1932, Hitler was running the largest political organization in Germany: it is impossible to think of such expansion of the movement without propaganda.

The anti-Communist campaign was carried on, and the Communists were outlawed and imprisoned after January 1933. Propaganda was still employed to secure maximum popular support for Hitler's régime, but, when it could be reinforced by other means of persuasion offered by the state, it lost some of its former value. It became one of the instruments for the maintenance of political power, rather than the most effective instrument for its achievement. Goebbels became the Minister of Popular Enlightenment and Propaganda; the heavy equipment—broadcasting, the film industry, mass-circulation press— passed under his control. The Minister ruthlessly exploited the opportunities offered him by the rise of his party to power. He interfered with the lives of the people to an extent unparalleled in history. The news and even the comments in their papers were centrally supplied; a dissenting opinion could never take the form of the legally printed word. The films they saw and the broadcasts they listened to, all carried an indelible Nazi stamp. The party took care of their leisure time, their travel, their social activities; it presented newly married couples with copies of *Mein Kampf.*

Against this onslaught, the Germans were on the whole defenceless. At the last parliamentary elections, not quite a half of the electorate voted for the National Socialists; soon after January 1933, the majority of the Germans disposed of neither the organization nor of the means for expressing anti-Nazi views. Goebbels's propaganda took great care to identify Germany with National Socialism, and National Socialism with Hitler: the campaign was highly successful, and it did untold harm to the nation. Although the Nazi propagandists often treated facts and political realities with disdain, they regarded it as their professional duty to keep in close touch with the mood, the shifts of public opinion, in Germany. The information on the various non-Nazi ways of looking at things, and on the reactions to the official propaganda drives passed, in the opposite direction, through the same channels—the propaganda departments in the party hierarchy—as the directives that were handed down to the last propaganda cell. The Nazis in fact conducted quite a precise 'audience research', and they were able to attack the remaining knots of resistance, or fill in the various propaganda gaps, as the situation required. The pre-war achievements of Hitler's régime at home and abroad, and their skilful exploitation by propaganda, doubtless gained Hitler new adherents. In the six years of peace, the cumulative impact of Nazi propaganda on the Germans was tremendous; it is of course difficult to judge how divided, or undivided, Hitler's Germany embarked on the war. Be that as it may, the impression of unity, of the degree of Germany's identification with National

Socialism, achieved by 1939, was indeed striking. Henceforth it would be difficult not to let the evil in National Socialism eclipse all that was good in Germany: it would be difficult for any judge of the National Socialist era, however detached, to regard the Germans and their system of government at the time as two quite distinct things.

After January 1933, new horizons opened before the Nazi propagandists. Their activities abroad suffered, however, from severe limitations. National Socialist ideology basically lacked international appeal; the leadership of the movement was also singularly short of men who possessed international vision or connexions. Goebbels thought of propaganda abroad as a mere extension of propaganda at home: this meant that the contents and the eccentricities of Nazi agitation in Germany were translated, indiscriminately, on to the international plane. The antisemitic charge in National Socialist propaganda abroad remained as high as that contained in the propaganda output intended for home consumption. At the same time, anti-Communism remained closely linked with antisemitism: whereas anti-Communism may have proved attractive to large sections of Europeans, antisemitism did not always find a receptive audience abroad. The antisemitic content of Nazi propaganda some times repelled rather than attracted potential sympathizers.

Although they were short of men with knowledge of the foreign scene, the National Socialist leaders, like the Bolsheviks, distrusted the diplomats: their relations with the outside world could not somehow be contained in traditional diplomatic channels. The clash between propaganda and diplomacy was reflected in the perennial conflicts between the *Promi* and the Foreign Ministry, which did not cease even after a party member—Ribbentrop—took over the direction of Germany's foreign policy. Propaganda and the most intimate relations between the two party organizations replaced diplomacy in the relations of Hitler's Germany with Austria, until the summer of 1934; propaganda also played an important role in the relations with the Soviet Union until the spring of 1939. And then, of course, propaganda had to make Hitler's Germany acceptable to the outside world, and especially to the Great Powers (here the *Promi* was helped by the fact that the large majority of German diplomates remained at their posts after January 1933), and it had to prepare the way for Germany's conquests before the outbreak of the war.

The unsuccessful *putsch* in Vienna in July 1934 taught the Nazi leaders that they could no longer behave irresponsibly: that they could not promise more than they could deliver, and that aggressive propaganda should, in the last instance, be backed up by the full might of the state. During the Saarland campaign, Goebbels exprimented, very successfully, with broadcasting. It created a 'bridge'—a feeling of community—that ignored both the frontier as it existed at the time, as well as the former political complexion in the Saarland. in the second Austrian campaign, and then in the drive against Czechoslovakia, Nazi propaganda achieved the peak of its efficiency. It was fully integrated in Germany's diplomatic and military manoeuvres, it helped Hitler to achieve his objectives without any wastage of troops or ammunition. Indeed, the intensive generation of a 'Saarland' or an 'Austrian', or a 'Sudetenland' atmosphere, and its effect abroad, may be described as the most notable achievements of the Ministry of Propaganda. Although the popular enthusiasm that accompanied these campaigns was in fact artificially contrived, German nationalism, seen from abroad, appeared as a spontaneous force. To this view of German nationalism Hitler owed most of his pre-war successes in the field of foreign policy.

They were confined to central Europe. Here, the National Socialists were prepared to use their connexions with the Nazi parties run by their compatriots. Their propaganda of course remained intensely nationalistic when it was aimed at the *volksdeutsche*. This predominantly German orientation of Nazi propaganda was its strength as well as its weakness. It was highly suitable for the subversion of the political order in central Europe established by the peace treaties. It lacked, however, a wider appeal: it could contribute nothing to Hitler's drive for 'acceptance', first for his regime and then for its expansion, by the Great Powers. Indeed, the Nationalist Socialist movement was lifted out of its exclusive parochialism only by the virtue of the 'international threats'—the Jewish and Bolshevik 'conspiracies'—it claimed to combat.

So long as Hitler's objectives remained limited to central Europe or, more precisely, to its German part, Nazi propaganda alone was sufficient to shatter the established order. But after the achievement of its most impressive victories, a certain exhaustion, a certain thinness, appeared in Nazi propaganda. In the summer of 1939, it was pursuing too many objectives: from having been ruthlessly concentrated, it was becoming diffuse.

And the publicity drive on behalf of the army marked the beginning of its decline. The army and military problems were fast becoming Hitler's main interests: there was room for nothing else in his mind. Although he had no intention of breaking up the apparatus Goebbels had carefully built up, civilian-conducted propaganda had to take a subordinate place. The *Promi* gave up some of its functions to the *Abteilung Wehrmachtpropaganda* in the *OKW*; central direction of the press was disrupted; the main function of Goebbels's Ministry was the dissemination of the material which was fed to it. Some of the secondary propaganda themes it initiated had to be either played down or abandoned. As far as occupied Europe was concerned, Nazi propaganda no longer operated in a vacuum, by remote control. The peoples of these countries came into contact with the realities of the German occupation, and their attitudes were affected by the direct contact rather than by the mellifluous outpourings of the propagandists.

Whereas Goebbels had succeeded in establishing some foothold for his Ministry in western Europe, he was unable to do so, until the end of 1943, in the occupied territories in the Soviet Union. Here, the propaganda of the National Socialist struggle against communism was exposed as an empty sham. The Nazis were less able to establish a *modus vivendi* with the local population in the east than in western Europe. They came as superior conquerors, and they intended to exploit every advantage the situation offered.

Finally, the war broke the Nazi monopoly of information in the Reich itself: the process coincided with the reversal in Germany's military fortunes. It wasn't long before the defenders of the besieged fortress found the feeling of claustrophobia, heightened by the centralized system of information, unendurable. Through foreign broadcasts, they were able to re-establish contacts with the outside world. The last phase of Nazi propaganda, exhorting the Germans to a fanatic resistance, intensified the chaos that accompanied defeat.

APPENDIX **A**

Lenin or Hitler?

A speech made by Joseph Goebbels in Zwickau, in 1926.

My dear German compatriots,

The poet Peter Rosegger once described the average German as sitting asleep in his armchair beside the stove, his tasselled cap pulled down over his ears. His enemies stand around laughing at him; they jeer and spit and grab everything in his possession. From time to time a good friend comes along and tries to rouse our German and draw his attention to the disgraceful behaviour of his enemies. And when Hans is then only half-awake he rubs his eyes and rises to his feet grumbling angrily and thrashes the very person who has wakened him.

We Germans are the most unfortunate people on God's earth. A nation of 60 million, surrounded on all sides by enemies within the country and outside its borders, bleeding from a thousand wounds, the hardest-working people in the world — sees its political duty in tearing itself to pieces. A people which would have every reason to close its ranks and, united, defend itself against its enemies, splits itself up into dozens of parties organisations and trade unions, and inspite of ardent endeavours cannot find the way to its own identity and to the recognition of its mission in world history. When one feels bound to this people in one's warmly beating patriotic heart and is forced to follow open-eyed the way of error to Calvary in the shaping of our national Will, one might well at times utterly despair for the future of Germany. One can then no longer believe that this people will ever find the path laid down inflexibly towards its own freedom.

And yet an unshakable faith rouses in us again and again one last hope. Then, seriously and objectively one tries to understand the dividing forces of the age and the nation, and one suddenly realises with a lightning flash that we are definitely not as unfortunate, lost, and at odds as perhaps it might outwardly appear. Perhaps we still recognise dozens of parties and organisations in the public life of this people but all at once we realise that nothing fundamentally separates the majority of these parties and organisations; they can be traced back to simpler basic forms and only seemingly, for quite definite reasons— namely the very reasons for their own existence— do they feign deep-seated differences. If we follow their train of thought more closely the whole picture of Germany's domestic politics is simplified at one stroke, and we recognise absolutely that in fact only three great movements shape contemporary German politics, three movements which of course differ fundamentally from each other since they are forms of expression of quite distinct types of political philosophy.

In the middle of all political parties and organisations we see the great 'status quo' bloc, the bloc of reaction, the bloc of the middle-classes, that conservative bloc, rooted in the system which conceives its duty to be the retention of the present-day state system by more or less skilful means, but at any price. That bloc which stretches from the Social Democrats up to and including the German Nationalists: that bloc which wishes the state to remain as it is to-day! To be sure, the other party within this bloc expresses its readiness for reforms, whether in the social or national sphere. The one party will press its claims with fanatical zeal, the other in more modest and discreet fashion, according to the outlook of its voters, but in fact they will all agree upon the preservation and protection of the system: Democracy, Liberalism, Capitalism— things which for them are sacred and inviolate.

At the sides of this *status quo* bloc of the centre are ranged revolutionary movements which have clearly recognised one basic thing, namely, that if we want the state of the future then it is not a matter of reform but of consistent revolution. The system of liberal-capitalist democracy is already internally so rotten and decayed that it cannot be patched and reformed any longer. It must be completely destroyed, mentally and politically shattered so that a new, young generation can build upon the ruins of the old. They have recognised the essence of a consistent opposition in the need for directing the spearhead of revolution not only against the perpetrators of the system under attack but also against the system itself. We are concerned in this revolutionary idea with the two intellectual movements which have found political expression in the Communist Party and in the National Socialist Workers' Party of Germany.

When I speak of Lenin or Hitler I don't mean these two men in their purely incidental human form or no longer incidental political form. It is a matter of more than this: we are concerned with these two men insofar as they represent the embodiment, the personification of an idea which, if I may say so, deeply affects us all. Let us rather consider these two men as conquerors of an old concept of the state and pioneers of a new one. That is our present task.

Politicians, men who make history, do not arise by accident. Man and the age are inextricably bound up. The age shapes the man and man gives the age its ultimate meaning and significance. This above all is true of the politician. He cannot be understood outside his own age. He arises from his age, is the child of his age, of his people, of his history. He represents in their clearest form the age, the people and its history.

Lenin and Hitler are children of the system, they became conquerors of the system. If we wish to understand them as they really are then we must investigate the obscure forces of their age, must learn to recognise what gave them birth in order to begin to understand whither they lead. Not only do they exist, they must exist. Everything in history, including the politician, has its historical cause, and only from the causes shall we find the path to the facts.

Which system must be overcome in Lenin or Hitler?

Let us begin with Germany.

If to-day we must painfully endure the humiliation of the present for the sake of the future, then we must seek causes and reasons as to why everything had to be as it is. Is the war, is 9 November 1918 or even the infamous system of Kaiser Wilhelm's age guilty of our latest collapse? No! a thousand times no! The causes lie much deeper, decades, almost a whole century back. I want to try to sketch them very briefly. With the growing industrialisation of Germany around the middle of last century German materialism grew up in the country and among the people of poets and thinkers. At that time enormous industrial ventures sprang up almost overnight upon our German soil, around which the new urban proletariat gathered in millions. These millions were urged along the fateful path of estrangement from state and nation. The ruling class of the people did not understand how to integrate them into the nation, to link them in joy and suffering to the soul of the nation. The larger these masses became the further they became dissociated from the compact unity of the state. They were forced towards the Left. And here the systematic saboteur of every genuine worker's movement, the Marxist Jew, was to lead the yearning masses along false paths—an all too easy game. The bourgeois-nationalist intelligentsia are tragically to blame for not having recognised this development, for having let events run their own course, instead of placing themselves at the head of the workers, fighting for their existence, and fighting with them for their rights, for the sake of the workers, and thereby the nation. The bourgeoisie observed this development and stubbornly rejected it; they did not even attempt to link the lowest class to the nation through sacrifice. Promptly and eagerly our Jew was able to steal a march on the socially reactionary bourgeoisie. From the very beginning he cleverly saw commercial and political opportunities for the future in the lowest class, always intending to exploit them for himself. He set himself at the head of the proletariat. He who had never worked presented himself to the worker as his leader, and the worker gladly and willingly accepted the only out-stretched hand.

The bourgeoisie watches this development smiling. It does not have the slightest idea that here events are being set in motion which gravely threaten its own existence. It turns its back on its social obligations from pride, arrogance and a lack of a spirit of national sacrifice; it subordinates its sense of responsibility to base mercantile instincts, goes to war for the sake of the nation when commanded yet studiously evades the unspoken dictates of its social future. Socialism and Nationalism are absolutely irreconcilable. The more rigidly Nationalist, the more brutally opposed to Socialist ideals. This people waged a hero's war in 1870-71 and through fighting won its political existence and greatness. It struggled for the ultimate concept of nationhood and failed to find it. What then followed constitutes the most horrifying lesson of German history. A people satiated. A people which had everything it could desire, power, riches, possessions. But this people was sick, it seemed, incurably sick. The seeds of death lay in its heart. It was inwardly decaying. It was no longer a strong organism, nor a united body-politic. It was bleeding to death from the great wound of social distress. Now and again the doctor diligently visited the sickbed of this people, saw the gaping wound, shuddered, shook his head and turned away in disgust. Perhaps too, out of pity, fear and shame he stuck the dressing of social welfare over the wound. At least it could no longer be seen.

But this wound grew and festered beneath the plaster, it gnawed into the very vitals of the body and was ready to destroy the whole organism.

'Germany is satisfied! Germany has no more political requirements! Germany wishes to conquer the world by peaceful competition!' Thus ran the latest political aphorism of a liberal bourgeoisie, corrupted by mercenary aims and the desire for profit.

But this sick people did pull itself together once again in August 1914,

donned its steel helmet and performed world-shaking deeds before which the
age and eternity held their breath. For four years this people stood unflinching
under a hail of bullets, only to collapse in the end as wretchedly as any other
people in history.

Terrible enigma! Just as terrible but no longer so mysterious when we
investigate the underlying causes.

Neither the system nor 9 November 1918 is solely to blame for the collapse.
They act together in tragic union. The word 'November-criminal' (*November-
verbrecher*) was like a curse to us. For long, fatally deluded, we saw them
solely as those who participated in that tragicomedy of 9 November. Today
we see further and deeper. The guilt remains the same in those miserable
wretches who promised freedom, peace, and bread and destroyed all hopes.
But equally undiminished is the extent to which atonement is demanded from
history by the guilt of those in the so-called Nationalist camp who, selfishly
deluding themselves, had created the historical foundations for 9 November
by excluding the masses from the community.

9 November represented treachery on both sides. The ruling class failed
from a Nationalist point of view. It cowered in mouse-holes and let the storm
rage past overhead. Marxism failed from a Socialist point of view. Willingly
it let itself be taken in tow by international Jewish-Capitalist interests. That
was not a revolution! That was mutiny; that was a miserable, wretched,
cowardly, mercenary revolt!

The revolt was already beginning during the war. While Germany's
heroic youth was sacrificing its thrice-sacred life for the nation in the
bloody battles of the First World War, Marxist traitors to the people journeyed through the land and preached negotiation. Preached negotiation
although they knew that the enemy's brutal flush of victory desired destruction and only destruction. The nation was crumbling for the sake of the Party.
Through the 9 November 1918 Marxist traitors were ready to help bless and
crown the social crime committed against the German people for decades
past. In their news-sheets, at a time when Germany was fighting for its
existence, this heroic people, before whose deeds the age held its breath,
was reviled, slandered, spat upon, and abused. Jewish helpers and accom-
plices aided Marxism to suck the people's marrow from its bones by means of
coarseness in art, the press and the theatre.

On account of the Party and only the Party! [i.e. the Socl. Democrat Pty.]
Thus morality, propriety, and strength were thrown to the winds. Yet one
never heard that a wave of indignation went through this nation when
Vorwärts—the so-called worker's newspaper, the most disgraceful word
in German history which has ever been uttered unchastised—wrote that it

was the sacred will of Social Democracy that the German people should strike their colours for ever, without having brought them home to final victory.

Can there be a greater act of hypocricy? Social Democracy permitted during the war—it had the means to oppose it without a general strike and without committing high treason—capitalist exploitation to descend on this people, of a kind as yet unknown to history. Why? Because it was to the advantage of the Party, because it was a means to an end in the hands of those who wanted to make use of it as a weapon against people and nation. One flatters it to describe it as intriguer, saboteur, enzyme of decomposition. For that it appears too small, too loud, too clumsy, and too domineering. Behind we see the whole pack of born destroyers, hyenas in the battlefield of German work, hungry for power and spoil.

Social Democracy was put at the head of the State by the trust of German proletarians, and then smugly and stupidly disguised this form of destruction, allowed the terrible act of murder to be committed unopposed against a whole people—for the sake of the Party.

Thus came, thus had to come 9 November 1918. Never has there been a more ridiculous, cowardly, and thoughtless revolt in the history of the world. Over and above all distress, all misery, all national and social humiliation, it has presented us with infinite disgrace in the face of history. That was not a revolution. That was theatre, lying, treachery, and baseness, a revolt of meanness and the pettiest Party urge.

Mr. Scheidemann stood on the stage of Parliament and offered the people peace, freedom and bread while far away in the west the evening cannon still thundered out the most brutal lust for destruction over his shallow phrases. He brought us freedom: for his Party, for the treachery of 9 November. He brought us peace: the Peace of Locarno with the very Capitalism which had been so sanctimoniously and zealously attacked. He brought us bread: the bread of slavery which we eat with tears.

He, yes indeed, he and his Party have won right along the line. But the German people has lost, has lost completely right along the line.

Let me ask one single question: What has 9 November brought to the German worker in purely material things, quite apart from imaginary values? Where are the gains of this base revolt? I hear the shout, 'Eight-hour day'. The shout rises of itself. You will soon see the time, my friend, when you won't need to work for 8 hours or even 6 hours, when you won't find even one hour of work in Dawes-Germany. At that time nonsense was talked about nationalisation. Certainly, some things have been nationalised: the posts of district magistrate, parliamentary President and Lord Mayor for Social Democratic Party bigwigs. At that time housing estates were mentioned. Certainly, some people have settled down: Mr. Scheidemann has established himself in a rich sinecure in Kassel, Mr. Leinert in Hanover. Mr. Severing in Prussia.

If the Marxist big shots meant this sort of nationalisation and housing estate, then they have gained their point, by God, they have carried out their programme in its clearest sense. Let us put ourselves, however difficult that may be, in the place of the leaders of the Social Democrats. They asserted that Capitalism must be destroyed, they saw Capitalism embodied in the system of 1914, they believed it their duty to overthrow this system to clear the way for Socialism. That would have been the historical significance of 9 November 1918. However, they know as well as anyone that Germany was surrounded by Capitalist enemies who had to hate a Socialist State like the plague, even one built on so modest a scale. For the protection of this State, for the protection of Socialism they needed forceful means—weapons, will, fanaticism. To enforce these means must also be for them as Socialists, as leaders of the workers, a requirement of the hour. 9 November 1918 might have gained historical significance if the Marxist leaders as its apostles had summoned the people to fight for the rights of the Socialist State. Instead of this they destroyed weapons, will and fanaticism; they systematically destroyed every activity of resistance and every instinct to resist. Why? Because they did not want revolution in this strife, because they did not even want Socialism, were not allowed to want it. Because of necessity, will and fanaticism would have been directed against those who counterfeited Socialism after 9 November, who only saw in it an easy way to the complete domination of Capitalism, who, as Marxist leaders of a foreign race, became the actual gravediggers of Socialism.

Thus 9 November had to become a revolt, a ridiculous, disgraceful revolt of swindlers on the stock exchange, and the Marxist leaders were stupid and simple enough for the gentlemen from the investment trusts to support this cunning swindler's trick with the necessary theatrical thunder of speeches and funeral oration.

Then the frightful and ridiculous happened. Window panes were smashed and storehouses burnt down. All in the name of the revolution. A Jew greeted the troops returning to Berlin, with stale phrases about freedom, beauty, and dignity. All in the name of the revolution. The way was prepared for an exploitation without precedent or parallel. All in the name of the revolution. Mr. Scheidemann spoke at the same time, starry-eyed, of incipient Socialism, sent paper protests across the Rhine and acknowledged with bows the

derision of the enemy for whom, by 9 November, he had forged the shar-
pest weapon for the fight against the German people. His hand did not
wither—and nevertheless Versailles was signed, was signed because he had
prepared the way through 9 November.

How infinitely brutal did the consequences of this treachery become,
especially for those for whom the "people's delegates" pretended to have
brought about the 9 November, for the German employees themselves. Let
us not beat about the bush! How empty and meaningless is the phrase: The
concept of Socialism is not feasible in a disrupted economy. How often did
Scheidemann and Ebert tell us the plausible yarn that nationalisation would
improve the economy and make the State more productive in every way.

Why then did they not carry out this nationalisation when they had the
power to do so; when every means had to be tried to secure the people's
existence?

Because they did not want Socialism—were not allowed to want it.

That is the crime which Marxism committed against the nation, the crime
of Marxism against the German workers. Treachery to the national principle,
treachery to the principle of Socialism. That is the significance of 9 November, that Marxism left both to the incessant plundering of its masters and
overlords, Capital and the hyenas.

Then everything happened as it had to happen, in ghastly, logical
sequence. A chain of national humiliations was fastened around the
neck of the German people and every national humiliation caused with
terrible consistency its new social distress. An enslaved people has no
right to, no time for, Socialism. It must work for its taskmasters.

We in Germany have descended to the lowest level of serfdom. We
starve and hunger under foreign oppressors, pay in full measure and
have no possibility for setting free the German spirit of the future on
its appointed path.

'First bread, then reparations', cried a recent German armchair-
politician, a dreary, retired mathematics teacher, now in the timber and
politics business, who travels through Germany under the historical title
of *Altreichskanzler*, dumping his political sophistry in front of torch-
bearing youth associations.

'First reparations, and still no bread!' We have felt, and will feel more
and more in the future how true is this distortion.

9 November 1918 is a stage. It is a black day at the beginning of
modern German history, from it everything which has come and is
still to come, results with brutal inflexible inevitability.

We signed Versailles—and no hand withered.

We let ourselves be humiliated in conference after conference as one would never dare humiliate a Negro people—and no one came and shouted 'No!'—not once.

The Ruhr district was occupied—and the German people concealed its middle-class cowardice behind passive resistance.

The Ruhr district was lost—and Mr. Gustav Stresemann kindled a spark of hope on the horizon.

The Dawes Plan was signed—His Excellency Mr. Herzt said he had almost no alternative.

Gustav Stresemann's spark of hope shone like a meteor. The Ruhr district was evacuated. High finance wanted it thus. France had played out its rôle of bailiff. The creditor paid voluntarily. Grinding their teeth, chauvinistic French generals had to abandon their beloved fat living. They were envied in Wall Street and the City.

The Moor has done his duty—the Moor can go.

Gustav Stresemann unswervingly pursued national *Realpolitik*. His fat hand signed everything that grinning enemies placed in front of him.

A new Bible was given to the people: the Dawes Treaty, the Bible of economy.

Then came Locarno—and Gustav Stresemann travelled to London filled with a sense of high purpose and leaving behind him doubtful rumours of attempted assassination—and signed.

A terrible line from Versailles to Locarno. How did it happen, why did it have to come about?

When Dawes threatened Germany warning voices were raised. But this people was assured that Dawes was the ultimate way of salvation. The great political questions were removed from the sphere of power politics and laid in the hands of the bankers.

And now the mysterious forces in world politics play one card after another. One has to have watched this game to gain insight into its terrible operation.

Public opinion dictates: The people's voice is God's voice. Public opinion is sacred to the people. What is public opinion in reality? A result of Capitalism. Money is public opinion. Money uses press and propaganda for its own ends. Public opinion created by Capitalism categorically demanded a signature to the Dawes Plan. One had played Münchhausen to this public opinion: it was taken in by the words; economic peace, reconciliation, compensation; tales were told of rivers of gold flowing towards Germany in a continuous stream—and public opinion signed through Gustav Stresemann.

For a mess of potage Germany sold all its sovereign rights, its financial sovereignty, its economic sovereignty, its transport sovereignty. We emasculated ourselves. After 29 August 1924 we no longer had the right to call ourselves a civilised people. Germany is only a colony of world-finance.

Thus the Dawes Plan brought us economic peace.

Political successes are infectious. Gustav Stresemann did not rest till he had added political peace.

He gave it to us through Locarno.

What happened.

One morning the sovereign people awoke and learnt through the process of public opinion that Gustav Stresemann wanted peace. Certainly he had already prophesied this peace after accepting the Dawes Plan, but now peace was to be made at last. And in fact, it was to be accomplished by having Germany give its former enemies securities. Can one think of a greater piece of political nonsense: Germany, disarmed down to the last toy pistol, to give its enemies, who are camped on its borders, armed to the teeth, securities. For what other purpose are these securities than for the unrestricted exploitation of German hard work?

And now the play began behind the scenes. A legal expert travelled to London. 'Informal discussions,' said Mr. Stresemann. In reality everything was a foregone conclusion. Then hasty preparations for Locarno turned up, over the head of the sovereign people.

We are the freest people in the world, because we obey absolutely the commands of high finance.

And now the leaders went to Locarno. Mr. Stresemann smiled once more into the cameras of the *Berliner Illustrierte* and then he went to make world history. The financial press plays skilfully on the instrument of the popular soul. It gives the German philistine the fodder he craves. To one man it speaks of everlasting peace: one part of popular opinion is ready. To another it speaks of the collapse and reconstruction of the economy: the second part of public opinion is ready. It reminds the worker of the spectre of being out of a job: the third part is ready.

There still remains the tough, viscous mass of the tea-party literati and coffee-house politicians, the last remnants of once-proud nation of poets and thinkers. The soft, the melancholy, the sentimental. The gossips, male and female. For them too, the Jewish press-bandit has a toothsome morsel. They are fed upon stories about the men, the heroes who practice politics in Europe today. These figures are presented to them in human and personal form. That has a pleasant and trust-inspiring effect.

We read that Mrs. Chamberlain was wearing a green silk dress. That causes a stir at the coffee-parties. We read that one day Luther and Briand went for a walk together to muse upon the profoundest matters in field and wood, at the breast of nature so to speak. That is moving. One really sees these men, these heroes, going on a pilgrimage through the dust of a country road and talking with fervent gravity of the peace of Europe. They entered a simple tavern, unknown, unrecognised; no one suspected that these simple, dusty wanderers held the fate of Europe in their hands.

A Jewish "shmok" interviewed the innkeeper's wife the other day and a few hours later deposited the whole lot in the German advertising and daily press before the beast of the German public. Innkeeper's wife's voice is the people's voice, is God's voice.

Enthusiastically this simple child of nature described her two guests. The man with a lot of hair had stroked the kitten, and the bald man, not to be outdone, had also stroked the kitten. The man with a lot of hair had ordered wine, and the bald man had ordered grapes. And then they had sat together for quite a while.

And finally a teasing quarrel broke out about who was to pay the bill. The man without much hair did not want to allow the man with a lot of hair to have the privilege, until finally the man with a lot of hair found the solution and said. 'I'll pay here, and you foot the bill in Locarno.'

When the security treaties were signed in Locarno gun salutes echoed from every hill, people embraced weeping in the street. Total strangers shook hands with one another saying, 'Peace on earth and goodwill towards men'.

At the statesmen's farewell dinner place cards were set out on which hovering angels of peace bore up the heads of Chamberlain, Briand, and Stresemann.

All that was told the German people, was allowed to be told it when its political death sentence was being signed. That was given to them as a substitute for political truth. Thus was fed the public appetite which demanded food. The last section of public opinion was ready: the soft, the melancholy, the sentimental, the gossips, male and female, were all for peace. And thus Locarno was signed. The tall house with the low reputation allowed the parties to give the necessary speeches out of the window—and accepted. Gustav Stresemann took leave of his weeping wife who on account of court mourning in London could not show off her new dress, journeyed with his retinue to London and signed the German death sentence to the accompaniment of music and flowery speeches.

The modern German Bismarck had given Germany economic peace. Now he gave it political peace. The film reached its end.

And what does Locarno signify?—not peace, but war!

Mr. Stresemann is not the father but the foster-father and lawyer of

Locarno—the security treaties originate in England and not in Berlin. World
Capitalism needs market outlets and loan possibilities in Russia and in the
Far East. England hates the Soviets as the perpetuators of the old Panslav
policy of Tsarism. To obtain credits France placed at its disposal its mercen-
aries of high finance. In the gigantic struggle which opened up between
World Capitalism and the producing countries in the East, England has no
use for an unsettled Europe. She desires peace for her policy in Asia. The
Western Democracies arm themselves for the general campaign against
Soviet Russia, and behind everything is the Jew, in Western Capitalism as
well as hidden in Russian Bolshevism, in order to stir things up between
Russia and Germany and have them seize each other more firmly and bleed
to death in one last warlike struggle. Then Jewish capital will have gained all,
then is the whole of Europe pacified and ready for international exploitation.
Mr. Stresemann is the means of securing this final aim. He must manoeuvre
Germany into the League of Nations in order to clear the way for the trans-
portation and concentration of Western Capitalist troops. As in the Thirty
Years War and the Seven Years War Germany is to form the ideal arena for
strife in Europe.

A new World War gathers like a threatening thunderstorm on the political
horizon. The Peace of Locarno is but the preparation of high finance for the
next war. The German worker is told today of everlasting peace. He will be
forced to go without bread and work in order to be the more readily degraded
by Jewish financiers to become the servant of high finance for its world-
Capitalist aims.

Already one can hear in the national camp the first siren-songs of the holy
Crusade against Bolshevism. Already the bourgeoisie is drumming up the
nation's youth for its own selfish reasons, for the fight against Russia. To be
sure the German Nationalists were still disposed against Locarno, but with
strong inner reservations. And anyway, it is nonsense to accept the Dawes
Plan and reject Locarno. For they are both one and the same thing. What the
Dawes Plan was in the sphere of economic politics, so is Locarno in the
field of power politics: voluntary surrender of all German sovereign rights
to world finance.

The next great world struggle is at hand. And in this world struggle
German youth from lecture-hall and factory will render yeoman's service
for their bitterest enemy, in the name of freedom, in the name of civilisation,
in the name of the rights of man.

That is the political development of Europe in the past and the future.
That is the system of equality and fraternity in which we live. The system
whose downfall we envisage and desire. All who have collaborated in this

system have become accessories to the crime, from the Social Democrats to the German Nationalists. None of these parties will be able to give Germany freedom. They will all be dragged together into the imminent collapse of the system. There will be no final argument between them and us about the state of the future, but rather between those who are in ultimate, bitterest, and most consistent opposition to this State, between Communism and National Socialism. This struggle develops in logical, historical sequence, it is being fought out on German soil and it will decide the ultimate fate of Germany.

The recognition of this imminent development compels responsibility. We have a duty to come to an understanding, earnestly, objectively, without demagogy, and without thought for the moment. We must come to one another, you of the Left and ourselves. For fundamentally we both probably want the same thing: our aim is freedom. We are only concerned with the difficult question of how to achieve this freedom and what form it will take. We cannot both be right. We have two basically different political ideologies: one is right and the other wrong. Against Capitalism we are both ever and always right.

From the system of collapse the will for freedom springs up. It finds its shape in basically new ideas: in Bolshevism and National Socialism. Both appear with the ultimate faith that freedom can be attained in the downfall of a whole world. Bolshevism and National Socialism take shape in two people who press on ahead of a resolute minority in the will for the future—in Lenin and Hitler.

We are concerned with each of them as supporters of an idea.

Man and idea are now under discussion.

Lenin—Ulyanov, the son of an impoverished petty Russian nobleman was brought up in the misery and social distress of a Russian intelligentsia already deep under the influence of the proletariat. He learnt to understand the meaning of hunger from his own body. Not in books, but in his own hard, cruel life did he study social distress, his own and that of his fellows. He became a revolutionary early and soon also a Marxist revolutionary. He studied at Russian Universities, in direst need he battled through; he gained insight into the social, economic, and political situation of his country and people, and was appalled at the terrible future which threatened the Tsar's enormous domain.

While a student he came to know hunger as a daily guest. He was a member of the young Russian intelligentsia, already completely proletarianised, which was utterly opposed to the Tsar's State. He lived in a country in which social distress cried out to heaven. Only think of this: in Russia before the war one could sail down the Volga for a week, passing all the time the enormous estate of the same owner, and on the fringes of this little kingdom were the cramped, foul cottages in which the Russian peasant lived, still half enslaved.

The Russian peasant, the unspoiled child of nature. Young, full-grown, bound to the earth, uncontaminated by Western civilisation, filled with faith, piety, fanaticism, and mysticism. Unawakened and uncultured. The smell of the soil clung to him. He carried his bondage like a destiny, like a fate. Quiet and devoted with an extraordinary capacity for bearing pain and suffering.

The Russian is still bound up with his destiny. He endures the distress of his age, half willingly, half reluctantly, with a dim, unclarified yearning for *possessions* and *freedom*. This people lacks the password to freedom, not only *the* password but any password. It will welcome and greedily absorb everything, devote itself passionately to whatever promises its freedom. Whoever guides it one day out of its distress will become its Saviour, its Apostle, its God.

Once this people tried to storm the Kremlin and the Tsar ordered volleys to be fired into the tightly packed crowd. It stood like a wall and would not yield. It had to be so. "They all ponder now in the streets and marketplaces about their faith," it says somewhere in Dostoievsky, the greatest Russian thinker.

Amongst this people Lenin became great. To this people he wanted to point out a way. To this people he was to become All.

He endured expulsion and persecution for belief in his idea. He bided his time. The war came. Russia sacrificed hecatombs of human lives for a West European phantom. Lenin waited. Kerensky came. Kerensky was swept away. He wanted Lenin to join in. He offered him posts, offices, money. Lenin said 'No'. He wanted to be the absolute ruler. His way could tolerate no compromise.

In 1917 his hour arrived. The Bolshevik revolution raised him to the head of the state, of a Russia destroyed after a bloody war—and he began the work of the Revolution.

I am concentrating here on the basic facts. Lenin went straight to the solution of the most burning question: the social question. He revolutionised the economy.

We differentiate in Russia between agrarian and industrial reform. The two progress at different stages and both must be regarded separately. The social problem in Russia lies in the agrarian problem. The industrial question, with which we are most concerned in Germany as an industrial country, only plays a subordinate rôle in Russia.

How did Lenin get to the heart of the agrarian problem? He expropriated all land and gave it into the possession of the Russian peasant. Not directly. He leased him the land for 99 years. But the Russian peasant today sees his land as his own property. With that Lenin slapped Marxist teaching right in the face. That demanded nationalisation of means of production. Lenin sacrificed Marx and gave way to the urge of the Russian peasant to own his soil.

Under the pressure of 90 million peasants Lenin in his agrarian reform had to show the impracticability of Marxism. Lenin fulfilled what the Russian peasant had always thought of as Bolshevism; he gave them land. In doing so Lenin made the most stable class, the peasant class, the real supporters of the new régime. The peasant, who received freedom and property from the new state, was henceforth ready to place himself on guard in front of this new State, *his* State to which he is closely tied through his own soil. And— loathed as is the Jew, especially the Soviet Jew, by the Russian peasant, so he is just as passionate a partisan of the agrarian reform, and equally ardently does he love his land and soil.

Is the fact that the Russian peasant turned against the Whites still a mysterious riddle? When the Whites advanced they were received by the peasants at first with jubilation. Yet the Bolshevik régime had also claimed countless victims among the Russian peasants.

But after the Whites followed the emigrés, the landowners who had mean-while been lounging about in Paris, Berlin, and London. Their watchword was 'Down with the Soviets! Down with agrarian reform!' Then the Russian peasant naturally turned against the Whites, 'Down with the Soviet Jews; long live Lenin's agrarian reform!' With that came the collapse of the anti-Bolshevik rising.

When a century ago Prussia lay in chains on the ground Baron von Stein coined the sentence 'In order to ennoble a nation one must give to the part of it deprived of rights political independence, freedom, and property.' He acted accordingly, carried out the liberation of the peasants. Prussia awoke and became free.

In practice Lenin rejected the theories of Marx; he followed the example of Baron von Stein, indeed, in agrarian reform he expressly referred to him.

Lenin's agrarian reform, therefore, signified for the Russian peasant a partial solution to the social problem.

But how is it with Lenin's industrial reform? For us Germans this question is much more important than the question of agrarian reform. In the last fifty years we have become an industrial people, the economy is, for our state of today, the decisive factor. Today the state of the economy deeply affects the life of the nation, and thereby the life of the individual.

Hence Lenin's industrial reform is the touchstone for us of the value or worthlessness of Lenin's system, Communism in Germany.

Certainly Lenin nationalised Russian industry. Nevertheless it drifted towards collapse. What was the cause?

Industrial reform took place in Russia on the lines that Karl Marx prescribed. A genuine effort was made to fuse industry and state. It failed. The Russian worker eliminated his Russian extortioners—only to leave the field open to the Jew. The Jew is master of Russia today, Jewish capital is the ruler, the Russian is slave to the dictatorship of the stock exchange.

When everything was so far nationalised in Russia that the economy tottered on the brink of disaster, a foreign country, America, had to step in with credits. Wall Street became the Saviour in distress. That was the result of implementing the teaching of Karl Marx! 'We must make concessions', said Zinoviev-Apfelbaum to his followers when, in dire distress, he desperately sought salvation from abroad.

It is interesting that these concessions were made to those very people whom we accuse of having financed the Russian revolution. Expressly in Lenin's industrial reform it is shown that Bolshevism was virtually nothing more than a pawn in the hands of Capital. It was only a stage towards the absolute dictatorship of the stock exchange.

Let it be clearly stated: capital and Capitalism are two different things. The struggle is concerned with Capitalism, not capital. The fact that there are factories and mines does not explain our plight; it is the way in which they are administrated and exploited against the common weal.

Capitalism is the immoral distribution of capital.

Marxism is also Jewish in this respect; it attacks capital in order to turn it virtually into Capitalism. Its theory is demagogic. Its practice is destructive.

It is certain that Russian industrial reform kept exactly to the teaching of Karl Marx; the basis of Bolshevism is Marxism. It has suffered shameful failure in Russia. It is therefore necessary first of all to examine the theory of Marxism. The basis of this discussion is naturally formed by the systematic summary of Marx's programme in his book *Das Kapital*. The bourgeois regards it as the cause, the fundamental evil, of our economic distress. Is this true?

Karl Marx portrayed only half correctly the causes of the Capitalist movements. Industrialisation of the European peoples leads to ever greater strata being proletarianised and the means of production being confined more and more to the hands of the few. According to Marx, the means of production are slowly lost by the working people. There develop two classes—the class of the cheated employee, and the class of the cheating employer. These two classes must wage a bitter war against each other. And thus the watchword of Marxism is, 'Class-war against Capital!'

Here we step in with our National Socialist criticism of Marx. Marx himself a Jew, knew only one kind of capital. And yet there is a vast difference between capital and capital.

There are two kinds of capital, and these two kinds of capital differ so basically that they must also be treated by us in a basically different way. We are not concerned with the holders of Capital, but with the Capital in itself represented by them. We National Socialists differentiate between a *working capital, a national state capital, and a rapacious, international loan capital.* Where does the difference lie?

What is Nation? What is National?

Nation is for us the organic union of a people into a working community of destiny. People — all of us who work in kinship for the whole, and National is everything that gives this people life, its national being. National capital is the working capital that toils for the nation: it is tied to the borders of the country, to the people, to the state. It consists of factories, railways, soil, land, mines, municipal and federal buildings; in short — national capital is state capital which is absolutely necessary to the life of the people; we cannot imagine it apart from the life of the people, without at the same time having to imagine the end of the people. National capital does not only create values, it is also something stable. Our mines, for example, cannot be transported abroad, they must remain in the country.

In contrast to national state capital is international loan capital. This loan capital no longer consists of factories, mines, railways, buildings; it consists essentially of money, better still, of gold. And this gold which has actually accrued from the profits of the economic system had been made an end in itself, mistress of the economic system. This gold has accumulated in the treasuries of the Jewish stock exchange. The stock exchange, however, with the help of this gold, seeks to gain power over the economic system; further still — political power, that is, power over the peoples. Dictatorship of bank and stock exchange over all peoples — that is the aim of loan capital. The gold is mobile, can be carried from country to country, is international, not tied to its country: that makes it easier for the stock exchange to realise its aim. How this realisation takes place is easy to recognise.

The main worry of the stock exchange must naturally be to clear the national states out of the way as quickly and completely as possible. And within the national states the national classes. It must wear these down in order to be able to erect on its ruins the worldwide dictatorship of gold. For the national classes will always react against any poison which threatens to destroy the body of the people.

Let us take Germany as an example because we have felt this poisonous process in our own body and must still experience it daily. Loan capital had to destroy five of our social classes in order to achieve its aim—the national bourgeoisie, the national intelligentsia, the German economy, German agriculture, and finally the German workers.

Each of these five classes, however, possessed definite weapons with which it could defend itself.

The stock exchange began with the middle-class. Its two weapons are mobile and immovable capital, money and property, land. Therefore, the stock exchange's war of extermination had to be directed against these two factors. And what happened? Swindlers created *inflation*, devalued the currency. The "German" government, the active willing agent of the stock exchange, placed such enormous taxes upon property that ownership is really no longer ownership, so that the bourgeoisie is left defenceless before the lust for power of the stock jobbers.

When the bourgeoisie was disposed of the national intelligentsia was also dead. The national intelligentsia came almost exclusively from the bourgeoisie. Now when this class had been battered to death, it was easy for the international stock exchange bandits to overcome the national intelligentsia and make them above all cowardly and receptive to Pacifism and Democracy. In Russia those who resist, and stir up opposition against the shameless extermination-work of the stock exchange are put to the wall; in Germany one sought to throttle economically those who spoke the truth when they could no longer hold their tongues. The system is the same— Bolshevik-Jewish.

The weapons of the economic system consist mainly in the possibility of gaining influence over wide spheres of the people. Their well-being is the well-being of the people, their distress is the people's distress. All the more horrible was the revenge of those who carried them, for believing, thanks to the baneful influence of Jewry, it would be better to go along with the Jewish financier than with the German worker. They did not notice how the Jew as industrialist, king of the stock exchange and the Jew as leader of the workers always skilfully widened the gulf between worker and employer, in order to pocket the profits from this quarrel as a laughing third party, smirking and rubbing his hands in delight—worker and employer became at the same time his hired slaves.

In order to stab the economy in the back the stock exchange needed an ally. This ally was the Marxist working class. For the stock exchange has put its middlemen into Marxism, who lead Marxism into opposing national capital and making national difficulties for it so that the stock exchange can drain this capital all the more easily. Certainly, industry and agriculture through their anti-social behaviour, only have themselves to blame for the fact that everything happened as it did. Only through the anti-social conduct of the bourgeoisie did the working classes become ready for the ideas of the Jew, Karl Marx, and ready for what Jewry wanted to achieve with them.

The sin of our forefathers is to have misunderstood and mistaken the legitimate unity of the working class, thus driving our workers into the hands of the Jews—a sin of the bourgeoisie, bloated, and unprepared for sacrifice, which has taken bitter revenge today.

We have seen all this quite plainly and terribly clearly at the time of the collapse of the Stinnes combine. Incidentally, I have absolutely no desire to defend Stinnes here, I've been fighting for years against combines of private capital, because I consider the accumulation of such huge economic wealth in a combine dangerous—Stinnes was a puppet. He liked it that way. The real, brutal enemy stood behind him, invisible as always, in order to be protected from all enmity.

Hugo Stinnes was ruined by the stock exchange; he owes his downfall to international loan capital!

The stock exchange had an interest in ruining him because he was not yet completely in its hands, because his output partly met the demand and was therefore not an end in itself!

What happened? The stock exchange advised him to corner the market; it promised to help him with credits. And Stinnes bought up; that done, the stock exchange withdrew its credits. The consequence was—the Stinnes shares plunged until finally the whole combine collapsed.

In this event lies a huge tragedy—the tragedy of the entire German economy!

Stinnes and his forebears, like the majority of industrial magnates today, unfortunately, did not recognise, did not want to recognise how foolishly they behaved in making their workers enemies and not friends. They treated the Jewish financiers, who wanted their extermination, as allies.

Young Edmund Stinnes saw the light when his father's lifework collapsed. When he stepped before his workers and offered them a share in his enterprise it was too late. Goaded on by their Jewish leaders, goaded on by their Jewish "labour" press, they became allies of the stock exchange, believing they were fighting *against* Capitalism when they refused the outstretched hand of young Stinnes, and yet only helping to realise the plans of the capital held by the international bank and stock exchange. The evidence? *Vorwärts* wrote at that time—'Workers, do not accept the shares offered by Mr. Stinnes. Why does Mr. Stinnes not go to the stock exchange and sell the shares there in order to give the workers hard cash? In this one sentence lies all:— everyone knows that an enterprise which suddenly sells its shares at the stock exchange is finished because selling is a sign of dire distress. The consequence—the price falls rapidly, the slaves are sold at a loss, stock jobbers with strong capital buy them for next to nothing and become masters of the enterprise!

Do we need any stronger proof that Marxism and stock exchange Capitalism work hand in hand? Both pursue the same goal because leadership is in the same hands. And one hand washes the other!

That is the tragedy of the German economy, the tragedy of the German employee.

The common aim of the stock exchange and Marxism is—complete elimination of every national economy, transferal of all economy to the domination of one thing—the stock exchange capital of Judah!

The pitiful 'revolution' of 9 November 1918, the Russian industrial reform, everything failed, had to fail because the masses did not recognise who was the true enemy with whom accounts had to be settled; because any attempts at solving the Jewish question were tactfully avoided. And just amongst the very bourgeoisie. Mental laziness and cowardice, the fear of perhaps having to give up well-loved views and habits, were faithful allies of the Jew. And he understood how to exploit them successfully for himself!

Thus we see that Communism passed over the question of international Jewish capital, had to pass it over since the very people who represent the stock exchange capital are its leaders.

Thus we see from a study of Lenin and his industrial reform that no salvation can come to the German people from this quarter because Communism, Marxism, as the ally of the Jewish swindlers on the stock exchange, never wants true freedom. It needs compliant slaves for its system of exploitation, for its plans to dominate the world, but no freeman. Indeed, real freedom spells its end.

Thus the final gigantic fight broke out, a fight which will bring us victory or defeat.

For us the essential problem of our day is the solution of the social question. Social question not in the sense of less work and more pay. For us the social question is the question of the possibility of and capacity for understanding between fellow Germans.

Germany will be free only when the thirty million of the Left and the thirty million of the Right can reach an understanding.

The bourgeois parties can never achieve this aim, Marxism does not want to achieve it.

Only *one* movement today is alone in a position to do so—National Socialism, personified in its leader, *Adolf Hitler.*

Who is this most hated man in Germany today?

Adolf Hitler does not come from the intelligentsia nor from the upper ten thousand. He is a man who has experienced all the social misery of his time, who has studied the social questions not in books, but through his own body. Hunger and cold, the misery of being without a job—he had to feel all this early in his life. Small wonder that he also pondered early why everything is so, that he began to search for the causes of this misery.

He took part in the World War as a volunteer, a simple soldier in the Bavarian army. And the war opened his eyes completely. He himself searched for the origins. And what he saw affected him deeply.

The treachery of Marxism to the working German people in November 1918, and the paltriness and cowardice of the national bourgeoisie, the enormous gulf between people who through their destiny belong together as fellow-countrymen—all this made Hitler's decision grow to dedicate himself to political work in the future.

Hitler recognises that a new idea, only the idea of the national will and socialist justice, is in a position to build the Germany of the future. He sees that the bourgeois parties are not capable of creating the new state since they could not even defend the old, since they crawled away as cowards in 1918 and thus betrayed Germany, their Fatherland, in its hour of need.

He sees that the Marxist Parties did not make 9 November 1918 a revolution for their freedom, but a revolution for the stock exchange, that they destroyed Germany in order to deliver it up completely to Western Capitalism.

Marxism did not *want* Socialism at all, because men lurked behind it and still stand there preaching phrases of freedom, peace and bread, who nevertheless did not want social liberation at all, but only used the workers as willing slaves for their own ends!

From bourgeois betrayal of the national principle and Marxist betrayal of the socialist principle results what we call National Socialism.

Once it was just the same in Prussia as it is today in Germany; once Prussia lay oppressed and there came a man, bearer of a powerful new concept of deliverance who liberated his people through realisation of his vision.

When Napoleon, the Corsican, burst into Prussia in 1806 the Prussian people had fallen asleep and there were also know-it-alls, politicians of compliance, who then said, 'We must make peace, we must yield, otherwise we shall be completely destroyed, absolutely ruined'.—And peace was made and Prussia yielded. And the Prussian people became enslaved.

Then *one* man struggled through who towered above everyone, who represented the will for freedom to the end—*Baron vom Stein.*

At that time the peasant had no bonds with the nation because he was no longer a property-owner in the nation. He was a serf. And then there came Stein and, in his search for future ways for Germany's rise, he recognised that the liberation of the people is only possible when it is made into a unified nation again; when the oppressed amongst the people are reintegrated into the fellowship of the nation, when they are given back the consciousness of being members of a whole, bound to this whole for better or for worse. Freedom and property—these were for Stein the only solution to the distress of his Fatherland. He made the German peasant free, gave him possessions, that is, administration of the nations material wealth and thereby, theoretical values. But the result of the Baron's action was the revolt of 1813.

It is our profound recognition of the facts that the German employee denied himself to the nation because he had no share in the nation. We have realised the profound causative relationship between the social emancipation of the employee and the national liberation of Germany.

We no longer believe in the International. We have seen it break up under the crushing blows of 9 November 1918. We have seen it break up under the disastrous collapse of the Ruhr campaign. We have recognised the enemy, the universal enemy—international Jewry, anonymous international loan-capital. We will no longer allow the universal foe to palm us off with the password to our own freedom since we know that this password is falsehood and deceit.

We want to take up the fight against this universal foe. We want to make Germany a state, the German people a nation. Our people shall be prepared to thrust the dagger deep into the heart of the foe.

The attempt is still being made to neutralise the workers' movement under the international watchword and to lead it into false paths. Whenever a régime became rotten and corrupt it became international, naturally and by force. The more corrupt a system is, the more international are its commitments. The International is the enemy. It tries to talk us into this idea of the International because it knows it is then invincible forever.

The International can only be eliminated by the National. Whenever the peoples rose against the international enemy they drew together more closely on a national basis. If we want to free the German worker then we must free Germany from the plague of the world—loan-capital. Here lies the enemy. We dare for the first time to name it publicly.

But if we want to make clear to the German worker the moral duty of his fight against this bane of the world then we must show him what he is fighting for. We must give him back what he had lost, what envious, irresponsible elements took from him.

Today this proletarian stands before us with the brutal accusation, 'I have no Fatherland called Germany'. We understand that. We no longer believe bourgeois ignoramuses and windbags who maintain the Fatherland is a thing in itself. We no longer believe that Germany can be liberated with cheering and beery pariotism. When the proletarian stands before us with the accusation, 'I have no Fatherland' then we know this accusation is profoundly justified.

What does this Fatherland give him? A life full of labour and toil, drudgery from early morning till late at night. All this might still be tolerable. But the final question, 'For what, for whom am I working?' demands an answer. And if this reply is lacking then the question engenders dissolution and accusation. I cannot require of a man that he does not respect; to respect something that he does not know. The German proletarian does not love his Fatherland because he has no share in this Fatherland.

We want to give him this share. We desire a share in property, a share in the management of this property, a share in the administration of the state; and to you, German proletarian, we shout, 'You do not hate Germany, you hate the form of this Germany, Democracy and Capitalism'. You are right to hate that. When you fight against that you will find us on your side. When you say, 'I have no Fatherland' we understand you. But it is false to say, 'I have no Fatherland and I want no Fatherland', but the password which can lead you to freedom runs, I have no Fatherland—it was stolen from me by men who had no right. They did not take it from me because they could boast of having the right of the stronger. They were not stronger, but cleverer, meaner, wilier than I. 'I have no Fatherland and I want to reconquer this Fatherland with my fists!' That is the battle cry which can lead Germany to freedom.

The social problem is the problem of making stable again the international proletariat in the cities. The German worker is not international from love of the International, but because he has no room to take root. Stability gives rise to feeling for the homeland. Feeling for the homeland is the germ cell of national consciousness. Let us take a simple example—when you arrive in a strange town you are a stranger in this strange town. You will go through the streets of the town without feeling any attachment to this town. You will yearn for the moment when you can shake the dust from these streets off your feet. When you see the towers of your home town in the distance your heart will beat faster. Why? Because you are attached to this town through something that belongs to you, whether land, a house, family, a mother. That binds you; here you can take root; here you are attached to your home in sorrow and joy. The German proletarian does not love his homeland because he has no homeland.

For this reason we want to give him room to put down roots; we want to give him a share in that for which he strives; we want to reintegrate him into the nation; we want to link him with responsibility to the sorrow and joy of his Fatherland; we want to make him a member of this Fatherland, a member of this nation. We have realised that without him it cannot work. We know that with him is bound up Germany's fate for the future. We do not approach him with bourgeois plaintiveness and social pity, but we approach him with the profound recognition that he is a part of Germany, perhaps even Germany itself. Germany is at stake, and ever Germany!

The social question is not one of bourgeois pity but a question of socialist, political necessity. We know that we shall have to fight with these principles against the solid majority in Germany. We know that the way which we want to follow is not the way of the ballot but a way of consistent destruction, a way of revolution. We desire this social revolution in order to set Germany free on a national basis, this national revolution in order to establish the social revolution forever. For us the guiding will is the saying of Lagarde: that he has not the courage nor the strength for the external revolution who is not man enough to complete the inner revolution within himself. We demand this inner revolution from the present-day German, this reconstruction and destruction within himself, this transformation from the old to the young citizen of the new Reich. What we want far surpasses bourgeoisie, far surpasses reaction. We want the conquest of the bourgeois, the conquest of the proletarian principle. Nothing binds us to this democratic Reich. Nothing binds us to the state of 1914. We have learnt from experience. We have seen a Reich created which stood for a thousand years, we have seen this Reich collapse because it had become old and rotten, collapse under the evil, envy, and incompetence of German princes.

The structure disintegrated, the principle remained! We have witnessed a hard period of transition from the First Reich to the Second. We have seen this Second Reich created under cannon fire before Paris. We had to witness the collapse of this Reich under the crushing blows of 9 November 1918; it collapsed because it became obsolete, collapsed because its supporters could not summon the courage or strength for defence. We live in the ruins of this Second Reich. What is happening around us is the process of decomposition of this state. The structure disintegrated, the principle remained!

We want to stamp the German principle in a new form, in the form of the Third Reich. We desire this Third Reich with the utmost ardour of our hearts; the Third Reich of a great Germany; the Third Reich of a socialist shared destiny. That far transcends ideas of brotherhood, far transcends the primitive doctrine of envy. We approach the German people with the final, most brutal charge. But this final, most brutal charge conceals within itself a final great reconciliation. We accuse the Right and conciliate the Left. We accuse the Left and conciliate the Right. Both sides were guilty of the German collapse. But the primary guilty party was he from the Right and therefore he must atone and offer sacrifice. If he wants to desire the Left to unlearn its proletarian thinking he must first have enough spirit himself to unlearn his bourgeois thinking.

We do not want a bourgeois state. We do not want a proletarian state. We want Germany! The nation is the ultimate and the greatest thing; the individual is as nothing beside it. But this nation is not completely unified until every individual has his place in it. It is not a shared destiny until the 30 million of the Left belong to it too, as a stable German working community.

We are National because we have realised that every great state concept has its origin in the soil of the homeland. We are National from a deep yearning for roots. We are not National because of remnants from the past, but from a purpose for the future. We want to deliver the world through Germany and not deliver Germany through the world. We are National because we know that no one will help us in our need, that only one single factor has the duty to set Germany free — we ourselves!

We are Socialist because we do not want to fight for the rights of our enslaved fellow countrymen as voluntarily or even reluctantly given gifts. We are Socialist because we want them to have their rights as a political necessity and out of popular justice.

We call ourselves 'Workers' Party' not because we cherish the delusion that only the manual labourer is called upon to save Germany. We call ourselves 'Workers' Party' because he is to belong to us, whoever is a German worker, whether by the head or the hand. Both belong to one another. To the one we say, 'You stand at the anvil and hammer out your destiny; you are nothing if the other man is not sitting in his study, making plans for the gigantic future of Germany. To the other we say, 'You sit in your study and make plans and schemes; you are nothing if the other man does not stand at the anvil, hammering your thoughts into an iron destiny.' Together you are everything; alone you are both lost.'

The fight has begun, not only in Germany but in the whole world. In the

Far East hundreds of millions are on the march. They do not fight for their freedom with the cry, 'Long live the Third International!' but with the cry, 'China for the Chinese!' The same fight has begun in India. The fires of freedom are glowing in the Colonies. Only Germany is thinking internationally. Only we are trusting in a right of mankind; are trusting in a right of love of peace which does not exist in the world.

Adolf Hitler once coined the phrase, 'Right is might!' Not until you have power will you receive the right! If you have no power then you can be right twenty times over and you will be wrong!

The 30 million of the Left and the 30 million of the Right are running up against each other. Only one thing gains advantage from it — the international scourge of the world. The 30 million of the Left and the 30 million of the Right rise up against each other. If the Right desires the freedom of Germany then the Left is ready to stab the Right from behind, and vice versa. Only when both stand together again, when from both a people of 60 million strong is formed again, can this people gain its freedom. The primary condition for German freedom is the will for freedom. To prepare this will is the task of our movement. Not until 60 million people want to become free with the deepest fervour of their hearts, will the destiny of the world, the God of history give his blessing upon it. This freedom is the last and greatest thing that we want.

Ask us our aim — freedom is our aim! Ask us our way — Socialism is the way to this freedom! Let the know-it-alls complain and cry for help; it is in vain. We shall not despair of freedom so long as one man still desires this freedom with this heart.

The Socialism that we want has nothing at all to do with the international-Marxist-Jewish levelling out process. We want Socialism as the doctrine of the community. We want Socialism as the ancient German idea of destiny. We want to make a people out of Germany, unified in a Socialist way, not only in joy but also in suffering. We want to make a people out of Germany, sharing its distress, its bread and its destiny. These are observations which do not stem from books, but rather from deep insight into the heart of things given to us by political instinct for the future.

We have lost a war. No people need succumb to that. We have lost a revolution. This lost revolution must be made good. Thus we no longer see a final division of the people into dozens of parties and dozens of organisations, but into two parts — the workers and the thieves, the hungry and the bloated. We shall have to discuss them in more detail. The bloated who before the war thought of Germany as a bundle of slaves; who turned the war itself into a business; who after the war rested comfortably on a foundation of facts. The hungry who before the war were excluded from the nation, who during the war sacrificed their health and their lives on the altar of the Fatherland out there in the trenches; who are now being pressed into a system more brutal and irresponsible than any that the history of world has everseen. They still rush past each other; the bloated still understanding well how to lead the will for freedom of the hungry into false paths. But the day of reckoning will come sooner or later when everyone will face the facts, that day on which the enemy will show himself in all his brutal nakedness, when the hungry will assault the bloated because they demand the concepts of Life, State, Nation, Germany.

Let them abuse and revile us. We know one thing: it brings no profit today to think and work for freedom. Let them laugh at us, this fast disappearing minority which, when the most brutal collapse comes, will unfurl the flag of freedom in a land rule by majorities. History is only ever made by a minority conscious of its aim, led on the path to freedom and rebirth by a radical will. Let them laugh at the young who rise against the old. We are proud that youth is found in our ranks. For us youth is not an error in itself nor age in itself a virtue. We want to urge on youthful enthusiasm and know that this very youth has the great task of completing the work of freedom. We do not give a damn for the experience and clear wisdom of old age. What we are going through has nothing to do with experience or wisdom. The collapse of a great people is so monstrous and so terrible that it strikes everyone, whether young or old, with equal brutality. What we are taking part in today, no living person has ever experienced before. But youth has always stood in the centre of things. In the terrible years of our past it has grown so early to manhood. For in their youth our young ones have seen more and suffered more than any previous generation. Who dares to cast the first stone at us? We have changed our colours before and will change our colours again. We know that fighting costs blood, and also that no drop of blood is in vain, but is seed upon German fields of yearning. We are this youth, driven by missionary zeal, driven by the necessity for action, formed by the task laid upon us by the history of the world. This youth is building up a Germany of the future. It laughs at the wise experience and smart-aleck superiority of the wise and old. What we desire is greater than experience and knowledge. Thus young National Socialist Germany steps forward, men who desire only to help, to discriminate, to clarify, and to work. Supporters of a new idea which will shape the future. Deliberate fighters for the spirit of the future Nationalist State in its clearest Socialist form and design. They are bound to this old State by nothing more than boundless hatred for its spirit and its supporters. They will be in the van of the fight against the Democratic-Liberal system. A movement for freedom does not have its profound origin in any cold powers of the intellect, but it is a thing of the will, of emotion, that will suddenly strike the people like a volcanic eruption and carry everything in its wake that was still half-hearted and cowardly. We are so terribly enslaved that neither intellect nor statistics can free us. Only the will for freedom can liberate us, and the final decision to subordinate all our thought and feeling and action to this single purpose.

Thus we do not fight against the International because we wanted to suppress the will for freedom of the slaves. The International recognises no will for freedom; but because we have realised the deceit of the International. An oppressed class, an oppressed people, has never freed itself through international protests, but always through national purpose for the future. The French citizen of the late eighteenth century did not wait for the solidarity possessed by the German and English citizen. He shook off his chains, unaided, with his own strength, and at the moment when they became unbearable for him. The powers of the old system tried to break his spirit but he defended himself and carried his principle, liberalism, victoriously through the whole world. It is the same today. The German worker will not become free until he frees himself, with his own strength, and he will do that when he can no longer bear the chains of slavery.

He is still enthusiastic about the International without having grasped its deepest meaning. His and our bitterest enemy, Democracy, money, is international. And money will not be overcome through Democracy, neither through money, but only through bloodshed.

The path to freedom is by way of the nation. The more unified this nation the stronger and more fervent the will for freedom. To give this passionate will for freedom its marching orders on a Nationalist and Socialist basis, that is the task of National Socialism. We desire freedom just like you, the German workers of the Left, only by other means, by means which will lead us to the goal. International solidarity is your programme. The solidarity of the nation, the community of the people is ours. They will come to believe us that our community of the people is not the pacifist slop that the middle-class supposes. The community of the people today is nothing other than the fight for the rights of the people for the sake of the nation. We desire this fight because it alone can bring us freedom.

There must be a fight for the future. You of the Left and we, we are fighting against each other without being real enemies. Forces are being divided in the process and we shall never arrive at our aim. Perhaps dire distress will lead you to us. Perhaps!—Don't shake your heads; in this question we are concerned with the future of Germany, and further still, with the future of

Central Europe. The new state or ruin and chaos, either is in our hands.

We young men of Germany, we are bearers of the destiny of generations. Let us never forget that! From the Left and the Right the way will be found to us when need has become greatest. A path from us to you does not exist. Why can we not unite with the bourgeois parties? Because we come from two different worlds. You are living in the collapse; we live in a prophetic conception of the future State. You are a hindrance in our way. Bourgeois admonishers, you preach at our back and want to dampen our will for freedom and want us to act with moderation in the name of Nationalism and Socialism. But this we have learnt in the years of the collapse: revolutions are never made in Parliament even though new motions and new resolutions are introduced every day. Out among the people, there the force is working which will build the new state, that force which the bourgeoisie in its political design cannot acquire, because it does not seriously want to acquire it. Organisation of this force, that is the task of the *Workers' Party*, so often reviled by the bourgeois parties.

However terrible and insoluble German need may be, we believe in the day which will come. This day will come because it must come. Germany's youth has not suffered in vain. History cannot ignore that a whole generation of fighters bled to death on the battlefields for an idea, unconsciously perhaps, but it lived in all of them, this idea, in the farsighted as faith, in the believer as a dim presentiment. A young Germany learnt there that we are on earth to offer sacrifice for the nation. And thus its thought and action revolve around Germany, around Germany alone.

Thus we regard the problem of Russia not as a problem of the present, but as a problem of the future. Russia lies embedded in the great problem of Europe and when Russia awakes, the world will see a miracle. We young Germans foresee this miracle with the instinct of a man of the present. We are not the withdrawn visionaries who set their last hope for the future of Germany upon this miracle. It is our duty rather to stop at nothing, but nothing, so that we can face this coming miracle as equal partners, or step to its side. There will be an awakening in Russia which will be more terrible than the war. This awakening will bring about the Socialist National State for which the young generation in every land, consciously or unconsciously, is longing so fervently.

We have learnt this from the collapse of the International: from the misery and deceit of an unnatural, foul pacifism, of a class-solidarity puffed up with words, the nationalist instinct is raising its victorious colours in the crumbling systems of Europe. Almost imperceptibly, the formation of a Nationalist State of Socialist character emerges.

Socialism cannot and will not deliver the world. The world will never be saved. It will save a people, perhaps the peoples; it is the political doctrine of the future nation.

We no longer believe in the proletariat's will for solidarity. We no longer believe in the world revolution, nor the salvation of the world. We believe in nothing more than our own strength. In this we believe all the more ardently, with the utmost fanaticism, with all the will for the future which burns within us. No one can save us except ourselves. If someone believed he could, we would not want it because we adamantly believe we can do it ourselves. We are Socialists, German Socialists. We do not want to have been such in vain. We are not satisfied with conviction. We seek to strengthen and deepen conviction through work and indefatigable striving. We demand clarity, clarity!

They do not know us yet! The docile, lukewarm and cowardly will be horrified at the radicalism of our demands, at the inexorable logic of what must be and what we intend to do just because it must be. Today they know in Germany that we allow no one to surpass us in our Nationalistic fanaticism for freedom. They will also soon come to realise that we stand just as firmly in the van in our will for Socialism. One thing still holds us firm in the fight, one thing still preserves our hope for the future and our passionate devotion to the people, to freedom and to the Fatherland: faith in the German worker, by mind and hand. In this we believe. We believe in the will for sacrifice, in the mad urge for freedom which slumbers in him and will one day awake. We believe in the Socialism in the worker, we believe in the mass rhythm. We believe in the future of history. That is our last consolation, our last hold.

If we ever have to say we no longer believe in this, then despair is our last refuge. But that cannot be, that must not be. We struggle for the soul of the German worker. It is there. Beneath distress, misery and hunger it slumbers and waits for him who will deliver it from death. Restorers to life! For this rôle has fate destined us. We are chosen for greater things than mere power. We are to bring the new State and with it the new man. That is no high-sounding statement, that is clear, sober truth. Already this new man is raising his still weary head, heavy with sleep and uttering words of universal significance. A time of such brutality that we still cannot envisage is approaching, indeed, we are already in its midst. In the face of these events all discussion turns to froth. Over all the confusion of empty words which wear us out to no purpose, over the shop keepers, literati and weaklings, the summons to action will sweep into the new Europe, a rushing tidal wave with a blood-red crest. For peace does not abide by the coward, but by the sword. Not all the fearless still lie buried beneath the ruins which engulf Germany.

That will be fulfilment. But to this fulfilment leads an unending path. We all seek it out with painful fumbling. One man is the pioneer who goes before us all — *Adolf Hitler*. The flag of freedom he unfurled again for the first time at a time of enormous cowardice, at a time of the most savage terror. He fought for this flag with the utmost passionate faith in freedom. He carried this flag at our head in the stormy days of November 1923. As leader of the idea he went before his followers into a shower of bullets from reaction. Let the Marxist decry us as bourgeois and capitalistic. Neither Marxist nor worker fired at us on 9 November 1923, but reaction. It fired at us because we did not want to take up our cowardly and comfortable position on the solid factual plane, because we set the passionate will for freedom on the march, because we did not preach as our ultimate goal, 'Maintenance of the peace is the primary civic duty', but, as a condition of freedom, the passionate demand for this freedom.

Thus we lead the way as those who still believe in Germany's future. Thus we let loose in the land the volcanic eruption of the new will for freedom and know that the volcano will one day become deed upon the barricades of revolution.

This is what we demand, this is what we are. We promise nothing other than the one thing: that we are honest fighters for what we desire.

Thus we are calling to battle. Before us flutters the flag of German revolution: a red background with a white circle and a black swastika. Under it we shall obtain by fighting what today is only empty talk and illusion: peace between mind and fist. Unity of the people!

APPENDIX **B**

Hitler's Secret Address to Representatives of the German Press Munich, 10 November 1938

The speech was made the day after the *Kristallnacht*, the pogrom against Jews in Germany. About four hundred journalists and publishers heard the speech.

This year of 1938 has had its successes, to be acknowledged with gratitude: the first of these being, of course, the immense programme undertaken by National Socialism to educate the German people. Slowly, the fruits of this educational programme are now beginning to ripen: the German people has taken its probationary test in the last few months and has passed brilliantly, we may well say, better than any other nation in Europe. These successes must further be attributed, of course, to the determination of our leadership. Nor, gentlemen—you can take my word for this—has it always been an easy task, first to take these decisions, and secondly, to stick to them through thick and thin. It has, of course, by no means been the case that the whole nation, and its intellectual strata in particular, joined in backing these decisions; on the contrary, there were, in the nature of things, a great many highly intelligent people—or people imagining themselves, at least, to be highly intelligent—who met these decisions with suspicion rather than with assent. It has, therefore, been all the more important to adhere with genuine, iron determination to the decisions taken—and taken as far back as May—

From *Es spricht der Führer*, pp. 268-86, edited by Hildegard von Kotze and Helmut Krausnick, 1966, Sigbert Mohn Verlag. Translated by Richard Thonger, April 1972. Reprinted by permission.

and to push them through against all forms of resistance. One further factor in the successful execution of these decisions, and therefore, also a direct cause of our general success, was the work of preparation which we have carried out in many fields, especially, it is clear, in those of military equipment. A very considerable number of measures have been taken this spring; they all had to become effective at a particular moment of time; it was imperative that they should become effective at that time; and they did indeed in fact become effective at that time. The mighty fortifications on our Western border took first priority. And one cause for our successes, perhaps the most important of all, has been our exploitation of the prevailing circumstances. The world situation in general appeared to me more favourable than ever for the successful assertion of our demands. None of all this, however, should let us forget one equally vital factor—the factor of propaganda, and not only propaganda directed *internally*, but also propaganda directed towards the outer world. If in fact the German people on this occasion—as I pointed out earlier—adopted an attitude quite different from the position taken by many other nations—different, indeed, from the attitude they would have adopted only a short while ago: this, I say, should be accredited to the continuous work of enlightenment—the propaganda—with which we have grasped the German people; and it is here that the press has done its great share of the work.

For the purposes of this programme we have in the course of this year set ourselves a few tasks which we mean to achieve by means of our propaganda—and here I will, if I may, place the contemporary press among the leading instruments for the purpose. *First*, the gradual preparation of the German people itself. The prevailing circumstances have obliged me to speak, for a decade or more, of almost nothing but peace. Only, in fact, by continuously declaring the German desire for peace and Germany's peaceful intentions was I able, step by step, to secure freedom for the German people and to provide Germany with the armaments which have, time and time again, always been the essential precondition for any further move. Peace propaganda of this kind, pursued for a decade or more, contains, it is clear, some questionable aspects; for an idea can thereby be planted, only too easily, in the minds of many people, the idea that the present régime is *itself* identical with the decision and the desire to preserve peace in *all* circumstances. This would, however, not only result in an erroneous appreciation of the aims of our system, but would also induce the German nation, instead of being armed and prepared for all events, to imbibe another spirit—defeatism—which, in the long run, would—nay, must—detract from the achievements of the present régime. It was sheer necessity that made me speak for years of peace alone. It has now, however, become necessary to submit the German people to a gradual change in its psychological state of mind, and to make it plain to the Germans that there are things which, if they cannot be achieved by peaceful means, *must* be achieved by means of force. In addition, however, it has been essential, while not advocating the use of force as such, for example, to spotlight certain happenings abroad in such a way that the *inner voice* of the people, the Germans themselves, would gradually begin to cry out for the use of force. This, then, has meant placing certain events in such a light that gradually, and quite automatically, a conviction has been kindled in the mind of the broad mass of the people— this conviction: 'If this cannot be put right by goodwill, then it must be put right by force; it cannot, however, be allowed to go on, in any circumstances whatsoever.' This work took months; it was systematically begun, systematically continued, and also intensified. Many people, gentlemen, did not grasp its significance; and many took the view that it was all somewhat exaggerated. These are those overrefined intellectuals who have no idea, in the final analysis, how to stiffen the mind of a nation to stand firm even when the thunder and lightning start.

Secondly, it has also been necessary to aim propaganda at the world at large, covering a substantial number of aspects. First of all, the problems which concern us have had to be represented to the rest of the world as naturally urgent and difficult. Secondly, it has been essential to show the rest of the world that the German nation is now reaching the point when it can no longer be trifled with; and a certain feeling that this was so must have gradually emerged from the way these problems were dealt with. And finally the world has had to be convinced of the *unanimity* of the German nation, and for this purpose, again, the co-operation of the press had to be arranged to a substantial degree. Further, however, it has been essential to use this same press and other propaganda to influence the enemy which first confronted us: that is, Czechoslovakia. There have perhaps been many people who did not grasp the significance of much of the action taken during these years. Gentlemen! Ever since May 21 it has been wholly clear that this problem had to be solved, come what may! Any further delay could only have made the problem more difficult and thus have contrived a still bloodier solution. And today we know, too, that that moment of time was, I should like to say, the very last moment at which this problem could be solved in the way in which it has been possible to solve it now. Of one thing, gentlemen, there is no doubt at all: any further delay, even of only a year or two, would have brought us into an exceptionally critical military situation. And our enemies in the world at large would still have been there. The "aircraft carrier" in the heart of Germany would have been dug in more deeply and equipped with still heavier armour, and all the additional weapons in our rearmament programme would have been swallowed up, in the event of any hostilities, by the task of finding a military solution to this problem alone.

For these reasons, therefore, a solution to this problem had to be reached this year, come what may. It was no longer possible to postpone even part of the action. The preparations which—for the first time, at that—had to be carried through and completed with the ultimate consequence in mind, were of such a massive nature that any question of camouflaging them seemed hardly imaginable. And as a factor of prime importance, it could no longer be assumed that in those circumstances the outer world would have continued to believe in it at all. Somehow I feel that this gramophone record, this pacifist record, has been played too often in Germany. People would probably not have listened to the tune any longer or if they did, they would not have believed what it said. I was firmly convinced that there was now only one other way open, that is, quite *brutally and ruthlessly*, to tell the truth, no more and no less. This, I was convinced, was bound in the long run, to exert a particularly paralysing effect upon that state which was most affected. I have frequently been asked the question: 'Do you think this right? For months now there has been continuous firing, by day and by night, on every rifle-range around the profile of Czechoslovakia; ceaseless firing at Czech fortifications; ceaseless firing with live ammunition; you are indeed drawing everyone's attention to it!' I was convinced that by means of these activities carried on for several months, I would in fact slowly but surely destroy the *nerves* of those gentlemen in Prague; and to this end the press, too, had to give its share of assistance. It had to help the process of gradually demolishing these people's nerves, and, their nerves did, in fact, not stand up to it. At the moment of ultimate and decisive pressure the nerves of the other side cracked, without any need at the final stage for us to take up arms. This was one of the most basic tasks of our press campaign, and this again, many people failed to understand. They would say; 'But this is all going much too far; and apart from that it is not fair; after all, the place is only a small state.' But only the intellectuals talk like that; the people, do not in any case use such language. The people prefer a trenchant, clear and, above all, well-seasoned diet. But certain intellectuals who—as is always the case in Germany—consider themselves the guardians of other people's morals and feel particularly responsible for what is called 'justice', and so on and so forth, and stand for moderation in anything and everything—many people of this type did not understand what was being done. But believe me, it was necessary: and after all, it is success that counts.

I should like to state now that his propaganda has in fact worked excellently this year, quite excellently, and that the press, too, has truly settled down to the job; and that it gave me, personally, great pleasure to peruse, day after day, these many German papers; and I really had to tell myself that this could not fail, in the long run, to have the desired effect on the German people; secondly, that this effect could not fail to make itself felt abroad; and thirdly, and most important of all, that the nerves of those responsible gentlemen, and particularly those gentlemen in Prague, would not be able to stand up to *it*. Praise and thanks be to God, they all know German and they all read our papers. I have been convinced that, in the long run, they were not going to *stand up* to it. Indeed I have received evidence to prove it. Since, obviously, Czechoslovakia was only able to possess telephone lines passing across German territory—to London or Paris, for example—and since we were, let us say, sufficiently prepared to help ourselves, or sufficiently lacking in conventional good behaviour—call it what you will—to do the natural thing and to tap telephone conversations, we were able to assess, every day, what effect our propaganda was having. And every day we were able to find things out, for example when Mr. Masaryk was talking to the press and said: 'There is nothing more that can be done—the Germans, of course, with their fantastic propaganda—no one believes a word we say any more—in fact, everything is lost—we may declare whatever we like—we can make whatever statements we like—we can say what we like, it all goes completely down the drain—it's all wasted effort, etc; they manage to cover up everything, etc.' Almost every day I have been able to ascertain the true impact of our propaganda, but particularly the impact of our press propaganda. As I said, it is success that counts and it is a success, gentlemen, a gigantic success! It is a fabulous success, so great that our present-day world is hardly able to assess its true significance. I myself became most aware of the grandeur of this success when I stood for the first time in the middle of the Czech fortified line. Then and there I realised what it means to take possession of fortifications representing a front almost 2,000 kilometres long without firing one single shot of live ammunition. Gentlemen, this time, by means of propaganda in the service of an idea, we have obtained 10 million human beings with over 100,000 square kilometres of land. That is something really magnificent.

This opens our minds, additionally, to understanding the victories of Napoleon; he did not merely win by being a strategist or a genius in the field; ah no, he was preceded by the Marseillaise and the ideas of the French Revolution, and he it was who reaped a portion of what this revolution had sown. From all this, however, one fundamental factor must be recognised: the press, gentlemen, can achieve *incredible* things and can exert an incredible influence whenever it serves as a means to an end. We live at a time where the opposite is also being demonstrated to an absolute degree. If a state contains 2,400 newspapers, and each one of them, guided by the thought-processes of journalists, is making its own policy, these 2,400 papers are bound to contradict one another. The only result achieved will be the Babel of voices which we are at present witnessing, for instance, in the French press. One paper repudiates another and in no time all the papers will be repudiating their own reports, again and again. If we pursue French press policy for the last six years, for example, we shall be unable to deny that this policy pursued by the press must bear a share of responsibility for the collapse of France, and that because of its total, entirely undisciplined disintegration. Each paper wrote down whatever it happened to think at the time. One paper was convinced that it was a crime to negotiate with Germany on the basis of an army of 200,000 and another paper was convinced that it was even a crime to negotiate on the basis of an army of 300,000. These very same papers were obliged to declare three years later: 'Why did you not then accept the offer of 300,000?' What is taking place over there is the continuous spectacle of people contradicting each other: and it goes to prove that in the world of today, when the greatest actions are being fought out, no battle can be won if the *most essential military forces* available are engaged, I should like to say, for purposes of self-glorification, instead of striking under one command and in one direction. When the press is a means to an end it is an enormously powerful instrument. And then, too, it is truly appreciated, because it need not contradict itself; because it is no longer possible for newspaper A to contradict newspaper B or for newspapers C, B, and A to contradict each other. But in the world of today, in which problems of such enormous size come up for discussion, the very moment that it deviates from the true course which I have indicated, the press will sink down into total, I should like to say, total insignificance—and this we see occurring in the other countries, before our very eyes.

Gentlemen, I have experience of this from my own youth. When I was a very young man and for the first time came to experience the actual forging of a country's history, in Vienna, the newspapers in that city were *exclusively* slanted in a liberal-democratic or Marxist direction: so that was all the big papers—the *Neue Freie Presse*, *Wiener Journal*, and still, at that time, *Die Zeit* as well, the *Wiener Tagblatt*, the *Extrablatt*, and so forth. These were the very substantial papers and the working-class papers. And by way of opposition to these, by way of anti-Semitic journals, there stood in fact only one, the *Deutsches Volksblatt* . . . . . [*a few words inaudible*] . . . . . on the agenda—a paper with a circulation of perhaps 20,000 or 25,000. And in the

Wiener Stadtrat, the Vienna City Council, there were, out of 148 members, *136 anti-Semites*, the Christian Socialists. So *slight* then had the influence of the press become. People no longer paid any attention to it. It wrote what it had to write and people read it, but it no longer exerted any influence whatsoever. And a similar situation exists today in other countries as well, where, I should like to say, popular opinion is certainly beginning to crystallize and is taking lines *quite* different from those whose existence the press is prepared to admit or, for that matter, even to report. Indeed, our own path, the road we have followed, is in fact the same. At the moment when I grasped the reins of power in Germany, we had *perhaps* 5 per cent of the German press in our hands; if indeed it was 5 per cent. Not even 5 per cent; 95 per cent against us. But *I* came to power, and I have the people behind me! From this can be learned how *mighty* the power of a press can be if it serves as an instrument of a leadership and how insignificant a press will be which, I should like to say, attempts on its own account to make history and with history, politics.

We for our part have attempted to fashion the German press into an effective weapon of this kind. And as we wind up this year, may I say to you all that I am more than satisfied with this attempt—more than satisfied. Its effectiveness has been tried and proved in a most convincing manner. Now, once more, we have very great tasks before us. And above *all*, Gentlemen, stands one vital task: we must now, with every means in our power, step by step, strengthen and increase the self-confidence of the German people! This is a task which cannot, I know, be realised in one or two years. What we need is a powerful, firmly rooted public opinion—extending, if possible, even into the ranks of our intellectuals [*movement and laughter*] . This, you will see, is the only way for a successful political line to be promoted in the long run. And when I say "in the long run", I am not thinking of spring 1939, or the summer after that, but of the decades to come, particularly, of course, of the years that lie ahead of us. Our people must be filled with *that deep self-confidence* such as in happier times, perhaps, suffused the German soldier— at the close, say, of the France-German War of 1871 and from then on until the middle of the Great War. That self-confident conviction—first, that in Germany the people itself is a standard of value, and secondly that this people's leadership is the right one. And here it is essential that in our programme of training in self-confidence, we should campaign against all those manifestations which I myself had plentiful opportunities to get to know as the greatest enemy of our national resurrection and revival: that is, mass hysteria, and here particularly, hysteria from the ranks of our intellectuals. Here particularly one must secure support from the broad mass of the people, in order to provide some counterweight against these degenerate intellectual, and hysterical elements [*laughter*] . Let me give you an example: On the . . . . . [*no date given by Hitler*] . . . . . February of this year the expressed conviction among these intellectual elements was: 'Our foreign policy situation is not very good, our foreign policy position is not good *at all*!' Towards the end of February this year it was: 'We are on the brink of disaster! Our foreign policy is disastrous, completely disastrous!' Middle of March,

'Tremendous victory! All has been achieved thanks to our courage and perseverance! Everything is in perfect order! Germany is invincible, a world power, etc.! Colonies are of course the next thing we are going to be presented with, and that quickly! Regrettable that the leadership did not push on straight away, the leadership was not quite up to the mark this time! [*Laughter and tumultuous applause*]. It should have done a left turn and then turned the enemy flank a little further still; that would all have been possible.'

Two months later: the problem of Czechoslovakia is starting to raise its head. 'That is really enough for this year', they say, 'you can't start tackling a brand-new problem straight away!' And another month later, 'This will lead to disaster! Germany is moving into economic ruin, we are being ruined financially! We have neither the money to pay for this nor the human resources to see it through.' And another week later: 'The whole world is against us, we are on the brink of a world war!' And another week later, 'Now we are on the brink of disaster; our defeat and disintegration are imminent!' And another week later, 'Triumph! Why has the leadership not taken possession of the whole of Czechoslovakia straight away? [*The beginning of the following sentence was drowned out by laughter*] . . . . . why . . . . . now . . . . . continue to negotiate?' Believe me, I *have* received many letters! . . . . . [*amusement and lively applause*]

It came to my notice once that a man who was sitting in an Office in Berlin, in connection with naval treaty negotiations, suddenly said:

This demand for 35 per cent is utter madness. To imagine that the British would ever agree to this is to have a completely false idea of them. They simply cannot do this, and they will never do it, never. This will lead to the breakdown of Anglo-German relations and to the isolation of Germany. The painfully won—that was in the German Foreign Office [*disturbance*]—painfully won Anglo-German understanding will be most gravely endangered.

Then the negotiations take place; 35 per cent is agreed to; in fact, 45 per cent for the U-Boat fleet; and as we announce it, it is even up to 100 per cent. About three or four months later I was finally obliged to throw this gentleman out of the Foreign Office for good and all. This time, this self-same person suddenly stated: 'I have no idea how Herr von Ribbentrop manages to talk so big. Well yes, if he had managed 50 per cent, that would have been something to talk about, but 35 per cent, what ever is that?' I then, as a matter of fact, fired this gentleman [*applause*] , the incident having been accidentally brought to my notice. He was a *Legationsrat*, a First Secretary.*

And, now, however, I have been experiencing the same thing again. I have recieved memoranda proving in black and white that all this was impossible, that it was bound to lead to disaster, etc., etc. And I have had memoranda on other occasions, memoranda which proved that between the southernmost point of our territory at. . . . .[*place-name inaudible*]. . . . .and the northernmost point of Lower Austria, there was a distance of only 60 kilometres, and why was I not going to take these kilometres as well? [*Laughter*] And then, there were actually linguistic pockets in the area, and I was reminded that all the people in them were supposed to be Germans, in case I did not know. [*Laughter*] Well, you know gentlemen: that is the *hysteria* of our upper ten thousand! And we must take particular care that this kind of hysteria does not get into the people, so that our people and, if possible, as I said earlier, even certain intellectual elements, are educated into a mood of truly self-reliant confidence. It is a task shared by the press to strengthen German self-confidence *systematically* and to avoid anything that might in any way, shall we perhaps say, gnaw at the roots of this self-confidence, or destroy it, or even cause it to falter.

I am fully aware of the voices coming from this or that quarter who argue that problems also exist which have to be subjected to criticism. Gentlemen, there are two possible objectives. Objective A means: I search all over Germany to see if I can't find something to criticize. If I once start doing that, Gentlemen, I shall in no time at all have turned into a real long-snouted snuffling pig. [*Laughter*] New things, you see, will crop up all the time, and I shall delve into them more and more deeply. This is, I suppose, a way of spending one's time, but in my view, not a satisfactory one. There is, however, another kind of activity which consists of recognising the great tasks which have been set for us. I shall not overcome the trivialities by running after each and every one of them, but by gathering the whole strength of the nation for the great tasks ahead and thus solving the secret of the great tasks themselves. For it is precisely the extent to which I solve the secret of these mighty tasks which will cause all the small detail to shrink to insignificant, nay, ridiculous proportions. No one will then mention it any more and thus I shall overcome it with the rest. No one will pay it any further attention; they will not even notice it. And, finally, the factor of human inadequacy: no one banished it from the world in times gone by; the press of the liberal states did not manage to do so either, nor shall we succeed in doing so. Human beings of inadequate

*Footnote apparently omitted.

strength, insufficient talents, faulty traits of character, and so on, will always exist, and have always existed, and we shall not remove them from the face of the earth. Another task, however, and of far greater importance, is not to draw the public eye to these *moments of weakness,* but to point out the nation's great *river of strength* which can be traced back hundreds and thousands of years. Once a man said to me: 'Look, if you do that, Germany will be ruined within six weeks.' I replied: 'What do you mean by that?—'Then Germany will disintegrate.' I replied 'What do you mean by that?' 'Then Germany will just cease to exist'. . . [*Sentence in the recording incomprehensible*]. . . The German people once survived the Roman wars. The German people survived the mass migrations of nations. Then, later, the German people survived the large-scale fighting of the early and late Middle Ages. The German people then survived a Thirty Years' War. Then, later, the German people survived the Napoleonic wars, the wars of Liberation, and it has survived even a world war, indeed even the Revolution—and it will survive me! [*Laughter and tumultuous applause*]

Our task is to find a successful way of filling our nation, by the example of our own history and by the strength of our faith, with *just that* confidence they need to enable them to carry out the immense political tasks which lie ahead. For, Gentlemen, a leader of the nation can do no *more* than the nation itself will give him. This is a law of unshakeable accuracy and significance. If I have behind me a people whose faith is weak, however shall I then grapple with the great tasks which the future has in store for us? It is not enough for *me* to believe, no, it is essential for me to have behind me a German people fervent in their faith, united, self-reliant, and confident in the future. To bring this about is the mighty work, the mighty task, which we all share in common, and it is truly a *wonderful* task. It is quite a different matter, you know, *making* history instead of . . . . [*words in recording incomprehensible*]. And today, we really and truly live at this wonderful period of time in which we may say history has really been made; and we can say further that we have wasted no time, that we have not exhausted our writing talent in favour of matters of no value, merely to write or speak for the sake of writing or speaking, and so that finally, one can say that one has spoken. All this has genuinely produced a result, and an historic result indeed, a result which enables us to perform a genuine *service* to former generations, Gentlemen! And this is our collective achievement, not only of my efforts, but the achievement of all those hundreds of thousands of people who stand behind me and march beside me and who, in the last resort, represent. . . . [*incomprehensible in recording*] . . . . and influence the people. It is essential to take the greatest pains to rouse the might of the German people by increas-

ing its confidence in its own strength and thus also bringing a *stability* into
the minds of our people to assist their appreciation of political problems.

I have often, and I have to add this in speaking to you, felt doubts on
one single matter, and that is the following: if I look at the intellectual
elements of our society, I think what a pity, unfortunately they are needed;
otherwise, one day one might, well, I don't know, exterminate them or
something like that. [*Commotion*] But unfortunately, one needs them. If now
I take a good look at these intellectual elements and imagine, and check,
their behaviour towards me, and towards our work, I feel almost afraid. For
ever since I began to be politically active, and in particular ever since I
came to lead the Reich, I have only had successes. And yet this amorphous
mass of individuals* grumbles and grouses about the place in a manner which
is often loathsome, really disgusting. Whatever might happen if one of these
days we had a failure instead of a success? That, even that, *could* happen,
Gentlemen. *How* do you think this "henfolk" would behave then? For even
now, when we are having nothing but successes—successes, moreover, that
are unique in the history of the world—even now these creatures are unreliable, but what would they be like if we had just one misfortune, one
failure? Gentlemen, I used to think with the greatest pride on having built
myself a party that would even in times of setbacks stand solidly and in
fanatical loyalty behind me—would stand behind me in fanatical loyalty
particularly at such a critical time. It was my greatest pride and it took an
immense weight from my mind. This is the state of morale to which we have
to educate the German people. The nation has to learn to believe so fanatically in final victory that even if we should one day suffer defeats, the nation
will only evaluate them from, I should like to say, the higher point of view,
saying: 'This is only temporary; the final victory will be ours!' There was once
a Prussian Commander-in-Chief in whom this trait of character was most
strongly marked; Blücher, the man who perhaps suffered the most defeats
of any military leader, but who had a fanatically firm belief in final victory:
and that was what counted. We must educate the whole of our people into
this frame of mind. The people must be educated to absolute, stolid, unques-
tioning, confident faith; in the end we shall achieve everything that we need.
This can only be built up, it can only succeed, by appealing continuously to
the strength of the nation, by giving prominence to the positive values of a
people and by doing all that is possible to disregard what may be called
negative aspects.

To this end it is also essential for the press, and particularly the press, to

*Footnote apparently missing.

acknowledge blindly the following maxim: 'The leadership's line of action is correct!' Gentlemen, we must all reserve the right to be allowed to make mistakes. Even newspapermen have not been liberated from this danger. But all of us can only survive if we avoid spot-lighting each other's mistakes, when the world is looking, but shine our torch on what is positive. That is to say, in other words, it is essential—*without in any way* disputing the possibility of mistakes being made, or even of discussion—it is essential that as a general principle the correct line taken by the leadership should always be emphasised. This is what matters. This is imperative, you realise, for the people's sake; for I hear so often—these are a sort of lapse into liberalism—I often hear the following question which I have in front of me: "Well, should one not now just for once leave this to the German people's own discretion?" Well, Gentlemen, you know, I imagine now that I have achieved a thing or two, more at least than many a cobbler and many a milkmaid. And yet it can, of course, come to pass that in assessing a particular problem with other gentlement who have also achieved a great deal, I do not see quite eye to eye. What is certain, however, is that *one* decision has now to be reached. It is wholly impossible for me, once *we* have failed to reach a clear line on this decision, that I should hand it over the dairy-maids and the dairy-farmers and the cobblers. That is impossible. It is, therefore, of no importance at all whether a decision of this kind is, in the final analysis, completely correct; that is *of no interest whatever*; what does matter is that the *whole nation* should fall in, like a single unit, behind a decision of this kind. There must be a front, and any feature of the decision which is not entirely correct will then be compensated for by the spirit of resolution with which the nation stands behind it.

   This, Gentlemen, will be important in the years to come! It is only in this way that we will be able, I should like to say, to deliver the people from a spirit of doubt that only makes them unhappy. The broad mass of the people *just does not want* to be burdened with it. The broad mass has one desire and *one only*: to be well led, to be able to trust its leadership, and to see the members of the leadership, not engaged in disputes with each other, but appearing before the people as a united body. Believe me, I know it full well, nothing gives greater joy to the German people than to see me, say for instance on a day such as 9 November, walking in the street with all my fellow-workers beside me; and then the people say: 'That is him, and that is him, and that is him, and that is him.' And the people feel secure from all danger at the thought: 'They all keep together, they all follow the *Führer* and the *Führer* holds fast to these men; these are our idols'. Many an intellectual may perhaps not understand that. But these little people out there somehow see, in *all* the men who appear before them in this way, an object worthy of their trust. And they cling to the idea of these men. When they can look like that at this scene, the *Führer* walking along with all those men by his side, it *comforts* the people so much, it makes them so *happy*! That in fact is what they *want*! And it was like this in earlier periods of German history too. The people are always happy when there are a few people at the top who stick together; it makes it easier for the people down below to stick together in there turn. This, however, we must grasp on a huge scale — we must understand our obligation to do everything to keep and preserve this impression in the people's mind. They, the people, must acquire the conviction that the leadership at the top is *taking the correct action*, and that *everybody stands behind* the leadership. And then, as far as the outer world is concerned, it will be psychologically very easy for the leadership to assert itself in critical situations.

Summing up, I should just like to say this, Gentlemen: In liberal countries the vocation of the press is conceived in such a way that the saying goes: *Press and people against the leadership*. And in our country it has to be: Leadership and propaganda and press, and so on, appearing before the people! All that is in fact leadership of the people. Every single individual is for this purpose a leading member of the people and should feel responsible for it. Every single individual has a primary duty to acquire this higher understanding of the principles of leadership. Whatever the leaders may perhaps discuss among themselves, before the people this leadership has to appear as one single bloc, a unanimous unit, quite irrespective of whether one man is producing propaganda here, another is with the press, a third is active at meetings and assemblies, a fourth presides as a leader, say, of political organisations, a fifth is commanding a military formation, a sixth is serving in an office or representing the nation abroad in dealings with the foreign world; *all this is the leadership of the German people*, and before the people itself this leadership has to appear as a united confederation. Among themselves, opinions may be exchanged. But in the people's presence, there is one opinion and one only. Gentlemen, this is a very clear principle! If we put it completely into effect, the German people, *through this leadership*, will grow great and powerful. And then we shall not be standing here in the year 1938 at the *end* of an historical period; then, we shall without doubt be standing only at the beginning of a great historical epoch for our people.

Now, Gentlemen, I firmly believe in this, the German people's future. Perhaps there has often been someone who used to ask himself the question: 'The *Führer* is just a visionary — how can he possibly believe in such things being possible?' Very simple, Gentlemen. The history of the world is made by human beings. It used to be made by human beings, and it is still made by human beings. What counts is the quality of these human beings and in addition to that, to a certain extent, their number. The quality of the German people is quite incomparable. I shall *never* allow myself to be persuaded that any other nation could be of *better* quality! I hold the conviction that our people, especially today, with its steady racial improvement, represents the highest possible value that exists anywhere on this earth at the present time. As regard the numbers, you should however always remember this: The United States has, it is true, a population of 126 or 127 million people. Nevertheless, if you deduct the Germans, the Irish, the Italians, the Negroes, the Jews, and so on, any other nationalities at all, you will not even have 60 million Anglo-Saxons, or even people who call themselves Anglo-Saxons. The Russian Empire does not possess even 55 or 56 million genuine Great Russians. The British Empire has not got as many as 46 million Englishmen in its mother country. The French 'Empire' does not even contain 37 million real Frenchmen. Italy possesses slightly more than 40 million Italians, Poland has only 17 million Poles left. But in Germany, from the year 1940 onwards, there will be living *80 million people of one race* and around us, nearly 8 million more who in fact belong to our race. Whoever has doubts regarding the future of this greatest of all blocs of human beings of one race, or does not believe in its future, is himself nothing but a weakling. I believe *unconditionally* in this future. We *were* once the greatest empire of all. Then we became weary and slack, we wasted our strength on a process of internal disintegration and thus lost our status and reputation abroad. But now after a crisis of perhaps 400 or 300 years, our people's restoration to health has begun. And I know full well that we now stand at the beginning of our German life and thus at the beginning of the German future. It must surely be for all of us the greatest good fortune to be allowed to assist in preparing, even shaping this future and in making this future come true. It must fill us with the greatest satisfaction, compared with which everything else shrinks to nothing, mere shadow without substance. It was this conviction that once led me forth from a military hospital, and it has stood by me up to this very moment when I now stand before you. And this is the conviction which must inspire us all on our German nation's way ahead, and this, I am convinced, will be a road to greatness, a road into the splendid future of our German nation. Once more, I should like to thank you for your co-operation.

Notes

INTRODUCTION

1. Max Domarus, *Hitler, Reden und Proklamationen 1932-45*, vol. 1, page 643. Wurzburg, 1962.
2. *Mein Kampf*, pages 474-5. Translated by James Murphy, London, 1939.
3. Ibid., page 476.
4. Ibid., page 478.
5. Chapter 6, vol. 1, deals with war and propaganda, and in chapter 11, vol. 2 the impact of propaganda on party organization is discussed.
6. *Mein Kampf*, page 156.
7. Ibid., page 94.
8. Ibid., page 161.
9. Ibid., page 158.
10. Ibid., page 158.
11. Ibid., pages 46 and 49.
12. Ibid., page 49.
13. See Bibliography.

CHAPTER I

1. Heinrich Hoffmann, *Hitler Was My Friend*, page 61.
2. See page 19.
3. Konrad Heiden, *Adolf Hitler*, page 199.
4. N.D. Fabricant, *13 Famous Patients*, page 43.
5. *Account Settled*, page 206. Cf. Alan Bullock, *Adolf Hitler, A Study in Tyranny*, 1962, page 68.
6. *Redeverbot*.

7. *Aktionausschuss zur Durchführung des Volksprotestes wider das Redeverbot Adolf Hitlers.*
8. *Sammlung Rehse*, page 254.
9. Ibid., page 268.
10. Hans-Jochem Gamm, *Der drame Kult*, Hamburg 1962, page 19.
11. Cf. George Masse, *The Intellectual Origins of National Socialism*, London 1967.
12. See page xvi (Introduction).
13. Karlheinz Schmeer, op.cit., page 9.
14. Philipp Bouhler, *Kampf um Deutschland*, pages 46-47.
15. Ernst Bayer, *Die SA*. *Schriften der Hochschule für Politik*, page 8.
16. Ibid., page 9.
17. See page 6 et seq.
18. Gunter D'Alquen, *Die SS, Geschichte, Aufgabe und Organisation der Schutzstafflen der NSDAP,* page 202. Neusüss-Hunkel, *Die SS*, page 7.
19. A Nazi *Gau,* which consisted of three Bavarian provinces: Oberfranken, Oberpfalz, and Niederbayern.
20. See pages 23-24.
21. E. Bayer, op. cit., page 8.
22. *Sammlung Rehse,* page 270.
23. K. Schmeer, op. cit., page 18.
24. Otto Strasser and Michael Stern, *Flight from Terror*, page 107.
25. *The Fall of the German Republic*, page 288.
26. See page 6 et seq.
27. Adolf Dresler, Der Führer und die Presse, *Zeitungswissenschaft*, *Monatsschrift für internationale Zeitungsforschung*, vol. 14, No. 5, 1939.
28. See the *Wiener Library Bulletin,* September-December 1954.
29. *Sammlung Rehse*, page 221.
30. Hans A. Münster, *Geschichte der deutschen Presse,* page 113.
31. See page 22.
32. H. A. Münster, op. cit., page 113.
33. J. Goebbels, *Vom Kaiserhof zur Reichskanzlei,* page 17.
34. Cf. E. Bramstead's article 'Goebbels and *Der Angriff '* in *On the Track of Tyranny*, a Wiener Library publication, edited by Max Beloff, page 49.
35. J. Goebbels, *Kampf um Berlin*, page 63.
36. Ibid., page 66.
37. Ibid., page 71.
38. R. Manvell and H. Fraenkel, *Joseph Goebbels*, London, 1960, page 77.
39. Dr. Wahrmund, *Gericht über Hugenberg*, page 37.
40. *Sammlung Rehse*, page 289.
41. Wolfgang Schaefer, *NSDAP*, page 12.
42. Ibid., page 19.
43. *Reichsbetriebszellenorganisation.*
44. W. Schaefer, op. cit., page 17. In comparison, the white-collar employers in private firms and self employed persons—12 and 9 per cent respectively of the total working population—provided the Nazi party with 25.6 and 20.7 per cent of its members.

45. Ibid., op. cit., page 17.
46. H. A. Münster, op. cit., page 113.
47. Entry on 8 May 1932 in Goebbels's *Vom Kaiserhof zur Reichskanzlei*, page 93.
48. Entry for 4 February 1932 in J. Goebbels's *Vom Kaiserhof zur Reichskanzlei*, page 38.
49. *Sammlung Rehse,* page 371.
50. *Vom Kaiserhof,* page 63.
51. Ibid., page 79.
52. Ibid., pages 17-18.
53. Ibid., page 82.
54. Hans Bausch, *Der Rundfunk im politischen Kräftespiel der Weimarer Republik 1923-33*, page 177.

CHAPTER II

1. *Vom Kaiserhof zur Reichskanzlei*, entry on 30 January 1933, page 251.
2. Ernest K. Bramsted, *Goebbels and National Socialist Propaganda*, London, 1965, page 198 et seq. In his book Dr. Bramsted analyses, in a detailed and convincing manner, the development of the Hitler myth.
3. Ibid., page 208.
4. K. Schmeer, op. cit., page 32.
5. Ibid., page 28.
6. See Chapter IV, *passim*.
7. *Vom Kaiserhof,* page 285.
8. K. Schmeer, op. cit., page 38.
9. See page 20.
10. W. Hagemann, op. cit., page 34.
11. From a speech to the journalists' conference at Cologne in November 1935, quoted by W. Hagemann, op. cit., page 39.
12. See pages 18-19.
13. *Reichsgesetzblatt*, 1933, part 1, page 714.
14. W. Hagemann, op. cit., page 37.
15. Ibid., page 40.
16. Page 272, Princeton University Press, 1947.
17. *Reichsgesetzblatt*, 1933, Part 1, page 483.
18. Quoted by W. Hagemann, op. cit., page 45.
19. Heinz Pohle, *Der Rundfunk als Instrument der Politik*, page 241. Hamburg, 1955.
20. Ibid., pages 239-40.
21. Ibid., page 257.
22. Ibid., page 399.
23. *Der Anteil des Rundfunks an der Schaffung Grossdeutschlands, Handbuch des deutschen Rundfunks, 1939-40*, pages 5-10.
24. See Chapter VI.
25. *Deutsche Grenzvolk in Not.*
26. H. Pohle, op. cit., page 409.

27. *'Unsere Saar—Der Weg freizur Verständigung'.*
28. *'Stunde der Nation'.*
29. H. Pohle, op. cit., page 412.
30. *Rundfunkhörerverband.*
31. Of the votes cast, 90.76 per cent were for the return of the Saar to Germany, 9 per cent for the retention of the *status quo*, and only 0.24 per cent for the transfer of the area to France.
32. J. Goebbels, *Nationalsozialistischer Rundfunk,* pages 12-13. Munich, 1935.
33. H. Pohle, op. cit., pages 416 and 417.
34. Ibid., page 418.
35. Ibid., page 432.
36. C. Searchinger, *Voice of Europe*, page 383. London, 1938.
37. See page 121 et seq.

CHAPTER III

1. See pages 10, 12-13, 26.
2. Paul Seabury, *The Wilhelmstrasse*, page 31. University of California Press, 1954.
3. Ernst von Weizsäcker, *Erinnerungen*, page 109. Munich, 1950.
4. *Docs. Ger. For. Pol.*, series C, vol. 1, page 483, Minutes of the Conference of heads of Departments, Wednesday, 24 May 1933 at 5.0 p.m.
5. Martha Dodd, *Through Embassy Eyes*, page 249. New York, 1939.
6. *Reichsgesetzblatt* of 5 July, no. 75, page 449.
7. N. G. Series No. 4062, secret report of the Ministry of Finance on expenditures of the departments of state, 17 July 1939. The report can be found among the material assembled in Nürnberg for the last of the major trials of war criminals. The accused were mainly German diplomats, and their trial took place in Nürnberg between 6 January and 14 April 1949. Cf. Paul Seabury, op. cit., pages 68 et seq.
8. Exhibit RF. 1147, Nürnberg trials, referred to in vol. 7, page 11.
9. See page 67.
10. See page 91 et seq.
11. *Volkischer Beobachter*, 5 April 1933.
12. *Memories of Alfred Rosenberg*, edited by Serge Lang and Ernst von Schenk, page 161. New York, 1949.
13. Cf. *The Brown Network*, pages 55 et seq.
14. See page 136 et seq.
15. *Das politische Tagebuch Alfred Rosenbergs*, page 129.
16. Ralph F. Bischoff, *Nazi Conquest Through German Culture*, pages 83 et seq. Harvard University Press, 1942.
17. Ibid., page 87.
18. Ibid., page 102.
19. *Docs. Ger. For. Pol.*, series C, vol. 2, page 49.
20. Ibid., pages 107-8.
21. That is, apart from the Foreign Ministry, those of Interior, Finance, Economics, Popular Enlightenment and Propaganda, and the Prussian State Ministry, the

Prussian Ministries of Interior, Ecclesiastical Affairs, and Finance.
22. *Docs. Ger. For. Pol.*, series C, vol. 2. page 36.
23. Louis de Jong, *The German Fifth Column in the Second World War*, page 227. London, 1956.
24. *Trials of the Major War Criminals*, Vol. X, page 13.
25. Nürnberg evidence, N.G. 5557, letter from Bohle to Schmeer, Hamburg, 4 April 1933.
26. *The Ribbentrop Memoirs*, pages 80–81. London, 1954.
27. *National Socialism, Basic Principles, Their Application by the Party's Foreign Organization, and the Use of Germans Abroad for Nazi Aims*, page 95. U.S. Department of State, Washington, 1943.
28. Emil Ehrich, *Die Auslandsorganisation der NSDAP*, page 17 et seq. Berlin, 1937.
29. Ibid., page 7.
30. *Der Parteitag der Ehre*, pages 124 et seq. Munich, 1936.
31. *Almanach der nationalsozialistischen Revolution*, edited by Wilhelm Kube, page 95. Berlin, 1934.
32. L. de Jong, op. cit., page 279.
33. L. P. Lochner, editor, *The Goebbels Diaries*, entry for 4 March 1943. London, 1948.
34. *Weltdienst*, 1 September 1934; Louis W. Bondy, *Racketeers of hatred*, pages 81-82. London, 1946.
35. 'Volksgemeinschaft und Völkerfriede', *Sitzungsbericht der Berliner Tagung*, page 8. Zürich, 1935.
36. *Am Internationalismus gehen die Völker zugrunde*, page 13. Zürich, 1936.
37. 'Volksgemeinschaft und Völkerfriede', *Sitzungsbericht der Berliner Tagung*, pages 19 and 20.
38. For a discussion of the role of the *Antikomintern* see pages 95-100.

CHAPTER IV

1. Cf. Z. A. B. Zeman, *The Break-up of the Habsburg Empire*, page 184. Oxford University Press, 1961.
2. H. Rauschning, *Hitler Speaks*, page 19. London, 1939.
3. Ibid. Apart from indicating that these conversations with Hitler date from the period between the beginning of the year 1932 and the end of 1934, Rauschning does not give the precise date of the pronouncement. It is likely, however, that Hitler was more concerned with this kind of problem after, rather than before, January 1933.
4. Ibid., pages 166-7 and 198.
5. Ibid., page 233.
6. Report from Rome to the *AA*, 10 October 1933, 8677H/E607177-92.
7. See Lionel Kochan's *Pogrom, 10 November 1938*; London, 1957; especially the last chapter, 'The Reaction Abroad'.
8. The dispatch was printed in the *Wiener Library Bulletin*, no. 1, 1962.
9. In Poland, there lived some 3,000,000 Jews; in Rumania, the number of Jews amounted to a figure between 500,000 and 750,000. Cf. Hugh Seton-Watson,

Eastern Europe Between the Wars, page 289. Cambridge, 1945.

10. *VB*, 5 October 1937; Cf. James B. Lunn, *Treachery and Antisemitism*, page 15. London, 1942.
11. *Fränkische Tageszeitung*, 21 January 1938; James B. Lunn, op. cit., page 19.
12. Ibid., page 21.
13. *Mein Kampf*, page 48.
14. Cf. Walter Laqueur, 'Hitler and Russia 1919-23', in *The Survey*, October 1962.
15. It was one of the posters reprinted in the first edition of *Mein Kampf*. The poster appendix disappeared from the subsequent editions of the book; in 1939, in the jubilee edition of *Mein Kampf* which marked Hitler's fiftieth birthday, the appendix was again reproduced, with the exception of the poster quoted above. The first moves were then being made in the direction of German—Soviet understanding. See C. Caspar's article—'*Mein Kampf* a Best Seller'—in *Jewish Social Studies*. New York, January 1958.
16. *Mein Kampf*, page 539.
17. Ibid., page 538.
18. Ibid., page 221.
19. Ibid., page 274.
20. Ibid., page 533.
21. H. Heiber (editor). *The Early Goebbels Diaries*, entry for 23 October 1925. London, 1962.
22. Ibid., entry for 15 February 1926.
23. *Unser Wille und Weg*. January 1932. Paul Meier-Benneckenstein, *Unser Angriff auf die marxistische Front*.
24. M. Domarus, op. cit., page 645.
25. Cf. 'Moscow-Berlin 1933', *The Survey*, October 1962.
26. 26 April 1933; *Presseabteilung*, 8677/E60698383-4.
27. Report from Moscow to the *AA*, 22 August 1933, 8677H/E607140-161.
28. See page 157.
29. A letter from Dr. Klein of the *Antikomintern* to the *Reichssendeleitung*, dated 16 October 1935. *Reichsrundfunkkammer* (*RRK*) papers, file No. 11980, at the Allied Document Centre, Berlin.
30. *Im Kampf gegen den Weltbolschewismus*, a publisher's report page 2. Berlin, 1936.
31. *Kampforgan der antibolschewistischen Weltbewegung*.
32. *Kampfblatt gegen Plutokratie und Volkerverhetzung*.
33. *RRK* papers at the Allied Document Centre, Berlin, File No. 11980.
34. Cf. Dr. R. Kommass, report of 24 January 1938, *RRK*, File No. 11980.
35. *VB*, 9 September 1936.
36. M. Domarus, op. cit., page 638.
37. *VB*, 11 September 1936.
38. *Aufklärungs und Redner-Informationsmaterial der Reichspropagandaleitung der NSDAP und des Propagandaamtes der Deutschen Arbeitsfront*, Lieferung 10 October 1937, Blatt 4/33.
39. *RPA*, 12 May 1939.
40. Ibid., 25 May 1939.

41. Cf. G. L. Weinberg, *Germany and the Soviet Union*, page 31, Leiden, 1954.
42. *RPA*, 30 May 1939.
43. Ibid., 31 May 1939.
44. Ibid., 22 August 1939.
45. *RPA*, 24 August 1939.
46. W. Hagemann, op. cit., page 272.
47. *VB*, 23 June 1941.
48. W. Hagemann, op. cit., page 273.

CHAPTER V

1. Ulrich Eichstädt, *Von Dollfuss zu Hitler*, page 22, Wiesbaden, 1955.
2. *Der Nationalsozialismus its jene Bewegung, die das preussische Schwert der Österriechischen Narretei zur Verfügung gastellt hat.*' W. Daim, *Der Mann der Hitler die Ideen gab.*, page 15.
3. Heinrich Benedikt (Editor), *Geschichte der Republik Österreich*, Vienna, 1954. An essay by Adam Wandruszka, "Osterreichs politische Struktur", page 406.
4. *Beiträge zur Vorgeschichte und Geschichte der Julirevolte*, page 4. An official publication, Vienna, 1934.
5. *Beiträge zur Vorgeschichte und Geschichte der Julirevolte*, page 4.
6. See page 13.
7. '*Wiener erwacht, gebt Hitler die Macht!*'
8. Cf. A. Wandruszka, op. cit., page 409.
9. U. Eichstädt, op. cit., page 24.
10. *Beiträge zur Vorgeschichte und Geschichte der Julirevolte*, page 9.
11. Ibid., page 11.
12. Ralf Richard Koerner, *So haben sie es damals gemacht*; *Die Propagandavorbereitungen zum Osterreichanschluss durch das Hitlerregime 1933-1938*, page 43. Vienna, 1958.
13. See page 51 et seq.
14. R. R. Koerner, op. cit., page 44.
15. Ibid., page 25.
16. Konrad Heiden, *Adolf Hittler*, vol. 2, page 16, Zürich, 1937.
17 H. Pohle, op. cit., page 404.
18. U. Eichstädt, op. cit., page 35.
19. The meeting between Hitler and Mussolini had taken place some six weeks before the *putsch*, on 14 and 15 June 1934. Hitler told Mussolini that it was impossible for him to come to terms with Dollfuss; at the same time, however, he informed the Italian dictator that the question of the *Anschluss* was of no interest to him because it was not internationally feasible. He went on to say that he had no particular person in mind as a replacement for Dollfuss, but that the future Chancellor would have to proclaim an election as soon as possible, and that the National Socialists would have to be taken into the government. *Docs. Ger. For. Pol.*, series C, vol. 3, page 10.
20. *IMT*, vol. IX page 294.
21. R. R. Koerner, op. cit., page 47.

22. U. Eichstädt, op. cit., page 56.
23. *Docs. Ger. For. Pol.*, series C, vol. 3, page 252.
24. Ibid., page 240.
25. Ibid., page 283.
26. R. R. Koerner, op. cit., page 54
27. *Docs. Ger. For. Pol.*, series C, vol. 3, page 229.
28. R. R. Koerner, op. cit., page 56.
29. Ibid., page 62.
30. *Der Hochverratsprozess gegen Dr. Guido Schmidt*, page 487. Vienna 1947.
31. *Guido Schmidt Prozess*, page 468.
32. A. Wandruszka, op. cit., page 410.
33. *Guido Schmidt Prozess*, page 469.
34. Ibid., page 471. Report of 4 April 1936.
35. M. Domarus, *Hitler, Reden und Proklamationen*, vol. 1, page 824.
36. R. R. Koerner, op. cit., page 69.
37. Ibid., page 70.
38. Ibid., page 72.
39. Ibid., page 79.
40. Ibid., pages 79-81.

CHAPTER VI

1. M. Domarus, *Hitler, Reden und Proklamationen*, vol. 1, pages 269 et seq.
2. *AA* Presseabteilung, 86774/E60698383-4.
3. *Mein Kampf*, page 525.
4. H. Rauschning, *Die Revolution des Nihilismus*, pages 363-4. Zürich, 1938.
5. *Docs. Ger. For. Pol.*, series C, vol. 1, page 26.
6. *Docs. Brit. For. Pol.*, Second series, vol. V, page 204.
7. Lord Vansittart, *The Mist Procession*, page 475, London, 1958.
8. See page 69 et seq.
9. *Docs. Ger. For. Pol.*, series C, vol. 1, page 761.
10. Third edition, page 1.
11. *Walks and Talks Abroad*, 3rd edition, page ix.
12. Ibid., page xi.
13. Ibid., page xvi.
14. Ibid., page 83.
15. Arthur Bryant's book *Unfinished Victory* belonged to this category; it was published in January 1940.
16. *AA*, K2113/K582609-616 and K528623.
17. *AA*, 5918H/E435115-132.
18. Ibid.
19. A letter from the press-section of the *Reichsleitung* of the *NSDAP*, 15 March 1935, to Dr. Gritzbach, Göring's personal assistant, *AA*, 5849H2/E428056-057.
20. *AA*, 5849H2/E428058.
21. A letter from Sir Leonard Lyle to the *News Chronicle*, 9 July 1940.
22. From a pamphlet published by the Fellowship in 1936.

23. By Werner Haas, Berlin 1936.
24. *Das politische Tagebuch Alfred Rosenbergs*, pages 129-36.
25. Cf. for instance, Prince Bismarck's report in June 1934; *AA, 5849H2 427978-982.*
26. See page 138.
27. See page 129 et seq.
28. M. Domarus, op. cit., page 802.
29. For an excellent, and definitive, analysis of the relations between the Germans and the Czechs between the wars see J. W. Brugel, *Tschechen und Deutsche*, Munich 1967.
30. W. J. Brügel, op. cit., page 527
31. Idem page 528.
32. *Docs. Ger. For. Pol.*, series C, vol. 3, pages 908 and 969, note 3.
33. See page 103.
34. In his autobiography, Hans Fritzche—*Hier spricht Hans Fritzche*, page 18. Zürich, 1943—points to the political reasons for the decline in the influence of Goebbels; in their biography of Goebbels, Manvell and Fraenkel deal with the Minister's personal entaglements at the time.
35. See page 103 et seq.
36. *RPA*, 25 and 26 August 1939.
37. H. Fritzche, op. cit., page 178.

CHAPTER VII

1. *Docs. Ger. For. Pol.*, series D, vol. 1, editor's note, page 520.
2. Ibid., page 588.
3. Ibid., vol. 2, pages 239-40.
4. See page 43 et seq.
5. *RPA*, 19 October 1938.
6. Helmut Heiber, *Goebbels*, page 286. Berlin, 1962.
7. *Docs. Ger. For. Pol.*, series D, vol. 8, page 30.
8. Louis P. Lochner, *The Goebbels Diaries*, page 235. London, 1948.
9. Cf. W. Hagemann, op. cit., page 440.
10. Ibid., pages 412 et seq.
11. H. Heiber, op. cit., page 292.
12. Ibid., page 290.
13. Ibid., page 296.
14. Cf. *Survey of International Affairs, 1939-46, Hitler's Europe*, page 47.
15. Cf. Paul Kluke, *Nationalsozialistische Europaideologie, Vierteljahreshefte fur Zeitgeschichte*, 1955, pages 235 et seq.
16. *Das Archiv*, edited by Alfred-Ingemar Berndt, page 735. Berlin, 1942.
17. See Hitler's declaration to the German nation on 22 June 1941, *Das Archiv*, volumes 85-87, pages 250-5.
18. W. Hagemann, op. cit., page 251.
19. *Vertrauliche Information R. Spr. Nr. 317, Infr. Nr. 49*, of 30 June 1941; quoted in a footnote of Paul Kluke's article *Nationalsozialistische Europaideologie*,

Viertelijahreshefte fur Zeitgeschichte, 1955, page 259.
20. *Das Archiv*, volumes 91-93, page 790.
21. *Hitler's Table Talk*, pages 37 and 34. London, 1953.
22. See page 98.
23. See page 91 et seq.
24. Rudolf Semmler, *Goebbels—The Man Next to Hitler*, pages 47-49. London, 1947.
25. *Trial of the Major War Criminals*, col. XXXIV, document 026-C, pages 191-95. *Weisungen fur die Handhabung der Propaganda in Falle 'Barbarossa'*, June, 1941.
26. Cf. A. Dallin, *German Rule in Russia*, page 66. London, 1957.
27. *Das Archiv*, vols. 91-93, page 579.
28. WL., Exhibit USA 723, 3064PS, A09584.
29. R. Semmler, op. cit., pages 54-55.
30. A. Dallin, op. cit., page 66.
31. *Das Archiv*, vols. 91-93, page 562.
32. Cf. A. Dallin. op. cit., especially pages 70 and 410.
33. See page 98.
34. Otto Brautigam, *Uberblick uber die besetzten Ostgebiete wahrend des 2. Weltkrieges*, pages 83 and 84. A publication of the Institut fur Besatzungsfragen, Tubingen, January 1954.
35. A. Dallin, op. cit., page 86.
36. Entry for 21 January 1942, *The Goebbels Diaries*, edited by L. P. Lochner.
37. Entry for 29 April 1942, *The Goebbels Diaries*.
38. R. Semmler, op. cit., page 63.
39. *VB*, 19 November 1942.
40. W. Hagemann, op. cit., pages 261-2.
41. Exhibit USA723, 3064PS, A095849-58.
42. W. Hagemann, op. cit., page 257.
43. See page 49.
44. *Reichsgestzblatt*, 'Verodnung uber ausserordentliche Rundfunkmassnahmen', September 1939, page 1683.
45. *Das Reich*, 12 October 1941.
46. H. Heiber, op. cit., page 302.
47. Entry for 24 January 1942, *The Goebbels Diaries*.
48. Cf. W. Hagemann, op. cit., page 302.
49. Undated and unsigned memorandum, National Archives, USA, Microcopy No. T81, Roll No. R-7, Serial 17/14491-14773.
50. E. Bramsted, op. cit., page 221.
51. Idem, page 225.
52. *Der steile Aufsteig*, Berlin 1944.
53. R. Semmler, op. cit., entry for 17 April 1945.

CHAPTER VIII

1. *Hier spricht Hans Fritzsche*, pages 27-28.

Bibliography

ORIGINAL SOURCES

1. *Unpublished*

Papers relating to propaganda from the *Reichspropagandaleitung*, now in the possession of the *Institut für Zeitgeschichte*, Munich; from the *Reichsrundfunkgesettschaft*, now at the Allied Document Centre, Berlin; diverse material filmed at the Alexandria (U.S.A.) repository, now at the Wiener Library; unpublished evidence submitted to the International Military Tribunal, Nürnberg, at the Wiener Library; speakers' directives, inserted into the *Promi* periodical, *Unser Wille und Weg*. A large part of the *Promi* papers was destroyed at the end of the war; most of the remaining material deals with the internal administration of the Ministry.

Documents from the archives of the Foreign Ministry (*Auswärtiges Amt*); film references were used throughout the book as additional indications to their placing.

2. *Published*

Documents on German Foreign Policy, Series C and D.

Documents on British Foreign Policy, 2nd and 3rd Series.

The Trial of the Major War Criminals before the International Military Tribunal, *Proceedings* (vols. I-XXIII), and *Documents in Evidence* (vols. XXIV-XLII). Nürnberg, 1947-9.

Trials of War Criminals before the Nürnberg Military Tribunals. Washington, 1951-3.

Domarus, Max: (ed.) *Hitler. Reden und Proklamationen.* Würzburg, 1962.

Mussolini, Benito: *Scritti e Discorsi.* Milan, 1938.

Der Hochverratsprozess gegen Dr. Guido Schmidt. Vienna, 1947.

Reichsgesetzblatt. A daily publication.

AUTOBIOGRAPHIES, BIOGRAPHIES, DIARIES

Asch, Walter: *Walter Frank. A study in Nazi Historiography.* Chicago, 1950.

Bade, Wilfred: *Joseph Goebbels.* Lübeck, 1933.

Beneš, Eduard: Memoirs. *From Munich to New War and to New Victory.* London, 1954.

Willi A. Boelcke (ed.): *Kriegspropaganda 1939-41: Geheime Ministerkonferenzen im Reichspropagandaministerium.* Stuttgart, 1967.

Borresholm, Boris: *Dr. Goebbels. Nach Aufzeichnungen seiner Umgebung.* Berlin, 1949.

Bouhler, Philipp: *Adolf Hitler. Das Werden einer Volksbewegung.* Lübeck, 1943.

Bramsted, Ernest K.: *Goebbels and National Socialist Propaganda,* London, 1965.

Bullock, Alan: *Hitler: a Study in Tyranny.* London, 1959.

Burckhardt, Carl J.: *Meine Danziger Mission, 1937-39.* Munich, 1960.

Chesteron, A. K.: *Portrait of a leader.* London, n.d.

Czech-Jochberg, E.: *Adolf Hitler und sein Stab.* Oldenburg, 1933.

— *Reichskanzler Hitler,* Oldenburg, 1935.

— *Wie Adolf Hitler der Führer wurde.* Leipzig, 1933.

Daim, Willfried: *Der Mann der Hitler die Ideen gab.* Vienna, 1958.

Dodd, Martha: *Through Embassy Eyes.* New York, 1939.

Doenitz, Karl: *Zehn Jahre Zwanzig Tage.* Bonn, 1958.

Drozdzynski, Aleksander and Jaborowski, Jan: *Theodor Oberländer. A Study in German East Policies.* Poznan, 1960.

Ebermayer, Erich and Roos, Hans: *Gefährtin des Teufels, Leben und Tod der Magda Goebbels.* Hamburg, 1952.

Fechner, Max: *Wie konnte es geschehen? Auszüege aus den Tagbüchern und Bekenntnissen eines Kriegsverbrechers.* Berlin, 1946.

Feierabend, Ladislav Karel: *Ve vládách druhé Republiky* (In the government of the Second Republic.) New York, 1961.

Frank, Hans: *Im Angesicht des Galgens. Deutung Hitlers und seiner Zeit auf Grund eigener Erlebnisse und Erkenntnisse. Geschrieben im*

Nürnberger Justizgefängnis. Munich, 1953.

Frischauer, Willi: *Himmler, The evil genius of the Third Reich.* London, 1953.

Fritsche, Hans: *Hier spricht Hans Fritsche.* Zürich, 1948.

The Goebbels Diaries. Translated and edited by Louis P. Lochner. London, 1948.

— *Vom Kaiserhof zur Reichskanzlei.* Berlin, 1934.

Greiner, Josef: *Das Ende des Hitler Mythos.* Vienna, 1947.

Haas, Werner: *Die nationalen Erneurungsbewegungen in Wort und Bild.* Berlin, 1936.

Hagen, Louis: *Evil Genius.* The story of Joseph Goebbels by E. Ebermayer and H. Meissner. (Based on the Original German *Gefährtin des Teufels.*) London, 1953.

Hanfstaengel, Putzi: *Hitler, The Missing Years.* London, 1957.

Hart, F. Th.: *Alfred Rosenberg, Der Mann und sein Werk.* Munich, 1939.

Heiber, Helmut: *Adolf Hitler, a short biography.* London, 1961.

—(ed.): *Joseph Goebbels. Das Tagebuch von J. Goebbels mit weiteren Dokumenten.* Stuttgart, 1961.

— *Goebbels.* Berlin, 1962.

Heiden, Konrad: *Der Führer, Hitler's rise to power.* London, 1944.

Hess, Rudolf: *Der Stellvertreter des Führers.* Berlin, 1933.

Heydrich, Reinhard: Oh the reign of terror in Bohemia and Moravia under the régime of Reinhard Hedyrich. Ed. by Czechoslovak Ministry of Foreign Affairs Department of Information, London, undated.

Heydrich, Reinhard: 7/3/04—4/6/42. Ed. by Reichssicherheitshauptamt, Berlin, 1942.

Hierl, Konstantin: *Im Dienst für Deutschland 1918—45.* Heidelberg, 1954.

Hinze, Kurt: 'Dr. Joseph Goebbels.' (In: *Jungdeutschland Bücherei.*) Donauwört, 1934.

Hoffmann, Heinrich: *Hitler was my Friend.* London, 1955.

Hombourger, Rene: *Goebbels Chef de Publicite du III eme Reich.* Paris, 1939.

Hunold, Hans: *Adolf Hitler und seine Männer.* Berlin, 1933.

Johst, Hanns: *Fritz Todt. Requiem.* Munich, 1943.

Jungnickel, Max: 'Goebbels.' (In: *Männer und Mächte.*) Leipzig, 1933.

Kersten, Felix: *The Kersten Memoirs, 1940-45.* London, 1956.

Knesebeck-Fischer, Alfred: *Dr. Joseph Goebbels. Im Spiegel von Freund und Feind. Sein Werdegang.* Berlin, 1933.

Krause, Willi: *Reichsminister Dr. Goebbels.* Berlin, 1933.

Krebs, Albert: *Tendenzen und Gestalten der NSDAP Erinnerungen an die*

Frühzeit der Partei. Stuttgart, 1959.

Kriesi, Hans: *Betrachtungen zu Goebbels Tagebüchern.* Frauenfeld, 1949.

Kuegelgen, Carlo von: 'Dr. Joseph Goebbels, Ein Charakterbild'. (In: *Die Fahne hoch!*) Berlin, 1934.

Langoth, Franz: *Kampf um Österreich. Erinnerungen eines Politikers.* Wels, 1951.

Leasor, James: *Rudolf Hess, The Uninvited Envoy.* London, 1962.

Lippert, Julius: *Im Strom der Zeit. Erlebnisse und Eindrücke.* Berlin, 1942.

—*Lächle und verbirg die Tränen. Erlebnisse und Bemerkungen eines deutschen 'Kriegsverbrechers'.* Leoni am Starnberger See. 1955.

Manvell, Roger and Fraenkel, Heinrich: *Joseph Goebbels.* London, 1960.

Mitford, Jessica: *Hons and Rebels.* London, 1960.

Moeller, Eberhard Wolfgang: *Der Führer.* Munich, 1938.

Muehlen, Norbert: *Der Zauberer. Leben und Anleihen des Dr. Hjalmar Horace Greeley Schacht.* Zürich, 1938.

Oven, Wielfried von: *Mit Goebbels bis zum Ende.* Buenos Aires, 1949-1950.

Papen, Franz von: *Memoirs.* London, 1952.

—*Der Wahrheit eine Gasse.* Munich, 1962.

Pick, F. W.: *The Art of Dr. Goebbels.* London, 1942.

Piotrowski, Stanislaw: *Hans Frank's Diary.* Warsaw, 1961.

Price, Ward: *I Know These Dictators.* London, 1937.

Rauschning, Hermann: *Hitler Speaks.* London, 1939.

Reed, Douglas: *The Prisoner of Ottawa: Otto Strasser.* London, 1953.

Renner, Karl, *An der Wende Zweier Zeiten. Lebenserinnerungen.* Vienna, 1946.

Ribbentrop, Joachim von: *The Ribbentrop Memoirs.* London, 1954.

—*Zwischen London und Moskau. Erinnerungen und letzte Aufzeichnungen.* Leoni am Starnberger See. 1953.

Riedrich, Otto: 'Dr. Joseph Goebbels'. (In: *Deutsche Führer—Deutsche Taten.*) Frankfurt, 1933.

Riess, Curt: *Joseph Goebbels, a biography.* New York, 1948; Baden-Baden, 1950.

Rosenberg, Alfred: *Das politische Tagebuch.*

—*Memoirs of Alfred Rosenberg.* edited by Lang, S. & Schenk, E. V. New York, 1949.

—*Letzte Aufzeichnungen. Ideale und Idole der Nat.-soz. Revolution.* Göttingen, 1955.

Schacht, Hjalmar: *76 Jahre meines Lebens.* Bad Woerishofen, 1953.

—*Account Settled.* London, 1949.

— *Abrechnung mit Hitler.* Berlin and Frankfurt, 1949.

Schellenberg, Walter: *Memoirs.* London, 1959.

Schirach, Henriette von: *Der Preis der Herrlichkeit.* Wiesbaden, 1956.

Schmidt, Peter: *Josef Grohé. Zwanzig Jahre Soldat Adolf Hitlers. Zehn Jahre Gauleiter. Ein Buch von Kampf und Treue.* Cologne, 1941.

Schuschnigg, Kurt von: *Dreimal Österreich.* Vienna, 1937.

Seeler, Hans O.: Goebbels. (In: *Die Reihe der deutschen Führer.*) Berlin, 1933.

Seidel, Erich: *Dr. Goebbels. Von einem SA-Mann geschrieben.* Leipzig, 1933.

Semmler, Rudolf: *Goebbels, the man next to Hitler.* London, 1947.

Seraphim, Hans Günther: *Das politische Tagebuch Alfred Rosenbergs.* Göttingen, 1956.

Stephan, Werner: *Joseph Goebbels—Dämon einer Diktatur.* Stuttgart, 1949.

Strasser, Otto: *Hitler and I.* London, 1940.

— and Stern, Michael: *Flight from Terror.* New York, 1943.

Vansittart, Lord: *The Mist Procession.* London, 1958.

Vaeth, Lore: *Johann von Leers. Ein Beispiel von pseudowissenschaftlicher Judenhetze.* Hamburg, 1960.

Viator: *Goebbels— Wer ist das?* Berlin, 1932.

Wahl, Karl: '. . .*es ist das deutsche Herz'. Erlebnisse und Erkenntnisse eines ehemaligen Gauleiters.* Augsburg, 1954.

Wenzel, Fritz R.: *Walter Darre und seine Mitkämpfer. Der Sieg von Blut und Boden.* Berlin, 1934.

Wighton, Charles: *Heydrich, Hitler's most evil henchman.* London, 1962.

Wulf, Josef: *Heinrich Himmler. Eine biographische Studie.* Berlin, 1960.

SECONDARY WORKS

Ball, Margaret M.: *Post-war German-Austrian Relations. The 'Anschluss' movement. 1918-36.* Stanford, 1937.

Bartlett, F. C.: *Political Propaganda.* Cambridge, 1940.

Bausch, Hans: *Der Rundfunk im politischen Kräftespiel der Weimarer Republik 1923-33.* Tübingen, 1956.

Beck, Joseph: *Dernier rapport Polonaise 1926-39.* Brussels, 1951.

Benedikt, Heinrich (ed.): *Geschichte der Republik Österreich.* Vienna, 1954.

Bierschenk, Theodor: *Die deutsche Volksgruppe in Polen 1934-39.* Kitzingen, 1954.

Bilek, B.: *Fifth Column at Work*. London, 1945.

Birch, Lionel: *Why they joined the Fascists*. London, n.d.

Bischoff, Ralph F.: *Nazi conquest through German culture*. Harvard, 1942.

Blake, Leonard: *Hitler's last year of power*. London, 1939.

Bodenstedt, Adolf: 'Sonderbericht der dt. Wochenschau' v. *Überfall auf Jugoslawien und Griechenland. Ein Beispiel nat.-soz. Film-propaganda im 2. Weltkrieg*. Hamburg, 1958.

Bohmann, Alfred: *Das Sudetendeutschtum in Zahlen*. Munich, 1959.

Bondy, Louis W.: *Racketeers of hatred. Julius Streicher and the Jew-Baiters' International*. London, 1946.

Braunthal, Julius: *The Tragedy of Austria*. London, 1948.

Breyer, Richard: *Das Deutsche Reich und Polen, 1932-37*. Würzburg, 1955.

British Union of Fascists and National Socialists, *Constitution and Regulations*. London, 1936.

Brook-Shepherd, Gordon: *Dollfuss*. London, 1961.

The Brown Network (Anon.): *The Activities of the Nazis in Foreign Countries*. New York, 1936.

Buttinger, Josef: *Am Beispiel Österreichs. Ein geschichtlicher Beitrag zur Krise der sozialistischen Bewegung*. Cologne, 1953.

Childs, Harwood Lawrence: *Propaganda by Short Wave*. Princeton, 1942.
 — *Propaganda and Dictatorship*. Princeton, 1936.

Clark, R. T.: *The Fall of the German Republic*. London, 1935.

Cross, Colin: *The Fascists in Britain*. London, 1961.

Driencourt, Jacques: *La propaganda nouvelle force politique*. Paris, 1950.

Ducloux, Louis: *From Blackmail to Treason. Political Crime and Corruption in France 1920-40*. London, 1958.

Edwards, Violet: *Group Leaders Guide to Propaganda Analysis*. New York, 1938.

Eichstädt, Ulrich: *Von Dollfuss zu Hitler. Geschichte des Anschlusses Oesterreichs 1933-1938*. Wiesbaden, 1955.

Ettlinger, Harold: *The Axis on the Air*. Indianapolis and New York, 1943.

Fabricant, Noah D.: *13 Famous Patients*. New York, 1960.

Fellner, Anton: *Wie es kommen sollte... Dokumentarische Belege für den Verrat Schuschniggs*. Linz, 1938.

Franzel, Emil: *Sudetendeutsche Geschichte. Eine volkstümliche Darstellung*. Augsburg, 1958.

Frisch, Sepp: *Die Saar blieb deutsch. Ein Rückblick 1680-1955*. 1956.

Frischauer, Willi: *Twilight in Vienna*. London, 1938.

Fuchs, Martin: *A Pact with Hitler. The Death of Austria*. London, 1939.

Funder, Friedrich: *Als Österreich den Sturm bestand. Aus der erfsen in die zweite Republik.* Vienna and Munich, 1957.

Garratt, Geoffrey T.: *The Shadow of the Swastika.* London, 1938.

Gedye, G. E. R.: *Fallen Bastions. The Central European Tragedy.* London, 1939.

Golding, Claud: *From Versailles to Danzig.* London, 1940.

Gordon, Matthew: *News is a weapon.* New York, 1942.

Goette, Karl Heinz: *Die Propaganda der Glaubensbewegung 'Deutsche Christen' und ihre Beurteilung in der dt. Tagespresse.* Münster, 1957.

Gregory, J. D.: *Dollfuss and His Time.* London, 1935.

Hagemann, Walter: *Publizistik im Dritten Reich. Ein Beitrag zur Methodik der Massenführung.* Hamburg, 1948.

Hájek, Miloš: *Od Mnichova k 15. březnu.* Prague, 1959.

Hargrave, John: *Words win Wars.* London, 1940.

Hartmann, Mitzi: *Austria still lives.* London, 1938.

Heiden, Konrad: *Geschichte des Nationalsozialismus. Die Karriere der Idee.* Berlin, 1932.

—*Adolf Hitler*, vol. 2. Zürich, 1937.

Heike, Otto: *Das Deutschtum in Polen, 1918-39.* Bonn, 1955.

Hepp, Fred: *Der geistige Widerstand im Kulturteil der 'Frankfurter Zeitung' gegen die Diktatur des 'Totalen Staates'.* Augsburg, 1949.

Hirsch, Helmut: *Die Saar in Versailles. Die Saarfrage auf der Friedenskonferenz 1919.* Bonn, 1952.

—*Die Saar von Genf. Die Saarfrage während des Völkerbundregimes von 1920-35.* Bonn, 1954.

Ingrim, Robert: *Der Griff nach Österreich.* Zürich, 1938.

'Les Instructions Secretes de la Propagande Allemande'. Ed. by *Le Petit Parisien.* Paris, undated.

Iwo, Jack: *Goebbels erobert die Welt.* Paris, 1936.

Jaksch, Wenzel: *Europas Weg nach Potsdam, Schuld und Schicksal im Donauraum.* Stuttgart, 1958.

—*Rhum und Tragik der Sudetendeutschen Sozialdemokratie.* Malmö, 1946.

—*Sudeten Labour and the Sudeten Problem; A report to International Labour.* London, 1945.

Jedlicka, Ludwig: *Ein Heer im Schatten der Parteien. Die militärpolitische Lage Österreichs 1918-38.* Graz and Cologne, 1955.

Jenks, William A.: *Vienna and the Young Hitler.* New York, 1960.

Jong, Louis de: *The German Fifth Column in the Second World War.* London, 1956.

Kleinwächter, Friedrich F. G.; *Der Deutschösterreichische Mensch und der Anschluss*. Vienna, 1926.

Klepetar, Harry: *Seit 1918. . . . Eine Geschichte der Tschechoslowakischen Republik*. Moravská Ostrava, 1937.

Kluke, Paul: 'Nationalsozialistische Volkstumspolitik in Elsass-Lothringen, 1940-45'. (In: *Festgabe für Hans Herzfeld*.) Berlin, 1958.

Kochan, Lionel: *Pogrom, November 10th, 1938*. London, 1957.

Koerner, Ralf Richard: *So haben sie es damals gemacht. . . . Die Propagandavorbereitungen zum Österreichanschluss durch das Hitlerregime 1933-38*. Vienna 1958.

Koszyk, Kurt: *Des Ende des Rechtsstaates 1933-34 und die dt. Presse*. Düsseldorf, 1960.

Kracauer, Siegfried: *From Caligari to Hitler*. Princeton, 1947.

Kreibisch, Karl: *Des Volkes Sache ist nicht Henleins Sache. Das Aussiger Programm der SdP und die Kommunisten*. Prague, 1937.

Kreisler, Fritz: *Wer hat Dollfuss ermordet?* Bodenbach, 1934.

Kriss, Ernst and Speier, Hans: *German Radio Propaganda. Report on home broadcasts during the war*. London, 1944.

Kun, Bela: *Die Februarkämpfe in Oesterreich und ihre Lehren*. Moscow and Leningrad, 1934.

Kunschak, Leopold: *Österreich 1919-34*. Vienna, 1934.

Lambert, Margaret: *The Saar*. London, 1934.

Lavie, Harold and Wechsler, James: *War propaganda and the U.S.* New Haven, 1940.

Lean, Tangye: *Voices in the Darkness. The story of the European Radio War*. London, 1943.

Leubuscher, Walter: *Der grosse Irrtum. Ein Beitrag zur Geschichte der nat. soz. Bewegung in Oesterreich*. Vienna, 1937.

Lennhoff, Eugen: *Agents of Hell*. London.

— *Last Five Hours of Austria*. London, 1938.

— *Thousand and one Nazi Lies*. London.

Lisický, K.: *Ceskoslovenskà cesta do Mnichova*. London, 1956.

Ludwig, Eduard: *Österreichsche Sendung im Donauraum. Die letzten Dezennien Österreichscher Innen-und Aussenpolitik*. Vienna, 1954.

Macdonald, Mary: *The Republic of Austria 1918-34. A Study in the Failure of Democratic Government*. London, 1946.

Mackenzie, J. A.: *Propaganda Boom*. London, 1938.

Maetzke, Ernst-Otto: *Die Deutsche-Schweizerische Presse zu einigen Problemen des zweiten Weltkrieges*. Tübingen, 1955.

Margolin, Leo, J.: *Paper Bullets, a Brief Story of Psychological War-fare in World War II.* New York, 1946.

Martin, Kingsley: *Fascism, Democracy and the Press.* London, 1938.

Mayer, Hans: *Frankreich zwischen den Weltkriegen.* Frankfurt, 1948.

Meerloo, A. M.: *Total War and Human Mind. A psychologist's experiences in occupied Holland.* London, 1944.

Micaud, Charles: *The French Right and Nazi Germany 1933-39. A study of public opinion.* Durham, North Carolina, 1943.

Mirbt, Karl Wolfgang: *Methoden publizistischen Widerstands im Dritten Reich.* Berlin, 1958.

Mullally, Frederic: *Fascism inside England.* London, 1946.

Mueller-Sturmheim, E.: *99.7%. A Plebiscite Under Nazi Rule.* London, 1942.

Münch, Hermann: *Bömische Tragödie. Das Schicksal Mitteleuropas im Lichte der tschechischen Frage.* Braunschweig, 1949.

Münzenberg, Willi: *Propaganda als Waffe.* Paris, 1937.

Murphy, Raymond E.: *National Socialism, Basic Principles. Their application by the party's Foreign Office and the use of Germans abroad for Nazi Aims.* Washington, 1943.

Nationale Frage und Österreichs Kampf um seine Unabhängigkeit. Paris, 1939.

Neusüss-Hunkel: *Die SS.* Hannover, 1956.

Niedermeyer, Albert: *Wahn, Wissenschaft und Wahrheit. Lebenserinnerungen eines Arztes.* Innsbruck, 1956.

Nobecourt, R. G.: *Les secrets de la propagande en France occupée.* Paris, 1962.

Österreich unter dem Reichskommissar. Bilanz eines Jahres Fremdherrschaft. Paris, 1939.

Pezet, Ernest: *Fin de l' Autriche—Fin d'une Europe.* Paris, 1938.

Pitt-Rivers, George: *The Czech Conspiracy—a phase in the World War plot.* London, 1938.

Pleyer, Wilhelm: *Europas unbekannte Mitte. Ein politisches Lesebuch.* Munich and Stuttgart, 1957.

Pohle, Heinz: *Der Rundfunk als Instrument der Politik. Zur Geschichte des dt. Rundfunks 1923-38.* Hamburg, 1955.

Pozorny, Reinhard: *Wir suchten die Freiheit. Weg einer Volksgruppe.* Munich, 1959.

Prago, Ladislas (ed.): *German psychological warfare. Survey and Bibliography.* New York, 1941.

Preidel, Helmut: *Die Deutschen in Böhmen und Mähren. Ein historischer

Rückblick, Gräfelingen bei Munich, 1952.

The Press in Authoritarian Countries. Ed. by the International Press Institute. Zürich, 1959.

Presse in Fesseln. Eine Schilderung des NS-Pressetrusts. Gemeinschaftsarbeit des Verlages auf Grund authentischen Materials. Berlin, 1947.

Propaganda Analysis: Ed. by the Institute for Propaganda Analysis. New York, 1938-40.

Quinn, Edward: *Mission of Austria.* London, 1938.

Radl, Emanuel: *Der Kampf zwischen Tschechen und Deutschen.* Reichenberg, 1928.

Raschhofer, Hermann: *Die Sudetenfrage. Ihre völkerreichtliche Entwicklung vom ersten Weltkrieg bis zur Gegenwart.* Munich, 1953.

Rauschning, Hermann: *Die Revolution des Nihilismus.* Zürich, 1938.

Renkel, Rudolf: *Staat und Nation.* Bonn, 1957.

Renner, Karl: *An der Wende Zweier Zeiten. Lebenserinnerungen.* Vienna, 1946.

Rieser, Max: *Österreichs Sterbeweg.* Vienna, 1953.

Rogerson, Sidney: *Propaganda in the next war.* London, 1938.

Roennefarth, Helmuth K. G.: *Die Sudetenkrise in der internationalen Politik.* Wiesbaden, 1961.

Rudlin, W. A.: *The Growth of Fascism in Great Britain.* London, 1935.

Rufolf, Karl: *Aufbau im Widerstand. Ein Seelsorgebericht aus Österreich 1938-45.* Salzburg, 1947.

Ruehl, Manfred: *Der Stürmer und seine Herausgeber.* Nürnberg, 1960.

Scanlan, Ross: 'The Nazi Rhetorician.' (In: *Quarterly Journal of Speech.*) New York, 1951.

Schaefer, Wolfgang: *NSDAP.* Hanover, 1956.

Schmeer, Karlheinz: *Die Regie des öffentlichen Lebens im Dritten Reich.* Munich, 1956.

Schneidmadl, Heinrich: *Grüner Weg in die braune Hölle.* Vienna, 1946.

Schumann, Wolfgang: *Oberschlesien, 1918-19, Vom gemeinsamen Kampf deutscher und polnischer Arbeiter.* Berlin (East), 1961.

Schuschnigg, Kurt von: *Austria must remain Austria.* n.p. 1938.

— *Austrian Requiem.* New York, 1946.

— *Farewell Austria.* London, 1938.

Seabury, Paul: *Wilhelmstrasse.* University of California Press, 1954.

Searchinger, C.: *Voice of Europe.* London, 1938.

Serant, Paul: *Le Romantism Fascist.* Paris, 1959.

Servaes, Franz: *Grüsse an Wien.* Vienna, 1948.

Shepherd, Gordon: *The Austrian Odyssey.* London, 1957.

Sington, Derrick and Weidenfeld, Arthur: *The Goebbels Experiment. A Study of the Nazi Propaganda Machine*. London, 1942.

Skalnik, Kurt: *Der Mann zwischen den Zeiten: Karl Lueger*, Vienna and Munich, 1954.

Soják, Vladimir: *O Československé zahraniční politice 1918-39*. Prague, 1956.

Starhemberg, Ernst Rüdiger: *Between Hitler and Mussolini*. New York, 1942.

Stránský, Jaroslav: *K otázce česko-německé*. London, 1955.

Taylor, A. J. P.: *The Origins of the Second World War*. London, 1961.

Teeling, William: *Youth on the Rhine. The Problem of the Saar*. London, 1934.

Turnwald, Wilhelm K.: *Renascence or Decline of Central Europe. The Sudeten German-Czech problem*. Munich, 1954.

Veale, F. J. P.: *Der Barbarei entgegen*. Hamburg, 1954.

Veuillot, François: *La Rocque et son parti. Comme je les ai vus*. Paris, 1938.

Wandruszka, C. F. A.: *Geschichte einer Zeitung. Das Schicksal der 'Presse' und der 'Neuen Freien Presse' von 1948 zur Zweiten Republik*. Vienna, 1958.

Webster, Nesta H.: *Germany and England*. London, 1938.

Weinberg, G. L.: *Germany and the Soviet Union*. Leiden, 1954.

Wieser, Georg: *Ein Staat Stirbt. Oesterreich 1934-38*. Paris, 1938.

Weizsäcker, Ernst von: *Erinnerungen*. Munich, 1950.

West, Rebecca: *The Meaning of Treason*. New York, 1947.

White, Amber Blanco: *The new Propaganda*. London, 1939.

Williams, Chester S.: *Ways of Dictatorship*. Evanston, Illinois. 1941.

Wiskemann, Elizabeth: *Czechs and Germans*. Oxford, 1938.

— *The Rome-Berlin Axis*. Oxford, 1949.

Zeder, Heinrich: *Judas sucht seinen Bruder. Schicksale aus dem Freiheitskampf Österreichs*. Vienna, 1948.

Zeman, Z. A. B.: *The Break-up of the Habsburg Empire 1914-18. A Study in National and Social Revolution*. London, 1961.

Zernatto, Guido: *Die Wahrheit über Österreich*. New York, Toronto, 1938.

Zoellner, Erich: *Geschichte Österreichs von den Anfängen bis zur Gegenwart*. Vienna, 1962.

Index